KV-339-482

Contents

PLAYING
FOR
KEEPS

SPORT, THE MEDIA AND SOCIETY

JOHN
GOLDLUST

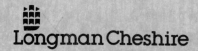
Longman Cheshire

Longman Cheshire Pty Limited
Longman House
Kings Gardens
95 Coventry Street
Melbourne 3205 Australia

Offices in Sydney, Brisbane, Adelaide
and Perth. Associated companies, branches,
and representatives throughout the world.

Designed by Vicki Hamilton
Set in 10/11 Plantin Light (Linotron 202)
Produced by Longman Cheshire Pty Ltd
Printed in Malaysia
by Vinlin Press Sdn. Bhd.,
Kuala Lumpur

National Library of Australia
Cataloguing-in-Publication data

Goldlust, John.
   Playing for keeps.

   Includes index.
   ISBN 0 582 71143 6.

   1. Television and sports. 2. Television broadcasting of
   sports – Australia. 3. Mass media and sports –
   Australia. I. Title.

302.2'345'0994

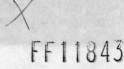

Acknowledgements

I welcome the opportunity to place on record my appreciation and thanks to my friends and colleagues in the Department of Sociology at La Trobe University for the strength of their encouraging support towards me throughout the somewhat extended time I have been engaged in the writing of this book. Also of great assistance was the leave granted to me by the university in 1985 to pursue an outside studies programme, which provided me with the freedom to concentrate on the research and writing required to bring the project to its completion.

In particular, I wish to thank Roger Wilkinson for his interest and practical assistance, both of which have proved invaluable. A formal note of appreciation is also due to my friend Phillip Lipton, who was happy to read sections of the material in draft form and who, throughout the endeavour, has continuously extended generous support, optimism and boundless good humour, all of which have contributed enormously in keeping me at my task.

For the transcribing of interview material from tape, the typing and preparation of the manuscript, I am indebted to the diligent work provided by Jill Gooch, Barbara Mathews, Judy Carr, Elaine Young, Bronwyn Bardsley, Helen Cook and Carol White. For the wonderful job they did as well as the cheery friendship they have provided over a number of years I am deeply appreciative.

A number of producers and on-camera personnel connected to the major television organisations — both in Melbourne and in Sydney — kindly agreed to be interviewed late in 1984 and provided me with much useful and interesting first-hand information on the practical operation of sports television. I thank them for their helpful co-operation and their forthright comments, a number of which are incorporated into the text that follows.

My sincere thanks to Neil Ryan of Longman Cheshire for the faith he has shown from the outset in my approach to the subject and for the friendly and positive manner in which he has overseen the publication of this book, as well as to Elizabeth Watson for applying her considerable editorial skills to my rough manuscript.

It goes without saying that the pressures are invariably the greatest upon those closest to someone who is labouring to complete a long and frequently frustrating task, so the wonderful support, patience and consideration that I received from my family—Ruth, Clare and Rachel—have been the most valuable, and deserving of my utmost gratitude.

November, 1986

For permission to reproduce stills from television sports coverage, the publishers wish to thank ABC (New York) for Super Bowl 1985 football; and PBL Marketing Pty Ltd for Nine network's cricket coverage.

While every effort has been made to trace and acknowledge copyright, in some cases copyright proved untraceable. Should any infringement have occurred, the publishers tender their apologies.

Preface

The subject matter of this study emerged from a developing interest in the increasingly evident interpenetration of two identifiably distinct institutions within contemporary popular culture—the mass media (more specifically in the form of television) and high-performance spectator sport. In the context of Australian society, my attention was particularly stimulated by two important developments of the past decade that highlighted the nature of the interrelationship between these two institutions.

The first was the apparent ease with which, in the space of a few years, the active involvement of commercial television interests acted as an important catalyst in bringing about radical changes to the structure, organisation and future direction of two of the more visible and prominent spectator sports in this country—cricket and Australian football—both of which previously had operated for more than half a century within securely entrenched and seemingly inviolable institutional frameworks.

The second was the noticeable expansion, from about the late 1970s, in both the quantity and variety of international sporting events regularly appearing on Australian television screens. Thus, for example, top-level European and Latin American soccer matches as well as highlights of the weekly inter-club games from many countries became a regular staple in the programming schedule of the new multi-cultural broadcasting network established by the Federal government. The commercial networks began filling their late-night programming with satellite transmitted replays of games from the American professional sports leagues (some, such as American football, were sports virtually unknown to most Australians) as well as direct telecasts of international motor-racing, skiing, tennis, golf, horse-racing and even show-jumping events.

The slickness of production techniques—employment of technological video gadgetry, extensive use of graphics, music and other elements signifying 'high production values' of such programmes—suggested the focus of my original investigation which was to analyse the 'state of the art' sporting telecast as a contemporary televisual form. A critical question at this stage was the extent to which the techniques of television production deliberately set out to intervene between the viewer and the sporting event itself. In which ways did they seek to transform the experience from that of the spectator in the stadium in order to suit the requirements of 'good television'? Chapter 4 presents detailed examination of these questions through an empirical analysis of a number of such sporting telecasts that attempts to 'deconstruct' the constituents of the form.

However, both in the academic literature and in public debate surrounding the relationship between television and sport, much of the discussion revolves around the issues of the extent to which television, as an institution and as a mediator of experience, 'changes' sport; and even further, whether through its increasing economic contribution to the financial profitability of high-performance spectator sport, television more and more comes to directly 'control' sport. Such discussions examine the extent of television's causal influence in bringing about changes to the internal structure of particular sports, television's role in the increasing professionalisation evident across many sports, the links between sport and the corporate business sector — the increasing annexation of sport for the financial interest of the marketing/leisure/entertainment industries in capitalist societies — and the political role of modern sport. These issues are considered at some length in Chapters 5 and 6.

Much of the discussion of such issues in the literature is premised on the unquestioned assumption that sport itself is a 'natural' or 'universal' activity that has evolved organically throughout the history of human social development, adapting itself finally to the significant structural changes caused by industrialisation into its contemporary form. This preconception assumes some 'ideal essence' of sport that is typically exemplified in the romanticised view that amalgamates the notions of sport as an avenue towards the higher cultivation of the human spirit (associated with Classical Greek civilisation) and the authoritative version of modern amateur sport (formulated in nineteenth century England, and institutionally universalised through the revived Olympic movement).

As this study seeks to challenge these assumptions, it seemed both important and necessary to present a somewhat extended socio-historical exposition of the broader context within which contemporary sport was socially constructed. Thus Chapters 1 and 2 seek to demonstrate that modern sport is a distinctive collective cultural creation, the structure and form of which was engineered by the dominant social class of Victorian England. Furthermore, the development of modern sport was part of the lengthy process of social reorganisation in which the 'problems' of labour discipline and the socially appropriate use of both leisure time and public space by the urbanised workforce were of tantamount concern to the dominant groups in the industrialising societies of Europe and North America. Organised sport, it is argued, on the lines formulated by such groups remained consistent with their broader social ideologies while also proving to be particularly popular with almost all sections of society. However, spectatorship at team sports emerged as an important focus for communal identity and group sociability. Popular sporting competitions developed local institutionalised support and provided an element of inter-generational, sub-cultural continuity. Thus, particular sporting clubs and competitions operated as important carriers of communal identity and came to symbolise various forms of group solidarity and cohesion. In many parts of the world, until well into the middle of this century, many high level spectator sports were considered a communal resource rather than a form of commercialised recreation.

The modern forms of mass communication, most notably radio and television, emerged at a time when a number of spectator sports were well established and, particularly in the United States, had already demonstrated their viability as lucrative commercial operations. Chapter 3 presents an outline of the political and economic context that determined the manner in which the possibilities for mass communication were translated into the working technologies of mass media organisations. That the latter became, almost universally, institutions centrally disseminating forms of popular entertainment meant that they were immediately attracted to the area of spectator sport. Similarly, there were pressures from within sporting institutions, particularly from those which began to perceive their sport's possibilities as an entertainment commodity, to embrace the potential of the mass media for expanding their financial and marketing base. As Chapter 6 seeks to demonstrate, the successful colonisation of many sports by television was facilitated by the increasing predominance of people who shared these ambitions within sporting organisations, in alliance with sporting professionals, business and marketing interests. Television was thus able to operate as a promoter of its own interests, and at the same time as an important broker in the process that helped transform in many cases indigenous, localised, community-oriented leisure pastimes into economically rationalised components of an internationalised popular culture industry.

Thus, hopefully, a study such as this, by focusing on the relationship between television and sport is able to elucidate upon the interaction of significant structural and ideological components in modern society that operate more generally in the broader process of the ongoing commodification of almost all available areas of popular culture. In doing so, the work that follows strives to adhere to the general premise recently enunciated as perhaps the most sociologically fruitful approach to the study of sport in society.

What is required then is a conceptual framework which goes beyond saying that the observable institutionalization of various games into sports manifests a process characteristic of any 'modern' society, and asks: What interests gave specific shape to the development of modern sport? Through what channels were these influences exercised, and for what purpose? What kind of institution is contemporary sport, and precisely how is its shape influenced by (and perhaps an influence on) developments in other, more obviously central, institutions?[1]

Notes

1 David Whitson, 'Structure, Agency and the Sociology of Sport Debates', *Theory, Culture and Society*, 3(1), 1986, p. 99.

1
The emergence of modern sport

Introduction

In its everyday usage the meaning of the term 'sport' appears at first to be fairly unproblematic. Almost anywhere in the world today one would find broad agreement that certain human physical activities, when they are expressed within well established, standardised forms, identified by such names as football, athletics, basketball and tennis are indisputably sports. Furthermore, we are aware that there exist a considerable number of these organised games and pastimes — some localised to certain areas or regions, others more widely practised — that fall within the generic category of sport. But what exactly is sport, and can we identify a particular set of characteristics that definitively sets apart those activities we call sports from all other forms of human behaviour?

Understandably, sport has come under considerable intellectual and academic scrutiny. While formal definitions proposed by historians, philosophers, sociologists and others vary somewhat in specifics, there would seem to be a general consensus that sport may be distinguished by the following:

1 the attributes of physical activity and the development of specific physical skills;

2 the elements of competition and opposition among participants or teams of participants in achieving particular ends or goals;

3 the authoritative codification of a clearly defined, formalised body of rules and conditions relevant to each sport, the adherence to which the participants feel morally bound.

Furthermore, while not denying that the particular form that sports take within different societies and in different historical epochs may be influenced by broader structural characteristics, the documented presence of sports in the culture of most tribal societies, in the ancient Graeco-Roman world, in the feudal period, as well as in contemporary times suggests to some scholars an 'essentialist' basis underlying the practice of sport. It is argued that the urge to develop particular physical skills and display such skills in competition against others represents a manifestation of certain expressive needs of the social human being; that is, that such activities are undertaken primarily for their own sake. In this way, sport is differentiated, on the one hand, from work, in which physical skills and abilities are developed and applied towards recognisably instrumental goals, but also, on the other, from those expressive human activities that are conventionally classified as crafts, hobbies, creative and performing arts.

A prominent version of this 'essentialist' or 'idealist' position identifies sport as a formalised expression of the 'play instinct', considered innate to all human beings (and many animal species) and typified by 'the suspension of the ordinary concerns of the everyday world'.[1] In an influential book entitled *Homo Ludens*, first published in 1938, the Dutch historian and philosopher Johan Huizinga wrote:

> Summing up the formal characteristics of play we might call it a free activity standing quite consciously outside 'ordinary' life as being 'not serious', but at the same time absorbing the player intensely and utterly. It is an activity connected with no material interest, and no profit can be gained from it. It proceeds within its own proper boundaries of time and space according to fixed rules and in an orderly manner.[2]

One might recognise a certain underlying philosophical communality between Huizinga's somewhat idyllic discussion of the 'play instinct' and the contemporary proponents of amateur sport. The latter argue that 'true' sport is undertaken by the individual for the intrinsic rewards of expressing skill, creativity and achievement in the spirit of human play without the necessity for any external reward. Yet, even in the case of the 'amateur' form of modern sport, Huizinga argues forcefully, 'we have an activity nominally known as play but raised to such a pitch of technical organisation and scientific thoroughness that the real play-spirit is threatened with extinction'.[3] More recently, in a similar vein Schmitz nominates three major tendencies in modern sport that operate towards extinguishing the 'spirit of play', namely, the exaggeration of the importance of victory, the rationalisation of techniques and spectatorship.[4]

A somewhat broader, but still fundamentally idealist, interpretation of sport draws its inspiration from Classical Greece through the philosophical conceptualisation of leisure found in the writings of

Plato and Aristotle. The Greek philosophers conceived of leisure as a 'state in which all necessity is absent'[5] thereby obligating the individual to 'cultivate' the self through engaging in activities that develop a greater consciousness and sensitivity to the 'higher' values of life. The extensive interest in sporting activities reportedly shared by the leisured citizens of the Greek city-states, as exemplified in the numerous, regularly scheduled sporting festivals celebrated throughout the region, is seen to reflect their belief that sport, undertaken as a freely chosen interest—as distinct from a trade or occupation—represents a legitimate pathway towards the higher cultivation of the self.[6]

Given the considerable intellectual respect accorded the philosophy and values of Classical Greece in the nineteenth century, it is not surprising that the Greeks' preoccupation with sporting endeavours was incorporated into a generalised view—widely shared by the intellectual and cultural vanguard of the rising industrial middle class throughout Western Europe—that the perspectives and lifestyle of the ancient world's patrician class exemplified a 'golden age' in the history of Western culture and civilisation. It was in this context that a new cultural movement emerged, centred in the British public school system. It sought to inculcate within the sons of the newly emerging dominant class the spirit of self-cultivation, through the pursuit of athletic and sporting excellence, consistent with a belief that the benefits of industrial wealth would facilitate a 'new golden age' and with it the potential for the modern attainment of the Greek leisure ideal.

Much contemporary journalistic and populist writing about sport is rooted in this 'classical' tradition, as is much of the continued pedagogic support for the inclusion of sport as part of the formal education curriculum. The major critique of modern sport expressed by those sharing this perspective takes the form of an exhortation to participants and supporters to help restore the practice of sport to a closer approximation of its 'imminent' or 'ideal' form. There is both hostility and dismay at the modern trend towards increasing professionalism and the ensuing substantial material and social benefits accruing to participants. Thus, for example, Maheu writes,

> sport as a job is not really sport. The only true sport is amateur. The moment sport becomes a utilitarian activity practised for profit it loses its connexion with leisure from which it originally sprang and which gives it its essential dignity and its close affinity with culture.[7]

Interestingly, similar assumptions also inform some of the leftist critiques that focus on the elements of corruption and exploitation in sport under capitalism. Writing in 1964, Max Horkheimer, the eminent German intellectual associated with the Frankfurt School group of critical Marxist theorists, equated sport with 'art, literature and philosophy and all that springs of the productive imagination'. He advocated that sport should be protected from those 'evil influences' that seek to harness it 'in the service of profit, politics, egoism' but maintained:

> the rules of sportsmanship and mentality of the sportsman, which it is true are violated only too often, constitute the modern expression of the former great cultural traditions, of Christianity, as also of the Age of Enlightenment in France and of the philosophy of Immanuel Kant.[8]

Whether sport is considered an outlet, albeit a corrupted one, for the 'play instinct' in human beings or as a means towards individualistic self-cultivation in the tradition of the Greek conceptualisation of leisure, the idealist view can provide us with only a limited understanding of its contemporary sociological connotations.

It helps us little when approaching the question of why particular sporting forms and skills are nurtured in certain societies while different ones emerge in others. How and why do the elements of competition become formalised into a specific body of rules? Are there significant variations between societies with regard to the social meaning of participation in sport, the implications of success and failure, the relationships between participant and spectator, the development of sport as an individual or team contest? Perhaps most importantly can we establish any systematic relationships between the role of sport within a society and broader structural variables such as the economy, political structure, class and status divisions and dominant intellectual and cultural values?

In order to satisfactorily approach some of these questions and to meaningfully focus on the increasing interpenetration of sport and the mass media that is one of the central concerns of this investigation, it seems pertinent to begin with a socio-historical survey of the developing role of sport over the past few centuries. Hopefully, this will lead to a clearer understanding of the significant forces and influences that have shaped the construction of the contemporary form of sport with which we are all familiar. Such an overview will also provide the opportunity to establish the range of academic domains and the leading theoretical perspectives within which the discussions surrounding the questions and issues outlined above have proceeded.

Sport as a sociological problem

As a focus for academic study, sport has attracted some attention from those disciplines concerning themselves with the study of *culture*, where this concept is considered, not in the popular sense of 'artistic and intellectual activities' but in the broader anthropological and sociological meaning of a 'whole way of life'.[9] In this context, anthropologists have accumulated substantial material on the variety of games and sports found in tribal societies. Lüschen, in a recent review of the anthropological literature on sport, notes that such reports first began to appear in the middle of the nineteenth century. Much of the work was essentially descriptive with some early concern exhibited in the diffusion pattern of particular games.[10] Attempts at interpreting the role of games and sports in tribal societies emphasised their supposed ritualistic, economic or political functions. No attempt was made to differentiate between games and sport, both of which were considered to be manifestations of non-serious play elements fundamental to human social life, although it was recognised that such activities might develop significant institutionalised functions associated with the maintenance of societal stability or the positive integration of sub-groups into the tribal culture.

As a number of anthropological field reports began to mount, the almost total absence of any society in which some games or physical contests were not present led some scholars to conclude that such forms of activity represented a 'cultural universal'. The interest of cultural anthropologists, as well as some cultural historians and philosophers turned towards first, the construction of a comprehensive classificatory scheme which could systematically incorporate the bewildering variety of games, sports and contests reported, and second, relating the presence or absence of particular types of games to broader structural characteristics of societies.

Perhaps the most inclusive and probably best known classificatory system was developed by Roger Caillois.[11] This schema sets out to subsume all human games under one of four 'rubrics'. The first type Caillois calls games of *agon* (he employs Greek nomenclature for his classificatory terms) incorporating all of those competitive contests in which there is an established body of rules and which draw upon the participants' intelligence and skill. This type most closely approximates those activities we conventionally refer to as sports. The structure of such contests, Caillois proposes, reinforces the ethics of personal responsibility, in direct contrast to those games included in his second category, *alea*, wherein the players have no control, surrendering the destiny of their outcome to fate. The latter activities include all games for which the result relies predominently on chance and luck.

Caillois' third category of *mimicry* includes those games that rely on make believe, role playing and invention, while the fourth he calls *ilinx*, the Greek term meaning vertigo or disorientation. In games of this type, the participants seek to experience sensations that destroy the stability of normal perceptions through activities such as jumping, spinning, tumbling and climbing. Such contemporary amusement-park pastimes as riding the roller-coaster as well as the more 'sports-like' recreations of skiing, hang gliding, diving and gymnastics would fall into this category.

This draws attention to one of the more obvious problems in applying Caillois' schema to modern sports. As Gruneau notes, a number of sports exhibit characteristics relevant to more than one category.[12] It becomes difficult to determine in relation to Caillois' taxonomy which aspect of a particular sport is the most predominant in determining its appeal to participants and spectators. The explanations offered for the presence of particular games waver between, on the one hand, the posited expression of innate psychological needs, motivations and essences and, on the other, a few unsystematic and unexplored sociological contingencies suggestive of possible social functions fulfilled by the presence of a particular 'rubric' in the culture.

Another approach to the problem, more firmly rooted in the empirical tradition of comparative anthropological studies, emerges in the work of Brian Sutton-Smith and John Roberts. After reviewing the available data collected from a large number of studies of tribal societies, they conclude that anthropological evidence so strongly supports the universality of games we should be highly sceptical of reports of cultures in which it is claimed none exist.[13] They propose a three-fold classificatory system consisting of (a) games of physical skill (b) games of strategy and (c) games of chance. Further, they suggest that the emergence of games of physical skill relates to environmental conditions that encourage 'mastery of self and the environment'. The presence of games of chance is related to the religious belief system, while tensions and hierarchies within the intra-group social system tend to be expressed through the development of games of strategy.[14] Again, such an interpretative framework has limited usefulness when applied to more complex modern societies in which all types of games appear to exist simultaneously.

Both of these approaches reinforce the notion that the rule-bound contest will emerge 'naturally' in any social grouping and would thus seem to be a cultural constant. The particular form that such activities will take, it is implied, will be specifically determined by the particular functional requirements for the maintenance of social subsystems and the integration of individuals and groups within the society's economic, religious and power structures. Furthermore, neither perspective seeks to posit any significant distinction between games and sports. Such a separation is seen to reflect the modern tendency to conceptually differentiate activities involving physical skills from other less strenuous forms of rule-bound contest.

However, contemporary sociologists of sport argue that the distinctions between the activites of play, games and sports *are* important and meaningful. Sport represents the transformation of play ('voluntary, non-utilitarian activity characterized by the freedom to innovate, by spontaneity and by a lack of externally imposed regulation') through games, being 'more rule-bound and formalized' activities incorporating elements of 'competition, skill, pretence, chance and vertigo' into a rigidly codified, highly regulated and institutionalised form of instrumental activity.[15] Furthermore, the contemporary nature of sport reflects the application of a number of broad tendencies associated with modern industrial society, notably rationalisation, specialisation, bureaucratisation and commercialisation, all of which undermine the element of play or effectively change its 'essence' as an unstructured, autonomous activity. The critical questions then focus on why and how these changes have come about.

At the risk of oversimplifying, the explanations provided are oriented around two contrasting theoretical assumptions about the nature of human social organisation which can be broadly characterised as the 'order' and the 'conflict' perspectives. In sociology, the order perspective has been most comprehensively articulated within the theoretical tradition of functionalism (as already noted also an influential explanatory paradigm in anthropology), an approach that has dominated the mainstream of the discipline for the major part of this century. As Gruneau has observed, from within this approach 'society is depicted as a natural boundary-maintaining system of action wherein individuals are shaped to existing patterns by virtue of the roles they are expected to play.' Consequently: 'The central problem of societies is system stability, thus transforming a concern for the *functions* and *dysfunctions* of particular units in the society into the major problem of sociological study'.[16]

Therefore, it is suggested that in pre-modern times particular games and pastimes found in any society occupied a training and socialising function for required military and economic skills (archery, shooting, unarmed combat, hunting, throwing the javelin—games requiring physical speed and agility) or were associated with religious rituals that symbolically integrated the social unit, legitimated hierarchical structures and expressively neutralised intragroup tensions and hostilities. From the functionalist viewpoint, the role of sport in contemporary society is metaphorically similar:

> It is one of the ways the social system integrates its increasingly differentiated components and one of the ways society socialises individuals into what is expected of them. Sport is thus said, among other things, to help in the formation of stable identities of personalities, and provide opportunities for tension release and for channelling aggression under socially sanctioned and controlled conditions. It is also said to be a means of integrating the elements of single institutions like schools, and of integrating the different institutions comprising the local community, and of harmonising potentially disruptive divisions in society.[17]

The diffusion of sport through society from above is seen as functional to the general movement extending democratic rights to the traditionally oppressed and underprivileged groups in society and, in the form of meritocratic professionalism, providing a viable avenue for upward social mobility for members of groups structurally disadvantaged by lack of access to capital and educational skills. So the very attributes that contribute to the particular nature of modern sport, namely increasing commercialisation, bureaucratisation and rationalisation operate together as a 'functional prerequisite, i.e. the very condition of its extension to the masses, and therefore the impingement of these phenomena on sport is not usually taken as problematic'.[18] Certain 'dysfunctions' of modern sport are recognised in the manifestations of hypercompetitiveness, violence, and overpoliticisation. But these are seen as pathological intrusions into sport that are capable of being contained and controlled through the responsible application of corrective moral pressures and socialisation techniques by sensitive educators, leading sporting role models and policy makers within the sporting establishments.

A very different interpretation of both the emergence of modern sport and the role of sport in contemporary society arises from an approach that is premised on the alternative conflict assumptions about society. While much of the work within this framework exhibits a broadly Marxist viewpoint, it also includes non-Marxist scholars who reject the functionalist postulates regarding, first, the essential self-stabilisation element inherent in any form of social organisation and, second, the presence of wide-spread consensus among the general populace on the central societal norms and values as the underlying mechanism maintaining social order. Rather, for those working within the conflict perspective, society is not an abstraction imposing its own powerful prerogatives, aims and needs on individual and group life but must always be conceived as a 'human construction' constituted and everchanging through the ongoing 'contested struggle between groups with opposed aims and perspectives'.[19] Against functionalism, the conflict theorists argue that the central premise of the former 'confuses the needs and interests of specific groups of people with the needs and interests of all . . .'[20] Whatever stability exists within a social system is based on the interactive combination of physical, psychological and moral coercion through which, in any historical epoch, the more powerful social groupings are able to maintain control of the central economic, political and cultural institutions within society and thereby shape the conditions of everyday life in a manner that is conducive to their group interests and world view.

There is a heavy emphasis, in keeping with Marxist tradition, on the critical role of the form of economic organisation overseeing the means of material production and distribution in, if not determining, then certainly limiting the possible shape and tenor of social and cultural life experienced by the entire populace. Therefore, any examination of a specific cultural phenomenon such as sport should be grounded in a sound understanding of the processes of social change that have resulted in the 'transcendence' of one historically specific economic 'mode of production', representing the struggle between dominant and oppositional groupings, by a succeeding form of social organisation in which new groups emerge, new realignments of forces develop and new cultural entities, consistent with these, take shape. Given this approach, the development of modern sport is considered in relation to the broad social developments that took place in European society between the sixteenth and nineteenth centuries, characterised as a transition between the feudal and the capitalist forms of social organisation, or by non-Marxists as the emergence of the modern industrial order.

Over three centuries the geographical and political expansion of capitalism has been associated with a number of important social trends. The first, directly connected with the movements of population out of rural and village life into cities and towns is generally identified by the term *urbanisation*. The growth of the existing urban centres and the establishment of new ones in accordance with the economic prerogatives of industrialism changed the demographic structure of Europe, then of the overseas colonies established by the European powers and finally, in this century, of those 'underdeveloped' regions of the world that only recently emerged from the domination of colonial control or had remained for various reasons resistant to industrial 'modernisation'.

Second, the authority of traditional religious beliefs and the temporal power of religious institutions was challenged by the growth of rational and scientific thought. The latter sought to demonstrate the facility of human beings to understand, interpret, manipulate and control the natural and physical environment for their own ends, without the necessity of positing supra-human or mystical explanations. This movement towards *secularisation* pushed religion and religious beliefs out of the centre of intellectual life and opened up the possibilities for theorising about society and politics without the constraints of theological premises.

Third, closely related to secularisation, came a generalised attack on traditional forms of political absolutism and increasing support for the principles of *democratisation*. By the seventeenth and eighteenth centuries, the political voice of the increasingly powerful industrial bourgeoisie, aided by a movement towards liberalism in philosophical and social thought, mounted a full-scale attack on monarchical and aristocratic authority that reached its watershed in the late eighteenth century with the successes of the American and French Revolutions. The institution of representative government organised along general democratic principles, if premised on a relatively narrow property-based franchise, became the conventional political orthodoxy eventually adopted by at least the 'progressive' elements within the bourgeoisie.

Fourth, *bureaucratic organisation* came to be seen as the most rational means of effective administration in both economic enterprise and public life. The growth of the civil service bureaucracy in the earliest industrialising societies actually preceded the movement towards representative government but was given a further impetus by the necessary development of an effective independent administrative apparatus for the democratic nation state. Bureaucratic procedures and organisational styles became increasingly more widely adopted within public and private institutions as well as in the large scale organisation of industry, commerce and trade. Indeed, writing at the beginning of this century, Max Weber concluded that it is the gradual extension of a bureaucratically based style of social organisation into all areas of social life, which in earlier centuries helped facilitate the successful rise of both the nation state and capitalism, that represents, more completely than the latter, the most significant, single characteristic distinguishing modern from pre-modern social formations.

Those adopting a conflict approach to the understanding of cultural phenomena would argue that all of these trends should not be understood merely as functional self-adjustments by an 'unseen hand', reflecting the survival 'needs' of an abstract 'social system' but as processes emerging from the uneven struggle between competing groups in society to structure economic, political and social conditions in a manner conducive to their general interests. In adopting a general conflict perspective in this book, it is therefore proposed that modern sport did not merely 'evolve' out of pre-modern folk games, rituals, regionalised group-based pastimes, but that its structure, social meaning and style of organisation were definitively shaped by influential groups in society in accordance with their group interests and their particular ideological and moral precepts. Such beliefs emanated from what we may identify as a 'naturalised' world view effectively propagated by the dominant bourgeois class in society, but generally represented by them as a rational and objective understanding of the underlying 'scientific' principles of economic, political and social order.

Sport and the rationalisation process in society

Underlying Max Weber's contention that the seminal process facilitating the transformation from pre-modern to modern society is the spread of the bureaucratic style throughout all levels of social organisation is the observation that such a form perfectly embodies and applies the principle of rationality that has become, over past centuries, the dominant source of validity for social thought and social action. Rationality, or the process of rationalisation, refers to the ability to determine the most effective and efficient means of reaching specified goals, a form of thought that Weber argues replaced the mystical and religious foundations of human understanding, providing, through its applications in science, technology, bureaucratic organisation and entrepreneurial capitalism, a powerful tool by the use of which 'man can gain mastery over nature and mastery over his own animal impulses'.[21]

However, as Weber also points out, while rationality, as manifested, for example, in the 'scientific method', embodies a technique to effectively achieve certain ends, it cannot be employed to 'objectively' determine the superiority of particular ends over others. Thus, as Marxist critics argue, the 'rationalisation' of industrial production spearheaded by the European bourgeoisie may have been incredibly successful in producing a dramatic increase in material wealth, but the form of social organisation constructed to serve this end embodied an 'exploitative rationality' at the expense of the mass of non-property owning wage labourers.[22]

Of major concern to the pioneers of capitalist industrial organisation was the securing of a reliable workforce to enable them to plan production schedules, meet marketing deadlines and establish effective cost-accounting procedures, all critical to the rationalising techniques 'making all the factors entering into the profit and loss equation subject to precise calculation and absolute control'.[23] This required a massive change in the traditional values affecting the individual's relationship to work. The struggle to develop effective 'labour discipline' had to fight against traditional rural work patterns established over many centuries and the general absence of social mores considering work a 'duty' or an expression of the human 'essence'.

In the main, work was considered an unpleasant burden necessary for survival, the routines for which were primarily determined by the natural agricultural rhythms of ploughing, planting, harvesting, milling and marketing. Even in the towns, it was difficult to persuade tradesmen or craftsmen to work regularly and continuously. Once the necessities of immediate material need had been taken care of, the urge to continue working dissipated rapidly, only to revive when lack of personal or family sustenance again threatened.

Furthermore, over the centuries, the typical pattern of the rural working year had become liberally scattered with numerous regular festivals, religious events, local fairs, wakes, not to mention other occasions for lengthy merry-making such as christenings, weddings, or the weekly Sunday holiday, such that, in the sixteenth and seventeenth centuries, non-working days constituted more than a third—sometimes up to a half—of the calendar year.[24]

From about 1500 onwards, social historians report a continuing widespread attack by 'respectable' groupings in society on the leisure patterns of the non-propertied classes.

In its earliest phase, this attack focused on the tradition of Carnival, the annual week or fortnight of pre-Lent merry-making that, in Catholic-dominated Western Europe, was celebrated by public gatherings attracted to the larger regional centres for the annual fairs and markets traditionally held during this period. As one of the few instances in the mediaeval year that occasioned the gathering of sizeable crowds, Carnival also became associated with occasional riots, disturbances, social protests and other attacks on 'public order'. This created increasing tensions and clashes with authorities as well as the attention of reformers led, in the early stages, by both Protestant and Catholic clerics who sought to eliminate the 'less desirable' manifestations of popular culture that emerged during Carnival celebrations. In the seventeenth century the position of the reformers was strengthened, particularly in England, by the austere moral attitudes adopted by the Puritans who vigorously opposed all forms of personal indulgence and licentiousness. This developed into a general hostility to most existing forms of popular recreation including public dancing, games and sport, all activities associated with both 'paganism' and 'over-indulgence'.

Consistent with such Puritan attitudes, a major aim of the reformers, it is suggested, was to proselytise the values associated with the Catholic and Protestant reformations to the 'upper echelons of the working class and to the peasants'.[25] The ethic being preached was 'one of decency, diligence, gravity, modesty, orderliness, prudence, reason, self-control, sobriety and thrift'.[26] While the success of the early reformers in inculcating such values into the consciousness and social behaviour of the labouring classes was, on evidence, somewhat limited, the general attack from above on popular leisure and recreation became both more urgent and more effective after 1650 when it became more closely tied to problems of industrial discipline and was taken up by 'moral reformers' from within the ranks of the rising bourgeoisie. The nature of the arguments against popular diversions became much broader, employing the logic of scientific rationality consistent with the new industrial ethic. To such men 'who especially valued industriousness, frugality and prudence, many of the traditional diversions were apt to appear scandalously self-indulgent and dissipated—wasteful of time, energy and money'.[27] While, as a religious movement, the severe moralism of Puritanism might have been rejected, 'many of its attitudes towards work and recreation survived' and 'were gradually incorporated into the orthodox thinking of educated society'.[28] If industry came to be considered a cardinal virtue then idleness was the most dangerous vice. The traditional calendar liberally dotted with 'antiquated' festivals and holidays legitimated the propensity towards idleness and dissipation. Both the amount of time taken away from work and the forms of recreation indulged in were seen as a 'threat of substantial proportions to steady and productive labour'.[29]

England and the birth of modern competitive sport

In Britain, by the middle of the eighteenth century, an authoritative view had emerged

> that annual holidays must be kept to a minimum, that unnecessary festivities — wakes, pleasure fairs, archaic rituals — should be reformed or eliminated; that boxing matches and other large assemblies should be curtailed; that public houses ought to be strictly regulated and prevented from offering recreational attractions.[30]

This attack on popular recreations was given further impetus by the rise, in the eighteenth century, of the Evangelical movement, which pursued a moral line on 'the evils of the flesh' not inconsistent with the earlier Puritan ethic. For the Evangelicals: 'Public assemblies for diversion were particularly suspect, for it was in these settings that temptations were most intense, the chances of contamination most likely, the sensual indulgences most extreme'.[31] They were very strong on the maintenance of the Sabbath and hostile to the use of public space on this day for games and sports. Overall they urged their followers to avoid public gatherings and elevated the home as the place for quiet recreation and spiritual contemplation. Methodism, the most prominent Evangelical sect, recruited strongly among the 'respectable' working class, actively combating the seductiveness of public entertainment by holding competing assemblies and prayer meetings.

Thus a number of forces combined in a concerted attack on the more 'objectionable' forms of public recreation indulged in by the poor. From the mid-eighteenth century, the authorities consistently began to use legislative power and legal authority to inhibit the practice of such activities as blood sports, street football and boxing. While at first these efforts were often far from successful, meeting with considerable popular resistance — in many cases the legal bans on activities were widely ignored — by the first half of the nineteenth century, the weight of persistent suppression and the imposition of harsh judicial penalties against offenders began to take their toll. Thus, for example, around 1830, in Birmingham:

> the police and magistrates had tried to suppress cock-fighting by seizing 40 spectators and tying them together with ropes, two by two. The men were then 'marched in procession through the principle streets of the town as an example, and then brought before the magistrates.' This kind of public humiliation suggests a

clash of cultures in which the victory of one culture over another was achieved more by force than by subtle means of acculturation.[32]

The class bias of the attack was most pronounced. The blood sports of the poor such as cock-fighting, bull-baiting and the 'pugilistic encounters' carried out in and around public houses suffered from the stern attention of the police and authorities, but parallel pastimes of the gentry such as hunting, horse-racing, prize-fighting and wrestling were left untouched. The rationale for this was that:

> Unlike the popular sports, genteel diversions had been incorporated into a code of sensibility and refined manners. Moreover, while fashionable pleasures were typically private, enjoyed within the confines of a personal estate, the amusements of the people were normally on public display, open to the view of delicate tastes, and consequently they were much more likely to violate the increasingly severe standards of public decorum.[33]

Concern with the control of public space contributed to the authoritative suppression of the numerous 'street football' games that had become traditional annual events in certain regions. In Derby, for example, the game, which took place over two days — Shrove Tuesday and Ash Wednesday — resisted Reformist attacks in 1731, 1746 and 1797, but was finally declared illegal by the Mayor in 1845.[34] The purposes of the town's streets were defined primarily in terms of benefits to ongoing trade and commerce which, the Mayor determined, have 'become of too much importance to be interrupted two days every year'.[35] In a gradual way all such 'unauthorised' usages of public space became prohibited so that:

> By the middle of the nineteenth century any kind of open space for recreation was very much at a premium. The custom of playing games on public thoroughfares was no longer tolerated; enclosure usually eliminated any public use of agricultural land; and the rapid growth of cities involved the appropriation of much open space, some of which had served as customary playgrounds, for commercial building.[36]

Thus, in England, a critical effect of the struggle to establish 'labour discipline' was an authoritative intrusion into the leisure patterns of the working class and a concerted attempt to eliminate cultural patterns considered by the dominant class inappropriate to the sort of public order and control necessary for 'social progress'. However, the extent of resistance to the repressive techniques employed strengthened the arguments that were becoming increasingly prominent among some of the more 'enlightened' within the bourgeoisie, that it was essential to make adequate provisions (meaning acceptable activities and the appropriate public space in which they could be undertaken) for the leisure pursuits of the working class. There emerged increasing pressures for positive action. It was felt that the combination of the workers' cramped living conditions and the systematic campaign to restrict the usage of public space might feed the simmering political dissatisfactions increasingly evident within the working class and contribute to the feared outbreak of serious social unrest.

Increasingly, more members of the middle class became 'alarmed at this process and guilty at their own class's role in bringing it about. They sought to create a new kind of public leisure to counteract it'.[37] In this they were joined by a substantial segment within the working class, particularly those influenced by the moral exhortations of the Evangelical movement, seeking to eliminate the 'debauched' tendencies in the popular culture of their peers. It was considered that the emphasis on excessive drinking, gambling, dancing, vicious and vulgar sports, apart from being offensive to their religious convictions, actively contributed to the widespread misery and poverty experienced by the working class, prevented the majority from improving their material and social position in society, and contributed to the dominant class's lack of sympathy to their needs. While the Puritan ethic, or at least its religious and secular successors, might be most securely rooted in the moral ethos intrinsic to, and championed by, the industrial bourgeoisie, by the nineteenth century its influence had effectively penetrated the social values and beliefs of a significant portion of the 'respectable' working class.

In Britain, from the 1830s onwards, leading representatives of both groups directed their energies towards what has become known as the 'rational recreation' movement.

Rational recreation was an attempt to forge more effective behavioural constraints in leisure. Popular recreations were to be improved, not through repression, but through the operation of superior counter-attractions. Within the new controlled environments, reformers would instruct workingmen in the elementary accomplishment of social economy — time-budgeting and money management — and introduce them to the satisfactions of mental recreation, thus immunising them against the contagion of the pub and the publican, and the animal regression of 'sensuality'.[38]

The 'counter-attractions' devised by the reformers included the promotion of workers' clubs, meeting-houses, public libraries and reading rooms, nature walks, the opening up of parks to the public. These were seen as avenues through which the poorer classes could partake of leisure activities that were 'uplifting', thereby stimulating intellectual improvement, and most importantly, keeping them away from the clutches of the publican. Despite some moderate successes, the bulk of the population to whom such activities were directed showed little enthusiasm to participate, often reacting against the paternalistic spirit with which the movement was imbued and finding little pleasurable for them in the activities being provided. The emphasis on temperance was particularly resented, but pehaps more so the earnest didacticism with which the middle-class organisers approached their task.

Implicit in the doctrines of the reformers, and understandably creating much resentment and hostility towards the movement by many among those they sought to reform, was the assumption that recreation which was 'rational' meant activities that involved public supervision and control by representatives of the middle class.

Apart from the recognisable resistance by a majority of the working class to the paternalism and 'wowserism' the rational recreation movement displayed, there had also developed significant commercial and entrepreneurial interests who sought to cater to — some would suggest exploit — more down-to-earth popular leisure pursuits and who had no motivation or desire whatsoever to 'reform' the morals or tastes of their potential customers.

With the decline of rural-based cultural traditions, the process of increasing authoritative control over the use of urban space and the limited appeal of the proselytising call to rational recreation, the rising influence of the commercial entrepreneur of popular entertainment comes increasingly to the fore. The prototype of this new breed of businessman was the publican. The dominant role of the English public house as the focal point of working class social life by the eighteenth and early nineteenth centuries is well documented. An old workman recalling conditions in industrial Yorkshire of the 1830s commented that of the places available to spend one's leisure time, church, chapel or ale house, 'the former were seldom open, while the latter was seldom closed. The first was not attractive, the second was made attractive'.[39]

In order to promote an increase in clientele, the publican provided space in and around the establishment for an enormous variety of diversions and social activities. Games and contests such as bowling, quoiting and pugilistic encounters featured prominently. But the pubs also became venues for 'glee clubs ... amateur and professional dramatics, fruit and vegetable shows, flower shows, sweepstake clubs and the meetings of trade and friendly societies.'[40] Although not in any systematic manner, the publicans were among the earliest promoters of modern sports events including occasional prize-fights and 'pedestrianism' — a somewhat crude form of 'street athletics' that flourished briefly in the first part of the nineteenth century. But with the competition from the 'rational recreationists', the pubs began to turn more to paid entertainers, some expanding into 'singing saloons' and later vaudeville music halls.

It is in this general context that we must place the development of the modern form of organised sport. While the major focus of rational recreation was directed at reforming the leisure habits of the lower orders, the movement's general principles might also be applied towards establishing more effective social control over other troublesome groups in Victorian England, notably the middle and upper class boys attending the public schools. While originally founded with the aim of providing free education to boys from the poorer classes, during the eighteenth century the public schools increasingly became the preserve of the male offspring of the 'landed gentry, the aristocracy and associated professional groups. By 1780, they had become essentially upper-class institutions with the poor virtually excluded.'[41]

Around this time, serious disciplinary problems manifested themselves in these schools. A primary reason, it has been suggested, was that the legitimacy of the authority of the teaching and administrative staff was seriously challenged by the boys who contemptuously rejected direction by those they considered their social inferiors. Between 1770 and 1820 there were a number of instances of open rebellion at the leading public schools. The situation was considered serious enough for the army to be called in at Rugby in 1797, and again at Winchester in 1818, where the authorities called in the militia armed with bayonets to quell a riot and regain control of the school.[42] The de facto power structure within the schools placed the oldest and strongest boys at the top, exerting a crude but effective arbitrary authority over the rest, particularly the youngest who were treated as 'fags', or personal servants, and often forced, at the whim of their 'masters', to suffer cruel and painful indignities. Nowhere was the hierarchy more clearly evidenced than in the playing of football, an activity frequently indulged in at the schools—particularly as many of the older boys rarely bothered to attend classes.

Each school had its own version of football, the basics for which were drawn from one or other of the regional folk games, but adapted to suit the particular physical and social circumstances, so that a form of game specifically identified with each institution began to evolve. From all reports, similar to the folk games from which they derived, the public schools' versions of football had few rules and generally consisted of two groups of boys contesting with each other to move a ball in one direction or the other as a vague premise for engaging in extensive physical pummelling, gouging, kicking and wrestling. The older boys made football compulsory for all and directed the younger boys to play roles that subjected them to the greatest physical danger and likelihood of injury.

> The fags, sometimes as many as 200 on a side, were forced to 'keep goal' for their seniors. They were arranged along the base line where they were expected to prevent the ball from being driven across. This defensive role was compulsory for them and inherent in their status as fags. The prefects retained for themselves the prerogative of attack.[43]

The masters were uniformly hostile or, at best, indifferent to the playing of these games, but given the tenuous control they exerted, did little or nothing to suppress them.

The increasing dissatisfaction from teachers, administrators and outside parties—notably middle class parents—with the general breakdown of authority in the public schools led, by about 1830, to strong pressure for action. Some of the leading administrators proposed that reforming and controlling the boys' games might prove a productive avenue for reasserting more general control over the students. The games would be sanctioned by the school authorities, but changed so that they could function positively; that is, to both prevent excessive violent and destructive activity by the boys and as useful educational instruments for character training. For these purposes the brutal adaptations of folk games were quite unsuitable so the students would be encouraged to 'regularise their football, to commit the rules to writing and to develop more regular procedures for settling disputes'.[44] This strategy was adopted at a number of the major public schools between 1845 and 1862. As much as possible the directly aggressive 'fight' component in the games was modified so that football might become 'a form of group contest which provided as much as possible the pleasures of a real fight without its risks and dangers'.[45] The technique proved to be enormously successful with the newly structured games finding considerable support among students, teachers, administrators and parents associated with the public schools. But more importantly for the history of sport, the existence of 'civilised' rules changed the image of football and athleticism, thereby turning them into pursuits eminently suitable for gentlemen.

The reconstruction of sport in mid-nineteenth century Britain came at a time when there was rising public dissatisfaction with what was seen as the 'aristocratic mismanagement' of the Crimean War. There were fears of a declining physical prowess and fighting character in British manhood; and organised sport, as exemplified by the public school experiment, might be the appropriate means of restoring the positive masculine virtues against the insidious threats of 'tractarianism and effeminacy'. Sport, previously despised as the idle recreation of the aristocracy or the debauched brutality of the 'uncivilised classes' might now prove amenable to 'rational' application for the positive benefit of the respectable middle class and therefore, of course, for the nation.[46]

But, unlike the earlier endeavours to spread rational recreation to the working class, 'civilised sport' was at first perceived as a form of leisure more aptly suited to the bourgeoisie, as evidenced in their appropriation of cricket, 'hitherto a game for gentry and their servants or a knock-about recreation for self-employed Midland weavers'[47] and in their new-found enthusiasm for football. With respect to the latter, it is indeed ironic, as one writer notes, that 'the game which had been consistently stigmatised as socially inferior and regularly outlawed ... came to the assistance of the class which had traditionally done its best to prevent the playing of football'.[48]

The enthusiasm developed by the public-school lads for football was such that they organised 'old boys' clubs in order to continue playing beyond their school days. They soon sought to extend their participation by challenging each other to competitive matches. This created some difficulties as there were significant variations in the rules formulated at the different schools. In particular, Eton had introduced a rule forbidding players to touch the ball with their hands while Rugby stuck to a form that allowed handling and carrying. The other schools tended to more or less follow one or the other of these two codes. It was the game formulated at Eton that became the basis of soccer and led in 1863 to the founding of the Football Association and the creation of a common set of rules and principles agreed to by all clubs that had adopted some version of the Eton game. Rugby persisted with its own game and, together with a smaller number of the clubs organised around old boys from public schools playing a similar game, founded the Rugby Football Union in 1871 for the purposes of standardising and promoting their game as a distinctive alternative to the Etonion version of football.

It is important to note that despite its eminently 'rational' qualifications, there was little enthusiasm by the majority of the middle class leisure reformers to spread the new gospel of sport to the masses. On the contrary, the middle class founders and promoters of the 'new athleticism' fought quite strongly to keep the lower orders from infiltrating their new pastimes. Outside the rarified public school environment there was little encouragement or opportunity for the children of the working class to participate. As one social historian notes:

> The Clarendon report on public schools in 1861 had recognised the value of sport in character training, but in terms of the State's provision it was training reserved for the society's leaders not the led. Physical education for working-class children meant not games, but drill.[49]

This was further reinforced within the act that introduced universal secular education to Britain in 1870 which suggested that drill 'would provide industrial training for each new generation of the labour force and paramilitary training for a potential citizens' army'. It would help teachers control unruly classes, make efficient use of space and was popular with children and their parents. Supplemented by occasional gymnastic exercises, one authority considered that this was all the working class children needed 'in as much as, after an early age, they have little or no time for recreation [un]like those socially above them'.[50]

In the adult world, working class involvement in sport was severely inhibited by the elaborate emphasis placed on amateurism. The Amateur Athletic Club formed in 1866 to promote 'gentlemanly' exercise and competition specified that the term amateur excluded anyone who had competed for prizes or money, taught or trained others in athletic skills for money 'or is a mechanic, artisan or labourer'.[51] Any member of the latter groups was also restricted from participating in other newly formed sporting associations of the period notably the Amateur Rowing Association and the Bicycle Union. The public rationales provided for such policies argued, first, that those who engaged in physical labour would have an unfair advantage in competition and, second, that recreation should be in direct contrast to regular work so 'the leisure needs of the muscular workman were best served by mental rather than physical exercise'.[52]

The middle class enthusiasts wished to separate their sports in both content and in style from the 'rude' contests engaged in by the urban masses, unpleasantly tarnished by professionalism, gambling and chicanery. Cricket, still predominantly a rural sport, provided a notable exception. Here the feudal values of the manor were maintained by allowing 'players', meaning a few of the more talented working-class cricketers, who received payment for their skills, to play alongside the 'gentlemen'. Such intermingling of the classes was, of course, restricted solely to the playing field itself.

A small number among the reformers certainly did recommend the advantages of physical exercise to the working classes. However, unlike the other avenues promoted by the rational recreation movement, actively, they did very little to provide opportunities for the workers to participate. Among the latter, many showed an enthusiasm and interest in the new sports and sought to organise their own competitions. At least until 1870, the only major institution to offer substantial assistance was the Church. A number of athletically minded churchmen argued in favour of promoting sports among their working class congregations, particularly as this might be effective in attracting new adherents. They endeavoured to provide the necessary facilities such as Church-owned lands and buildings for use by the congregation to play competitive sport and encouraged the formation of sporting clubs under the Church's patronage.

'Muscular Christian' and 'Christian Socialist' priests, many of them educated at public schools, played a central role in the diffusion of Rugby and Association Football to the working classes. They regarded them as means of moral and physical salvation, as activities which would help the denizens of slums to become strong and physically healthy and to develop traits of character which would enable them to improve their miserable lot. Indeed, many of the new, working-class clubs founded after 1870—some of them the ancestors of present-day professional teams—were founded by Muscular Christian and Christian Socialist priests in association with church or chapel.[53]

As an indication of the significance of church patronage for working class entry into football, in 1885, twenty-five of 112 football clubs in Liverpool had religious connections, and this trend was replicated in other industrial cities in the north.[54] Similarly, it is reported that in 1867, a third of the cricket clubs in Bolton were connected to a religious body.[55]

Other avenues for working class participation in sport opened up after 1870. Organisations such as YMCAs, friendly societies, Workingmen's Clubs, as well as public houses, schools and employers responded more positively to working class pressure for opportunities to play organised sport by sponsoring or otherwise materially assisting in the foundation of new clubs.

Despite the publicly stated emphasis on the wholesome, healthy and character-building attributes of sport, football, and many of the other sports initially most attractive to workers, incorporated aggressive, vigorous and combative elements spiced with direct physical clashes. Such inbuilt characteristics allowed significant variation in the way a sport could be played and there were strong indications that working class football incorporated tougher physical clashes and more frequent brawling than its middle class counterpart. Football, particularly the Association style, proved most popular with the workers, especially in the north of England. The early dominance of the game by public school old boys was challenged—especially after the establishment of the Football Association Cup in 1871 allowed the workers' clubs to compete in open competition, and in a short space of time, consistently defeat their middle class opponents. After 1880 the middle class presence in English soccer rapidly receded. The signs of incipient professionalism intruded, especially in the northern clubs, and—after a half-hearted attempt by the Association to outlaw paid players collapsed—was officially sanctioned in 1885. The public schools and their sporting affiliates hastily abandoned soccer and switched their allegiance to rugby.

In the interim the middle-class passion for organised physical competition produced an interest in new games such as lawn tennis and yachting, as well as a renewed enthusiasm for modernised forms of older ones such as cricket and golf. For a while these proved to be safer havens for the amateur ideal and could more effectively screen out the participation of the lower orders.

Thus, with the aid of an institutional socialising structure represented by the public school system, the middle class operated as a
collective cultural entrepreneur promoting a form of physical activity
that presented an opportunity for individuals to develop and hone
certain expressive and combative skills; that provided adequate satisfaction for outdoor recreation within controllable urban spaces; that
remained consistent with dominant social values such as discipline,
hierarchy, competition, personal achievement and group identification; and yet had intrinsic appeal to a significant segment within
all social classes. The new form of sport which they created incorporated many of the rationalistic and egalitarian principles consistent
with that combination of political liberalism and *laissez-faire* capitalism
that formed the ideological constellation adhered to by the dominant
groups of nineteenth century British society.

An important, though not the sole, source of the appeal of sport lay
in the 'doctrine of fair play' and in the universalistic premises under-
scoring the rules of competition. In contrast to the old sports, rationalised sport was 'now a laboratory in which men could test themselves
under precise and uniform rules, not an arena where... men were
incited to "outrage nature"'.[56] Modern sport subjected participants to
strict institutionalised control and authority; it glorified the ethic of
competitive striving and purposive rational activity towards a goal; it
exemplified the positivistic notions of physical and mental exertion,
the disciplined control of both body and pysche; it emphasised symbolic and personal satisfactions of success in activities not constrained
by structural inequalities, such as class, wealth, education or social
power; in team sports, it offered sources of communal sociability and
identification; and not least importantly, it provided an alternative
hierarchy of esteem, achievement, material and status rewards that in
no way threatened or challenged the existing economic, political and
social order. With such an attractive combination of diverse attributes,
this collective cultural creation of mid-nineteenth century Britain
rapidly established itself as the basic model for the universal organisation of modern competitive sports.

Notes

1 Kenneth L. Schmitz, 'Sport and Play: Suspension of the Ordinary', in
Ellen W. Gerber (ed.) *Sport and the Body: A Philosophical Symposium*, Lea
& Febiger, Philadelphia, 1972, p. 28.
2 Johan Huizinga, 'The Nature of Play', in Gerber (ed.) p. 57.
3 Johan Huizinga, 'The Play Element in Contemporary Sport', in Eric
Dunning (ed.), *Sport: Readings from a Sociological Perspective*, Frank Cass
& Co., London, 1971, p. 14.
4 Schmitz, p. 31.
5 Neil H. Cheek, Jr. and William R. Burch, Jr., *The Social Organisation of
Leisure in Human Society*, Harper & Row, New York, 1976, p. 222.

6 However, despite the idealistic halo that surrounds the modern view of sport in Ancient Greece, historical evidence suggests that it was neither free from politics nor professionalism. Winners at the ancient Olympic Games received a substantial monetary prize in addition to the symbolic laurel wreath. See Peter C. McIntosh, 'The Sociology of Sport in the Ancient World', in Günther R. F. Lüschen and George H. Sage (eds), *Handbook of Social Science of Sport*, Stipes Publishing Co., Champaign, Ill., 1981, pp 33–6.

7 Rene Maheu, 'Sport and Culture', *International Journal of Adult and Youth Education*, 14(4), 1962, p. 171.

8 Max Horkheimer, 'New Patterns in Social Relations', in E. Jokl and E. Simon (eds), *International Research in Sport and Physical Education*, Charles C. Thomas, Springfield, Ill., 1964, pp 184–5.

9 Raymond Williams, *Culture* Fontana, Glasgow, 1981, p. 13.

10 Günther Lüschen, 'Sociology of Sport and the Cross-Cultural Analysis of Sport and Games', in Günther Lüschen (ed.) *The Cross-Cultural Analysis of Sport and Games*, Stipes Publishing Co., Champaign, Ill., 1970, p. 7.

11 Roger Caillois, 'The Classification of Games', in Gerber (ed.), pp 36–43.

12 Richard S. Gruneau, 'Sport as an Area of Sociological Study: An Introduction to Major Themes and Perspectives', in Richard S. Gruneau and John G. Albinson (eds), *Canadian Sport: Sociological Perspectives*, Addison-Wesley, Don Mills, Ont., 1976, pp 16–17.

13 Brian Sutton-Smith, 'The Social Psychology and Anthropology of Play and Games', in Lüschen and Sage (eds) p. 461.

14 John M. Roberts, Malcolm J. Arth and Robert R. Bush, 'Games in Culture', in George H. Sage (ed.) *Sport and American Society*, 2nd edn, Addison-Wesley, Reading, Mass., 1974, p. 147.

15 Gruneau, p. 19.

16 Gruneau, p. 32.

17 John Hargreaves, 'Sport, Culture and Ideology', in Jennifer Hargreaves (ed.), *Sport, Culture and Ideology*, Routledge, London, 1982, pp 35–6.

18 Hargreaves, p. 36.

19 Gruneau, p. 32.

20 Hargreaves, p. 37.

21 Robert Goldman and John Wilson, 'The Rationalization of Leisure', *Politics and Society*, 7(2), 1977, p. 164.

22 As Richard Ashcraft observes, 'Weber's dichotomization of rational/irrational was itself the product of a specific view of rationality, one which was tied to and which provided the rationale for a particular socio-economic system, namely capitalism'. See, 'Marx and Weber on Liberalism as Bourgeois Ideology', *Comparative Studies in Society and History*, 14, 1972, p. 156 f.n.

23 Goldman and Wilson, p. 164.

24 It is reported that in the fourth century, under the administration of the Roman Empire, there were 175 officially designated non-working days each year. Even medieval craftsmen in Paris worked less than two hundred days each year. See Thomas M. Kando, *Leisure and Popular Culture in Transition*, C. V. Mosby Co., St Louis, 1975, pp 69–82. As one writer has observed: 'Estimates of annual and lifetime leisure suggest that the (contemporary) skilled urban worker may only have regained the position of

his thirteenth-century counterpart.' S. Parker, *The Sociology of Leisure*, George Allen & Unwin, London, 1976, p. 24.
25 Peter Burke, *Popular Culture in Early Modern Europe*, Temple Smith, London, 1978, p. 208.
26 Burke, p. 213.
27 Robert W. Malcolmson, *Popular Recreations in English Society 1700–1850*, Cambridge University Press, London, 1973, p. 89.
28 Malcolmson, p. 90.
29 Malcolmson, p. 94.
30 Malcolmson, p. 98.
31 Malcolmson, p. 103.
32 Keith Cunningham, *Leisure in the Industrial Revolution: c1780–c1880*, Croom Helm, London, 1980, p. 24.
33 Malcolmson, pp 155–6.
34 Anthony Delves, 'Popular Recreation and Social Conflict in Derby, 1800–1850', in Eileen Yeo and Stephen Yeo (eds), *Popular Culture and Class Conflict 1590–1914: Explorations in the History of Labour and Leisure*, Harvester Press, Sussex, 1981, p. 90.
35 Delves, p. 106.
36 Malcolmson, p. 109.
37 Cunningham, p. 76.
38 Peter Bailey, *Leisure and Class in Victorian England: Rational Recreation and the Contest for Control, 1830–1885*, Routledge, London, 1978, p. 170.
39 Bailey, p. 9.
40 Bailey, p. 9.
41 Eric Dunning, 'The Development of Modern Football', in Dunning (ed.), p. 135.
42 Dunning, pp 135–6.
43 Dunning, p. 136.
44 Dunning, p. 143.
45 Dunning, p. 144.
46 Cunningham, pp 110–17.
47 Cunningham, p. 113.
48 James Walvin, *The People's Game*, Allen Lane, London, 1975, p. 30.
49 Bailey, p. 130.
50 Bailey, pp 130–1.
51 Bailey, p. 131.
52 Bailey, p. 131.
53 Dunning, p. 147.
54 Walvin, p. 57.
55 Bailey, p. 137.
56 Bailey, p. 133.

2
The growth and institutionalisation of competitive sport

Alternative models

The competitive sports model so successfully implanted into the cultural mainstream of mass leisure and entertainment in nineteenth century Britain was not the only form of organised physical exercise to emerge at this time. An alternative approach evolved in Europe where the political turbulence and instability of the early nineteenth century saw the formation of first, the *Turner* movement in Germany and, shortly after, the *Sokol* movement in neighbouring Bohemia. Both sought to prepare and mobilise the populace to fight for national political independence through the organisation of clubs ostensibly devoted to gymnastic training.

The Turner movement was founded in 1811 by Friedrich Jahn, a professor at the University of Berlin, and an active propagandist for an emerging pan-German nationalism that sought political unification in the wake of the recent revolutionary and Napoleonic upheavals. Jahn was also a leading proponent of the concept of 'Volkstum', a term connoting the 'mystical, integral nationalism founded on the racial doctrine of a transcendental German "essence"'.[1] A central pillar of this view was that a strong united nation could only be forged by a virile and healthy populace and, towards this end, Jahn sought to mobilise and train the youth of Prussia through massed gymnastic exercises and displays. Apart from physically toughening young men in preparation for the military task of combating the Napoleonic armies, Jahn considered that both the 'participants and spectators alike would be awed by the massed formations of his followers, known as Turners, and feelings of patriotism and loyalty would be aroused'.[2]

While the post-Napoleonic period did not bring the sought after unification of the Germanic states, the Turner movement did establish a firm foothold in German popular culture, an effective advocate of a political ideology devoted to the development of massed gymnastics as the pathway to a strong, healthy and vital 'body politik'. Numerous Turner clubs propogated Jahn's philosophy throughout the German states, and significant support for the physical and spiritual benefits of gymnastic exercise and synchronised calisthenics began to emerge in other areas of Central and Northern Europe, particularly in Sweden. By the middle of the nineteenth century, organised gymnastic displays, presented in the form of regularly scheduled festivals ('Turnerfeste'), attracted participant clubs from all over Europe. German and Scandinavian emigrants carried the Turner philosophy with them to the United States and the clubs they formed there helped popularise group gymnastics and calisthenics as an adjunct and an alternative to competitive sports for the purposes of developing and maintaining physical health and bodily vigour.

In Prussia and the other Germanic states, the Turners continued to be closely linked to the political unification movement and remained dedicated to the rise of the German 'Volk' as a coherent military-political entity. They contributed significantly to the Prussian war effort against France in 1870–71, and with the subsequent establishment of a unified German state, 'they became one of the mainstays of the new imperial government of the Second Empire'.[3]

Strongly influenced and impressed by Jahn's ideas and by the popularity of the Turners, Miroslav Tyrs (1832–84), an art history professor in Prague, founded a pan-Slavic movement along similar lines, to be devoted to the aims of 'physical fitness and the reawakening of national consciousness'.[4] Originating in Bohemia, his organisation known as the *Sokols*, was committed to building a sense of national identity among the Slavic minority within the Austro-Hungarian empire.

> Denied political representation under the structure of the Austrian- and Hungarian-ruled state, the Sokols offered politically active Slavs an outlet for their energies. Mass gymnastics, colourful costumes, and lectures on national independence gave many Czechs a new meaning in their lives . . . Patriotism and physical fitness were the dominant themes of Sokol lectures.[5]

During the First World War, the Sokols found an opportunity to effectively pursue their cause. Thousands of movement members who had been drafted into the Austrian army deserted *en masse* and re-formed to fight on the allied side. They received their reward after the war when the government of the newly independent Czechoslovakian state provided the movement with generous financial assistance 'thus becoming the first modern government to officially endorse sports'.[6]

International diffusion of the British competitive sports model

However, despite the considerable support developing for the style of physical exercise advocated through the European gymnastics movements, it was the British version of competitive amateur sport that demonstrated the stronger popular appeal and took a firmer root, particularly in those countries advancing most rapidly towards industrialisation by the middle to the end of the nineteenth century. A useful guide to this process of diffusion is provided in Table 2.1 below which lists the founding dates of the national associations set up to administer eight of the earliest organised competitive sports in Great Britain, the USA, Germany and Sweden.

Table 2.1 Years in which national sports associations were founded

	Germany	USA	Sweden	Britain
Association football (soccer)	1900	–	1904	1863
Swimming	1887	1878	1904	1869
Cycling	1884	1880	1900	1878
Rowing	1883	1872	1904	1879
Skating	1888	1888	1904	1879
Athletics	1898	1888	1895	1880
Lawn Tennis	1902	1881	1906	1886
Skiing	1904	1904	1908	1903

Source: Peter McIntosh, *Sport in Society*, C. A. Watts Co., London, 1963.

In these, and in other countries, the bourgeoisie and the upper class pioneered the introduction of competitive sports, enthusiastically setting up the required organisations, clubs and competitions. The practice of competitive games became *de rigueur* at colleges and universities and as a leisure facility provided for members of private clubs — the preserves of the status conscious, well born and newly rich. Almost everywhere the 'English sports' were taken up within an organisational framework and style that followed closely that formulated in Great Britain with the concommitant emphasis on restricting participation to 'gentlemen amateurs'. In the sports listed in Table 2.1, apart from soccer, an affinity for which the British working class demonstrated from the 1880s onwards and which similarly became the sport of the 'masses' elsewhere, participation and organisational control remained firmly in the hands of the bourgeoisie (with a healthy representation of titled aristocrats) until well into the twentieth century.

The successful spread of the British competitive sports model was greatly enhanced by Britain's international position, both as the leading industrial nation and major imperial power. The social and cultural style associated with the British gentleman of the Victorian era served as an influential model flatteringly adopted by the rising bourgeoisie in many other countries.

A close identification was exhibited by the social and political elites of Britain's planted colonial dominions (Australia, New Zealand, Canada and South Africa) with the values, styles and customs fashionable 'back home'. It is not surprising then that this also included the enthusiastic adoption of many of the 'English sports'. As almost all of the leading administrative, professional and business positions in these colonies were filled by recent British immigrants, or descendants of earlier British settlers, family, business and cultural links with Britain remained close. For those whose wealth or station placed them within the colonial establishment, it became customary to send their sons to be educated at the leading British public schools and universities, from which they not infrequently returned eager to spread the new gospel of sports. Even in those outposts of the British Empire where a sizeable indigenous population vastly outnumbered the colonists, such as the Indian sub-continent, Africa and the West Indies, many aspects of middle-class British culture, including the newly established passion for sports, held out a strong socialising attraction to local elites, particularly to those recruited into administrative service by the colonial governments.

Further assisting the spread of competitive sport throughout the world was the ubiquitous presence of the British navy, British merchant ships, expatriate colonies of British traders, planters and entrepreneurs. For example, it is reported that soccer was first introduced to Latin America by British sailors in the 1860s. Despite the sport's early appearance in Brazil, 'for many years it was played only by employees of British and German firms who later were joined by a few young men from the country's upper class'. It was only towards the end of the century that soccer in Brazil, and elsewhere in Latin America, began to acquire a working class following.[7] This pattern was typical of the manner in which many of the new sporting codes, first formulated in nineteenth century Britain, were exported to other countries and also representative of the process whereby they became further disseminated throughout the receiving society.

But what was being internationally distributed here were not only specific sporting forms such as soccer, tennis, athletics, and so on, but a modern cultural ethos that vigorously expounded the positive social benefits of organised, rule-bound contests based on physical skills. The significance of the British contribution lay in the creation of a universal model for the organisation of competitive sport. In addition to the formal rules and organisational styles associated with particular sports, the British model presented an approach whereby any traditional game or pastime could be transformed into a legitimate sport. This required the application of certain principles which would make the game a goal-directed contest operating under formalised rules that seek to ensure *equality of conditions of competition for all participants*. It is perhaps this characteristic that most clearly differentiates modern sport from those sports-like activities present in tribal societies, practised in Greek or Roman civilisations or appearing in the Middle Ages, that in many conventional approaches to the history of sport are considered the direct precursors of contemporary games. While conditions of equal competition were not unknown, even in Greek and Roman times, as Guttman points out this was restricted to equality *within* each competition but not *across* competitions in the same sport.[8]

However, the natural localism of traditional games could be transcended by the modern approach that defined a sport in terms of a universalistic set of rules and conditions. So, if it followed the same set of precepts a game of soccer on the Argentinian pampas was essentially, at least in formal terms, the same cultural experience as a game of soccer in the suburbs of Manchester. Such a formality of structure provided a viable foundation for the development of an international hierarchy of competition in which the relative standing of individuals or teams in any sport might be 'objectively' evaluated.

Throughout the last decades of the nineteenth century, the British, and to a lesser extent the Americans, were at the forefront in codifying the rules to numerous games, some of which were adapted from indigenous pastimes, others based on activities first observed among peoples in other parts of the world, and a few, consciously invented by particular individuals, following the established guidelines of the universal sports model. Soccer, rugby and cricket are successful examples of the first type. Hockey, mountaineering and skiing, all of which had their origins elsewhere, were first formalised as sports in Britain. With regard to invented sports, a few notable examples are badminton, a game originating with English army officers stationed in India in the early 1870s; basketball which was formulated by a Canadian physical education student in 1891; and volleyball which was originated in 1895 'as an indoor sport for businessmen who found basketball too strenuous'.[9]

Hybrid sports were also constructed, often influenced by peculiar local conditions. Thus ice hockey combined skating with field hockey and produced an outdoor game that tends to be most popular in countries that generally experience long, cold winters. An indigenously Australian version of football was constructed in the 1850s, ostensibly to help cricketers keep fit during the winter. Water polo crossed swimming with the landbased team sports of soccer and polo.

In America the English games of rounders and rugby evolved into baseball and American gridiron respectively. With regard to the latter, while both soccer and rugby were played in mid-nineteenth century America, a former student at the English Rugby School who entered Yale University in 1873 is credited with creating a revived interest in the rugby style of football and popularising it with his classmates. Because of certain cultural differences the American college boys found in the English game 'many uncertain and knotty points' in the rules 'which caused much trouble in their game, especially as they had no traditions, or older or more experienced players to whom they could turn for the necessary explanations'.[10] Thus, the process of tinkering with the basic structure of rugby eventually produced grid-iron football, first a college and subsequently professional sport that has proved enormously popular in North America, while neither soccer nor rugby developed a significant following there.

At this point it might be useful to digress somewhat and outline a few of the more pertinent aspects associated with the parallel growth of organised sport in the United States up to the latter part of the nineteenth century. In the early years of European settlement, the religious and moral Puritanism that influenced the British and European attitudes to leisure and popular amusements were also important in forming basic authoritative attitudes to sport and games in the American colonies.

However, as was the case in England, the Puritans' ability to effectively enforce such a dour lifestyle in North America, except among their most faithful adherents, foundered very quickly. As one historian has observed, the effectiveness of Puritan controls had diminished by the mid-1600s and 'at no time after the very first years of settlement was the New England scene actually as devoid of all amusements as it is so often said to have been'.[11] However, the strength of Puritan attitudes remained a focal point for continuing hostility directed towards any diversionary pastimes that were considered 'unproductive' and, it has been suggested, this may have acted as an inhibitory barrier to the growth of sports in pre-nineteenth century America.[12]

From the middle of the eighteenth century there is evidence of the developing interest in exercise and sport. At this time a significant influence on American intellectual life, particularly with regard to educational views, derived from European sources, most notably Rousseau's *Emile*,[13] the writings of Pestalozzi and the German advocates of the gymnastic movements, the most prominent of whom, Johann Muths, was also the inspiration for Friedrich Jahn. In the early decades of the nineteenth century, American educators

travelling abroad visited Pestalozzi's Yverdun and Emmanuel Fellenberg's Hofwyl, where gymnastics and outdoor exercise were featured. The gymnastic movement gradually penetrated American school circles in the twenties as knowledge of Prussian educational reforms spread.[14]

The leading secondary schools and universities of the north-east eagerly embraced the practical teachings of the European advocates of gymnastic exercise, encouraging the building of facilities and the incorporation of physical training into the formal curriculum. In this they also found strong support among the medical profession, some of whom even went so far as to advocate the positive benefits of exercise for young women.[15]

There is evidence to suggest that the American enthusiasm for gymnastic drill had begun to wane by the 1840s. But concern for the nation's physical vitality found a new outlet in competitive games. The general development of competitive sport, though less comprehensively organised than in Britain, certainly began to take off in America at this time.

> Rowing clubs in Boston, New York, Philadelphia, Savannah, and Detroit; throngs attending thoroughbred racing and trotting; matches between runners, pedestrians, and prize fighters; formation of numerous hunting and fishing clubs; sailing and yachting clubs in Atlantic coastal communities and on the Great Lakes; adoption of mass football, gymnastics, cricket, or crew at eastern colleges — all bore witness to the sporting fever.[16]

But, as with soccer in Britain, it was the development of a populist sport — one that had little initial association with the influential elitist minority centred in the eastern educational establishments — namely, baseball, that served as the focus for the significant spread of competitive sport that took place in late nineteenth century America.

The origins of baseball can be traced to the seventeenth and eighteenth century bat and ball game known, in one of its variants, as rounders or townball (also a direct predecessor of cricket), which, as a game called 'base', was already popular prior to the American revolution. But as a game with the rules and structure of its contemporary form, baseball emerged in the early 1830s. The first formal baseball organisation appeared with the founding of the Knickerbocker Club by a group of New York businessmen in 1842.[17]

Similar to the rational recreation movement in Britain, but with a less didactic interpretation of the term rational, the early supporters of baseball in America included those who sought to morally reform mass recreation: 'The promoters of baseball were among those who campaigned for the suppression of cockfighting, gambling and dog-fighting and presented their own game as a suitable alternative both for working men and the middle classes'.[18]

However, baseball's early popularity and the prospects of attracting paying spectators — the first recorded game with gate receipts took place in 1858 — also stimulated the immediate interest of businessmen and entrepreneurs.[19] Businessmen entered the organisation of baseball by promoting amateur clubs and giving their employees time off to play for them. Some considered that this was beneficial to their business as it 'provided cheap advertising, and improved labour-management relations'.[20] As greater benefits accrued to the bene-factors of winning teams this consideration stimulated the early move towards the professionalisation of players. Despite the initial ban on payments, by 1869 all leading clubs had some players who were receiving surreptitious remuneration, and the practice of enclosing grounds to increase takings from gate receipts was well underway.

The trend after 1869 was for groups of capitalists to withdraw their support from the amateur and company teams, to develop city-wide teams, often sponsored by joint-stock companies.

The larger and more ambitious plans of the business groups proved advantageous for a number of reasons. A businessman in Cincinatti, for example, could get more publicity by promoting a city team rather than concentrating on his own company team. Through sponsorship of the city team his products were given nationwide exposure, while at home his civic involvement in the development of his own region was emphasised; he appeared as a civic booster. It was for these considerations rather than from the idea of profits in the game itself that the first openly professional team, the Red Stockings, was formed in Cincinatti in 1869. Among its founders were most of the city's leading businessmen, including the proprietor of the largest sporting goods firm in the West, George B. Allard. 'Glory', said one merchant upon the return of the Red Stockings after their unprecedented eastern tour on which they were undefeated, 'they've advertised the city, sir, advertised us, sir, and help(ed) our business, sir'.[21]

The immediate success of the Red Stockings in Cincinatti did not pass unnoticed by businessmen in other cities. A year later, the first professional team in Chicago was financed by that city's Board of Trade. In the six years to 1876, a number of other cities followed the trend, but the rapid switch to professionalism was financially risky as eleven of the twenty-five major professional teams formed during this period folded within a year. 'The reported cause of this massive financial failure was high salary payments to entice players away from semi-professional and other professional clubs.'[22] Throughout this period, players were centrally involved in the administration and business decisions of the clubs, but in 1876, a new organisation calling itself the National Baseball League, led by businessmen and entre-preneurs, set about reorganising baseball on a professional *and* a commercial basis. This organisation, still in existence today, totally dominated major baseball until the end of the nineteenth century and established an important principle in the commercial operation of spectator sport — 'separating the playing of the game from its manage-ment and ownership'.[23] They wrested control of the game from the players by introducing the 'reserve rule' whereby any club that first contracted a player could prevent that player from accepting employment with another club, thereby successfully eroding the players' bargaining position over salaries.

While maintaining a strong interest in securing financial profitability, the businessmen controlling baseball also exhibited a strong concern with the moral and national significance of the sport. In this they were supported by the nation's press as evidenced when 'a string of editorials all over the country greeted the arrival of business-dominated baseball as a means of promoting morality in America's national game'.[24] Contrary to the beliefs accompanying the British approach that treated professionalism as corrupting and unworthy of sport's primary role as a vehicle of social discipline and character training for young gentlemen, 'Americans welcomed the domination of money'. Consistent with the institutionalisation of *laissez faire* political and economic beliefs, the business community vigorously supported by the press championed 'free contractual relations and a career open to talent. Provided the influence of money on sport was, like everything else in the society, subject to the discipline of market forces, only good could result'.[25]

Professional baseball certainly proved to be a financially successful operation as the National Baseball League 'achieved unparalleled commercial success in the 1880's'.[26] The example of baseball encouraged entrepreneurs and skilled practitioners of other sports in North America to develop their commercial potential leading to the introduction of professionalism in grid-iron football, ice hockey, basketball, golf and bowling, all between 1894 and 1903.[27]

Thus, by the end of the nineteenth century, competitive sport had become firmly institutionalised as a popular cultural form 'naturally' suited to the structural characteristics of modern industrial society. The benefits of regular physical exercise, both for the individual and for society in general, to the goals of developing a stronger healthier population, better able to cope with the stresses and challenges of modern life, had received increasingly widespread intellectual support from within the liberal, rationalist movements that, from the middle of the eighteenth century onwards, provided influential theoretical paradigms for Western philosophy, education and science. The linking of such ideas to broader political concerns had produced both the European gymnastics movement and the pedagogic principles that elevated the importance of physical training to a vital component of the formal educational curriculum.

The process of transforming a feudalistic rural society into an urban industrial capitalist society, in which Britain was at the forefront, required, from the point of view of the bourgeois class that had risen to power, the creation of industrial discipline and social order consistent with a capitalist organisation of production. The perceived need to overcome the traditional attitudes and values relating to both work and

leisure resulted in campaigns to reconstruct the lifestyle of the wage
labouring 'masses', and through a combination of authoritative control
and persuasion, to socialise the latter into adopting the cultural mores
deemed to be 'rational', and 'civilised'—not surprisingly the very
characteristics considered to be best exemplified in the values and
lifestyle of the middle class. While the intellectual and literary based
approach of the rational recreation movement met with some resistance from the working class, the competitive sport movement that
grew out of the middle class public schools provided more substantial
appeal. If the code of the gentleman amateur proved to be somewhat
alien to the 'lower orders', the physical aggressiveness, partisanship,
group identification and masculine vigour inherent in team sports such
as soccer found fertile ground. The elements of rule-boundedness,
equality of conditions of competition, competitive struggle and institutionalised control could be accommodated to—although with considerable variation in style and emphasis—by both middle and working class cultures.

Competitive sport, more comprehensively than gymnastic drill,
incorporated the authoritative concerns regarding the need for regular
physical exercise, for the general improvement in the health and
muscular capacity of the workforce which might improve productive
output, and for ensuring a better standard of military preparedness
among the youth of the nation. As such, it contained most of the
positive attributes described by the gymnastic training movement but
was more flexible, taking many different game forms; more dynamic,
in its directly agonistic basis; more indigenous, in the sense that it
drew on widely known traditional games and pastimes; and, overtly at
least, detached from broader political concerns.

But it was the elements of competition and the unpredictability of
outcome of any particular contest that greatly expanded the potential
spectator interest in sport. Competition within the rules of the game
focused the physical activity of all the participants upon the goal of
victory. Unlike many traditional and tribal games in which the result
is often preordained by social ritual,[28] modern competitive sport is
designed to establish hierarchies of success, to encourage invidious
comparisons among competitors and to establish the absolute superiority of one individual or team over others. As such, competitive sport is
available as a direct index of achievement level and as a metaphor for
broader hierarchical ranking of individuals, communities, racial
groups and nations. The early linkage of sporting abilities with strength,
masculine virility and, in team sports, collective achievement inevitably loaded upon sporting contests a broader symbolic significance
that encouraged partisan support and attracted spectatorship. A central
appeal of the sporting contest to spectators was that for each new
competitive confrontation the opponents began their struggle afresh
with a blank scoreboard. Such formally structured equality of op-

portunity for success, generally absent from most other social endeavours, aroused the curiosity and involvement of spectators, stimulating renewed interest or partisan hopes with each new confrontation. It also presented attractive opportunities for gambling on the possible outcome, an activity that has long been associated with any kind of structured competition.

The creation of institutionalised teams, of fixtures and competitions, all stimulated spectatorship further. The formalisation of rules limiting participation to a specific number of players in each team encouraged competition between aspirants in the refinement of skills in order to secure a regular place in the side. In British soccer and American baseball, teams took their identities from their local communities from which they also tended to draw most of their players and supporters. Regular contests against teams from other communities generated substantial interest and partisanship. Each sport became associated with a fixed period in the year during which, every second weekend or so, the local team played a 'home' game. Following the fortunes of the community team became the basis of a regular social activity, an outdoor entertainment event, an acceptable way to spend some of the weekend leisure hours. A general shortening of working hours—in particular the institution of the Saturday half-day holiday—made Saturday afternoons the most appropriate time for scheduling major sporting events, thus avoiding a direct confrontation with the restrictive Sabbath laws. The growth of metropolitan and inter-city transportation made it possible for supporters to follow some or all of their teams' 'away' games. While participation in sport was overwhelmingly a masculine activity in the nineteenth century, spectatorship could be a family affair, and the major team sports certainly developed a considerable following among women and children.

Institutional and political support in the growth of competitive sport

The latter half of the nineteenth century was a period in which competitive sport entrenched itself securely in the cultural mainstream of industrial society. Throughout this process of diffusion, sport was greatly assisted by the institutional support it received from a number of critical sources.

Initially, the general support for both physical training and later for competitive sport by the educational systems in the leading industrialising societies was of vital significance. The establishment of universal education, as an obligation of the state to its citizens, emerged as an important political priority across the ideological spectrum. Full-time formal schooling for all children for a minimum of six to eight years became the established norm. This expansion of education from privately funded institutions catering, in the main, to the elite and middle class segments of the population, stimulated the rapid emergence of a body of trained professionals to staff and administer schools and to determine the appropriate curricula. From the end of the eighteenth century, the growth in support for physical training in the formal educational curricula of the established private schools, academies and universities, and the positive experiments with competitive sport in the British public schools ensured a fairly uncontroversial acceptance that such activities should be incorporated into any universalised system of education.

Thus, by the late nineteenth century, almost every young boy was provided with the opportunity to participate in competitive sport through the educational curriculum. Development of the physical skills required was encouraged and in some cases formally taught. Interschool competitions in various sports soon developed and with these a keen rivalry for success. Most notably in American high schools and colleges, sport took on an important social and economic role. The institution's success in certain sports competitions enhanced the status of the school in the eyes of the community, attracted support (attendance at games, financial donations) and reflected favourably on the social standing participating students achieved among their peers. Among other benefits, educational administrators and policy makers considered the inclusion of popular sports in the curriculum a useful tool of social control and cultural socialisation. Thus, for example they saw 'baseball as a means of communicating ideas of teamwork, discipline, efficiency, and competition among the young, especially among the vast numbers of immigrant children who entered or were born in the United States in the period 1900–20'.[29]

While the more popular sports such as soccer and football were considered inappropriate for girls, there were pressures to develop more suitable sports so that they too could participate. Even if they did not become involved in competitive sports, girls were required to partake of some physical exercise, generally in the form of calisthenics or gymnastics. From the outset, there was a strongly held taboo against 'mixed sport', although girls were sometimes allowed to participate in some of the more 'genteel' sports — those not requiring bodily contact — but only in competition with other girls.[30]

The underlying masculinity and physical aggression central to many of the more popular sports together with the muscular toughening supposedly derived from regular participation attracted strong support for organised competitive sport within military organisations. The outward resemblance of many pre-industrial games to mock military encounters, as already mentioned, also helped to create a strong natural affinity between the goals of military training and the discipline of focused physical aggression present in the structure of certain sports. The growing popularity of contact sports, most notably the various codes of football, found further support in the military as a suitable peacetime activity for young men sequestered in an institutional all-male environment. More popular among some officers and most enlisted men than traditional drill-type physical training, competitive sport supplemented the former as well as diverting aggressiveness and heightened desire for physical confrontation into activities believed to promote the military virtues of tenacity, ferociousness, collective endeavour, team discipline, positive group morale, strategic and tactical resourcefulness and the ultimate goal of all combat activity—comprehensively vanquishing the opposition.

The nineteenth century was redolent with organised collective aggression as manifested in the growth of regional nationalism and the jockeying for colonial expansion among the European powers. There were also ominous threats to internal order as evidenced by the wave of 'revolts' that swept Western Europe in 1848 and the general rise of revolutionary socialist and anarchist movements. For each nation or political movement, military strength and readiness for combat were important concerns so any form of activity that might prove beneficial to the increase of physical prowess found strong support. The pioneering role of Britain in the promotion of competitive sport was duly noted and admired by the political and military leadership of both its allies and rival powers. A commonly articulated belief attributed imperial success, in no small part to the physical and mental advantages that a strong sporting culture made to the fighting capabilities of the British military services. For example, in 1895, an English sporting paper cited 'an eminent German military authority' who reportedly

> offered the opinion that it [football] satisfies a craving which renders conscription unnecessary in this country. It does not make trained soldiers of our young men, it is true, but it enhances in them the spirit of pluck, opposition, competition, never-know-when-they-are beaten, never-say-die, play up Wednesday or United kind of feeling, which tends to the greatness of our national character.[31]

Thus, competitive sport found willing and enthusiastic patronage among the military. As competitive sports spread from country to country the military were invariably among the first institutions to organise teams, provide facilities and equipment and encourage the participation of the troops in such activities. In England a number of clubs in the infant football association originated in military installations. The American military enthusiastically took to grid-iron football when it started to become popular in the late nineteenth century, and the annual contest between the Army and the Navy—the teams being drawn from the cadets at the officer training institution associated with each branch of the service—became a highlight of the season, and still remains a prestigious event in the American sporting calendar.

A number of sports, more directly associated with nineteenth century military training, such as fencing, equestrian contests, modern pentathalon, rifle and pistol shooting, still draw a substantial proportion of their participants from the career military personnel in many countries who continue to practise what are now considered somewhat antiquated arts of combat. Thus, overall, military organisations everywhere, regardless of the level of industrial organisation or political culture of the society, have provided significant institutional strongholds of support for both the principles and the practice of competitive sports.

The important institutional role played by religious organisations in the diffusion of competitive sport may at first appear contradictory considering what has already been observed regarding the Christian Church's theological antipathy to idle diversions and amusements and the longstanding hostility to sport exhibited by a number of the non-conformist Protestant sects. One of the earliest manifestations of organised sport—the Hellenic tradition of the quadrienniel Olympiad—which had been celebrated continuously for more than a millenium, was prohibited by the Emperor Theodosios in 394 AD, just three years after he had adopted the Christian religion as the official creed of the Roman empire. The English Puritan movement of the seventeenth century entered into a protracted conflict with King James I over his Book of Sports (1618) which listed and encouraged the practice of certain games in the realm. The Puritans' hostility was so intense that while they held brief political power during the English revolution they had the Book of Sports publicly burned by the common hangman.[32] Similar attitudes to sport were exhibited in the Puritan dominated American colonies throughout the early years of settlement.

However, it has been suggested that the hostility to sport by reformist Protestantism was not directed towards the physical training aspect but, rather, to its traditional association with amusement, brutality, licentiousness, gambling and the desecration of the Sabbath. Thus, Meyer argues that,

> the Puritans' attitude towards the human body and towards physical training had been basically positive, that Puritanism had antagonized only the corruption of physical training, and that Puritanism had played an important part in the development and forming of physical training.[33]

In the Puritan ethos, physical training should not be an end in itself, but rather a relaxant from work and a means 'to get the "physical desires" under the control of mind and soul and to lead man away from sin'.[34] In this sense there was nothing in Protestant theology, even of the Puritan or Calvinist variety, that would be opposed to the precepts of the German Turner movement in which physical training was to be put to work for the political and spiritual salvation of the

'Volk', or of the more idealised expression of the British competitive sports movement that aimed to develop strength, character and discipline in youth through organised games.

Outside certain of the fundamentalist sects, the nineteenth century Churches—both Protestant and Catholic—saw little evil in the new competitive sports and indeed found them to be theologically and socially more acceptable than most of the indigenous leisure pastimes attractive to their working class parishioners—gambling, drinking, brawling and blood sports. By encouraging the formation of sports clubs under the patronage of the Church, they sought to maintain or even expand Church attendance in their parishes and to exercise some authority over the manner in which sport was played. Particularly, as already noted, the Churches' positive involvement in sport was welcomed by working class congregations. It provided one of the few avenues of their participation, given the reluctance by the gentlemen's clubs to facilitate inter-class social mingling.

The Churches' acceptance that sport should be accommodated to, and might even enhance a good Christian life, is further evidenced by the general support given by most mainstream Protestant denominations for the YMCA and YWCA movements, both founded in the United States in the 1850s. As a loose network of localised branches catering specifically to young people, the movement sought to attract youth by providing in their centres facilities and organisers for sports programmes. While they were also involved in other activities such as hostels, summer camps and study groups on religious and general themes, sports became a pivotal focus through which the movement helped to promote a healthy life based on Christian values and ideals. Its growth into an international organisation has proceeded through a generally non-didactic, low-key approach to religious matters together with the movement's continuing strong emphasis on sport and social welfare.

The Catholic Church has, in general, taken a more flexible position on leisure and amusement from that of the Protestant denominations. While it had participated in the suppression of the more licentious and brutal aspects of popular culture in the post-Reformation period, the Catholic Church, through its elaborate educational system, and at the level of local parishes, has happily accommodated to the popularity of competitive sport and provided enthusiastic institutional patronage for the widespread growth of sporting subcultures.[35]

The role of the state and formal political institutions in the growth and spread of competitive sport is an indirect but generally positive one. The enthusiasm for the personal, social and national benefits of competitive sport that manifested itself through such significant secondary institutions as the education system, the military and religious bodies was provided greater force and legitimacy by the ideological and occasionally practical support evinced by politicians and public administrators of the more industrially developed societies at local, regional and national levels.

Governmental support and assistance to the playing of competitive sport came under the general rubric of providing public facilities for leisure and recreation, akin to the establishment of zoological gardens, public parks, playgrounds, swimming pools and consistent with the commitment of public land and monies for the provision of more cerebral cultural venues such as museums, art galleries, concert halls and libraries.

As in the early stages most sporting competitions were fairly localised, the direct contributions took the form of leasing or donating sections of public lands for use as sporting fields. Also, through the medium of government funded schools, sporting facilities and equipment for use in educational institutions were incorporated into budgets and planning. As commercialisation entered top-level sporting competitions and they expanded into national leagues, entrepreneurs took some advantage from the benign acceptance by local authorities that there were broad economic and social benefits to having a major sports team located in their city or region. They benefited through the granting of lease subsidies, reduction or elimination of tax requirements, provision of roadworks and public transportation for ease of access to the arenas and other financial arrangements contributing to the economic viability of both non-profit and commercial sports leagues.[36]

With the emergence of international sporting competitions, stimulated by the establishment in 1894 of the Olympic movement, national governments became more directly involved in sport. Throughout the twentieth century success on the sporting field has more and more come to represent an index of national strength and a vindication of the ideological validity of competing political systems. Governments have assigned enormous amounts of money and resources towards developing top-level competitors through the setting up of coaching programmes, sports institutes, training camps, grants, subsidies and international trips for sports officials and competitors in the belief that international sports successes will be reflected in the boosting of the 'national morale', increased economic productivity and the solidifying of popular support for the regime or political party associated with any rise in fortunes on the international sporting field.[37]

Sport in the twentieth century — the creation of an international sporting culture

By the year 1900, competitive sport had emerged as a youthful but vigorous transnational cultural entity with well entrenched roots and significant institutionalised support. In the process of its emergence throughout the nineteenth century, sport had spawned a number of major structural variants, each of which continues to have its adherents and critics and each of which has been subject to significant further development throughout this century. The three major streams may usefully be identified as: 1 the participatory amateur concept of sport; 2 sport as high level professionalised display — commercialised, spectator entertainment; and 3 sport within the socialist movement.

Participatory amateur sport

In a reappropriation of the Classical Greek ideal of sport as an avenue to self cultivation, the British formulated the modern amateur ethos. In the high-born literary and cultural environment of the Public Schools and Oxbridge from within which modern sport was championed, competitive games had meaningful value only if they were undertaken purely for their own sake, for the joy of participation and the challenge of refining one's physical skills and prowess. Any obsessive concern with victory at all costs or the notion of receiving monetary reward for sporting performance were denigrated as unworthy of 'true sportsmen', and most certainly of the true gentlemen. As it was invariably those who identified strongly with this conceptualisation of sport who were at the forefront of the processes of codification and organisation of competitive games in the late nineteenth century, it is not surprising that such a perspective predominated and that the numerous clubs, competitions, tournaments and leagues that were created around each sport in Britain and in other countries were firmly committed to amateurism.

It was certainly out of this amateur ethos in sport that the Olympic Games movement emerged and to which it owed its allegiance. It is well documented that the French aristocrat, Pierre de Coubertin, credited with being the 'founder' of the modern Olympic movement, was greatly impressed with the role sport played in the British public schools. He attributed an important causal role to sport both for Britain's imperial successes and the superior 'moral climate' he considered existed in Britain in contrast to France. The Baron de Coubertin's somewhat monomanic endeavours led to delegates from fourteen nations convening at the Sorbonne in 1894 to formulate a programme for the revival of the classical Olympiad. Ostensibly, the idea of a periodic international sports festival was presented as a positive avenue for improving international harmony and goodwill. But the Baron was apparently also concerned with mobilising support for his belief that a greater emphasis on sport would assist in the task of revitalising the national fortunes of France, recently suffering from the aftermath of military defeat in the Franco-Prussian war, political instability and a depressed economic climate. Significantly, no delegates from Germany were invited to attend the founding conference of the Olympic movement.[38]

However, Germany was one of thirteen nations represented by competitors at the first Olympic Games of the modern era held in Athens in 1896. Of the 311 participants, 230 came from the home country.[39] The competitive programme of the first Olympic Games provides a rough guide to those amateur sports that already had established a sound organisational base in a number of countries by the end of the nineteenth century. The heaviest programme was in track and field athletics, followed by gymnastics, which had developed a competitive format, despite the longstanding opposition to this from the hard-core of the European Turner clubs. The seven other sports included were cycling, shooting, swimming, wrestling, fencing, weightlifting and tennis. Notable for its absence was soccer, a sport already 'tainted' with professionalism and a predominantly working class following, neither of which endeared it to the group of well-born sporting 'purists' who made up the founding committee of the Olympic movement. However the extensive popularity of this sport and the desire to expand the base for competitors to secure the continuation of the Olympics saw soccer, along with seven other sports added to the list for the second Games held in Paris in 1900.

The Olympic Games have continued to be an international focus for the amateur sports movement throughout this century. The Games have operated continuously at four-yearly intervals, except during the two world wars. The number of sports has steadily increased (although a few included in early Olympics have been dropped) as has the number of nations and competitors participating. By the twenty-third Olympiad in Los Angeles in 1984 there were 8000 competitors representing 140 nations in twenty-four sports.

The Olympic movement has also operated as a stern, self-appointed, institutional guardian of the nineteenth century amateur ideal. The original strict guidelines laid down for eligibility to Olympic competition exclude from participation anyone who has received direct monetary recompense as the result of their involvement with any sport at any time. This concept of the amateur was conceived in an era when competitive sport was dominated by the middle class gentleman and has persisted despite the significant social changes that have taken place since. As one writer has pointedly observed, 'By and large the line between amateur and professional is mainly a line between the unpaid members of a privileged class and the paid members of an under-privileged class'.[40] The extension across class lines of the opportunity to participate in most sports, the increased intensity of competition requiring extensive years of training and preparation to even qualify for Olympic selection, the organised mobilisation in a number of countries of scientific, medical and political resources devoted to the task of producing top-level sporting performances and the substantial commercial enterprises that have developed around sport have together persistently operated to subvert the original amateur ideal. Enrolments in educational institutions, military or government paid jobs, nominal employment by sporting goods firms, media organisations or businesses with some financial involvement in sports have been used as convenient devices for 'officially' maintaining the amateur status of promising sportspersons, while in reality allowing them to focus most of their time and energies on refining their competitive abilities.

Until recently the Olympic movement through most of the national amateur sports associations affiliated with it attempted to police the regulations and effect punitive measures against the most blatant violations of the amateur code—most notably in instances of competitors receiving payment for displaying manufacturer's names on clothing and equipment—on occasion banning the offender from further participation in amateur competition or even, in a few celebrated cases, stripping them of medals or championships already awarded. However, the institutionalised subversion of the amateur rules, most blatantly, but not exclusively, practised in the socialist countries put pressure on the amateur movement to retreat from its position of uncompromising hostility to the encroaching commercialisation of amateur sport in the West. They have now almost completely capitulated. The rules have been amended so that a sportsperson can now nominally remain an amateur, but still accumulate commercial payments or endorsements, so long as such earnings are deposited in a trust fund administered by a recognised amateur sports organisation. The athlete may withdraw 'essential living and training expenses', the remainder to be claimed by the recipient after he or she retires from active competition.

Outside the Olympic movement, a number of amateur sports developed large spectator followings for regular or top level contests and the profits from gate money in these circumstances applied towards subsidising or covering participants' personal costs (equipment and travel), general overheads (venue rental, maintenance, publicity) and other aspects determined by the administrators to assist in the promotion of the sport, such as junior development programmes, paid coaches and officials and general administration costs. For certain sports that remained nominally amateur, but still capable of consistently drawing large paying crowds to their events, most notably athletics and tennis, it became common knowledge that sizeable 'under-the-table' payments were made to outstanding competitors whose publicised presence in a contest was likely to bring more paying customers through the gates.

Thus gradually, despite persisting with the increasingly more meaningless distinction between amateurism and professionalism in

high-level sport, the organisation and administration of amateur competition (outside the socialist countries), from local club level right
through to the pinnacle of the Olympic Games have become increasingly intertwined with marketing and commercial organisations. In
recent years, it has become the conventional wisdom in the international sports community to actively co-operate by negotiating with
commercial interests for the sale of almost every marketable aspect of
sporting competition. While amateur sport, being an activity that
entails economic costs, has always required some method of raising
finance, this has traditionally relied upon the direct contributions of
participants and supporters at the local level, with the assistance of
administrators of publicly owned resources and occasionally private
benefactors. With regard to the latter two sources, assistance was
usually provided primarily because those concerned held generally
positive beliefs about the social and/or moral benefits of sport to the
community, although in some instances support was calculated to
bring with it reciprocal benefits that flowed back to those offering
financial aid—in the form of political support or increased business.
However, the establishment of top-level sport as a form of spectator
entertainment generating substantial income, particularly as demonstrated by the increasing popularity and financial success of commercially oriented professional sport, have become influential factors
enticing the organisers of amateur sport in a similar direction.

As, particularly since the 1950s, the cost associated with the staging
of large-scale sports festivals such as the Olympic Games escalated, the
capital expenditure required began to grow beyond the public resources of even larger cities. However, the indirect returns to the host
city and country as manifested in the inevitable stimulation to the
construction industries, tourism, a variety of business interests and
more recently, television royalties, make the Olympics a mouth-
wateringly attractive entrepreneurial venture. After the financial de-
bacle of the Montreal Olympics in 1976, which almost sent the host
city into bankruptcy, the International Olympic Federation agreed to
hand over the financial organisation of the 1984 games in Los Angeles
to private enterprise. According to published reports from the committee responsible for administering the event, as a business venture
the Games made a profit of around two hundred million dollars.[41]

The almost total commercialisation of the Olympics, together with
the *de facto* professionalism of a substantial proportion of the competitors, suggests that the direction of top-level amateur sport will
continue to become increasingly governed by the forces and interests
that dominate the professional sport it has for so long despised as mere
'vulgar entertainment'. At the time of writing (early in 1986) the
executive board of the International Olympic Committee has publicly
supported a proposal to 'throw open' both the summer and winter
Games to 'all athletes'—which would effectively hammer the last nail

into the coffin of the concept of amateurism in top-level sport.[42]

But the vestiges of the nineteenth century amateur ideal remain alive among those millions of individuals throughout the world who participate in organised competitions at local club levels in an enormous variety of codified sports. Throughout the century this kind of participation in sport has grown to become, internationally, one of the most popular forms of recreational activity—a source of sociability, a means of regular physical exercise, a socially sanctioned avenue for self expression, for non-vocational achievement, for the release of physical aggression and the application of competitive striving.

However, central to this somewhat diffuse international sporting culture, providing it with an important source of meaning as a worthwhile social activity, lies the extensive infrastructure of high-achievement sport. To those involved with the latter, the primary goal is the quest for continuously improved performances by the more proficient participants who have filtered through a complex hierarchical structure of graded competition. Almost everywhere, the meritocratic process of selection, training and competition is highly organised in order to identify, encourage and channel those with potential ability through the well institutionalised structures, towards the pinnacle of international success represented by victory in the Olympic Games or the regularly scheduled regional and world championships now operating for many sports.

That such high-level competitions arouse considerable spectator interest, which in turn can be significantly boosted through modern mass communication technologies—most effectively television—has encouraged increased entrepreneurial growth within high-achievement sport. The marketing potential of such sport, (notably the commercial entertainment value of the sporting spectacle) has substantially changed the economic relationships between sporting organisations, competitors, spectators and the business world. These trends will be elaborated in subsequent chapters. At this point it is sufficient to note the distance that amateur sport has moved from its foundations in the middle of the nineteenth century. One of the major reasons for this shift has been the parallel development of sport as commercial entertainment practised by paid professionals. It is to a brief examination of this process, since the end of the nineteenth century that we will now turn.

Sport as high level professionalised display

If the British were largely responsible for the ethos, codification and diffusion of competitive sport as an amateur pastime, then certainly the locus for the expansion of professional sport in this century has been the United States. Professionalism in sport existed prior to the modern era, even, according to historians, in ancient Greece and

Rome. Also, in nineteenth century Britain, horse-racing provided employment for trainers and jockeys; cricket had paid professionals playing alongside gentlemen amateurs; and soccer rapidly moved towards a fully professional game at the highest level of competition by the last decade of the century.[43] However, even well into this century, professionalism was only disdainfully tolerated in Britain. It was accepted as an unfortunate necessity once working class involvement in sport brought in individuals whose background and lifestyle encouraged them to seek a modest recompense for cultivating sporting skills as an avenue of economic survival far preferable to almost any alternative form of employment open to them. As evidenced by the turning away of the middle class from soccer at the time it started to become increasingly dominated by working class teams and supporters and increasingly professionalised, it was a widely held belief that the value and authenticity of the sport quickly dissipated once it began to be played not purely for its moral and social benefits, but as a medium of entertainment and as a form of paid work. Furthermore, as most English soccer clubs were strongly rooted in working class communities who provided the gate-money from which professionals were paid, there was little scope or interest in entrepreneurial activity beyond the necessities for maintaining a successful team and paying salaries and expenses. The imposition of maximum wage payments by the Football Association and the residual control by the original employer over a player's services severely limited the potential for commerical expansion or exploitation of professional soccer in Britain until well after the Second World War. This situation was similar in other countries in Europe and Latin America where, until well into the latter half of this century, soccer was one of the few popular sports able to develop even a rudimentary professional basis.

But in the United States, there existed both a notable absence of authoritatively held cultural values that would discourage the growth of commercialised sport, together with a number of social circumstances that proved extremely supportive. In a society without a hereditary aristocratic class, a founding doctrine of egalitarianism and a strong ethic supporting economic development through free entrepreneurial activity, the rapid industrial expansion, massive immigration and urban growth after the Civil War facilitated the rise and expansion of new forms of commercialised leisure. A decline in working hours,[44] together with a rise in the real living standards of the workforce attracted business capital into the provision of popular entertainment economically rationalised on a national scale. In the late nineteenth century there was a significant increase in the number of travelling circuses, vaudeville, variety and repertory theatres. Astute 'leisure entrepreneurs' began to organise these into regional or national touring companies to maximise revenue. Professional sport, as evidenced by the success of the National Baseball League demonstrated a further avenue in the entrepreneurial competition for the consumer's 'leisure dollar'. Indeed the game was so successful for its backers that a rival American Baseball League was formed in the early 1900s.

Clearly the very emergence of modern professional sport and the extent of remuneration sportsmen could expect to receive was closely tied to the costs/income relationship associated with the running of particular sporting competitions or contests. The capacity of arenas, the social class attracted as spectators to particular sports, the overhead costs associated with the sport were the primary factors determining the potential income of sporting professionals. Certainly, until the 1960s, with the notable exception of a few 'superstars' in team sports and the occasional highly successful golfer, boxer, or jockey, a sports professional might expect, at best, an income approximating that of a well paid skilled manual worker or perhaps a low level white-collar employee.

Where commercial interests were not so prominent, notably the more popular spectator sports outside of North America, there developed a semi-professional format through which participants received an established payment per game played. Such a system meant that due to the seasonal nature of most team sports, the modest game payments received, and the insecurity of a variable income, most regular players also maintained other forms of employment, training and playing outside normal working hours. Yet, in North America by the first decade of the century, even relatively minor sports whose popularity was restricted to one geographical region were able to organise fully professionalised competitions. Thus, professional grid-iron football 'emerged in the mining and mill towns of Ohio and Pennsylvania in the late nineteenth century',[45] while ice hockey, extremely popular in Canada, was able to organise a professional competition incorporating teams based in Toronto and Montreal with a few centred in the larger American cities of the north-east where the game had evolved a reasonable following.

The steady increase in attendance at tertiary institutions assisted the growth of professional sport providing a training ground for recruits to the professional ranks. The colleges built huge stadiums for their football teams further escalating the popularity of the sport and providing the base for another wave of expansion of professional sport in the 1920s.

The salience of professional sport was greatly enhanced by the attention paid to it by the popular media. First newspapers, then radio and television, involved themselves significantly in the coverage of popular sport, and in the American context this meant an equal if not greater emphasis on the professional team sports than the college or predominantly amateur competitions. In the main, the moral and social distinctions in sport between amateur and professional were considered of little significance in North America. Those operating professional teams in major sports leagues understood the importance of ensuring there could be no serious accusations of immorality or lack of authenticity in the contests. Baseball had become so well enshrined as the national sport that the scandal surrounding the alleged 'fixing' of a crucial game in the 1919 World Series stimulated the appointment of a respected jurist to the position of the first independent Commissioner of Baseball, an action designed to assure the public that the moral rectitude of the professional game would be strictly monitored in the future.[46]

The boom years of the 1920s saw the consolidation of professionalism in what has come to be known as the four major team sports in North America — baseball, football, basketball and ice-hockey. The number and home location of teams making up each of the professional leagues and regional divisions established during this period remained fairly stable until the 1950s. Considering the general economic and social turmoil associated with the Depression and Second World War, spectator support for the major professional leagues was maintained (and in some cases steadily increased) sufficiently to allow them to remain viable as economic enterprises.

A number of individual sports also developed a spectator subculture large enough to support a growing core of practitioners able to make a full-time living exhibiting their skills. Golf, at which professionals had participated since 1894, began to develop a substantial following among the wealthier segment of the population. Despite its British origins, it was the growth in American support for the game that resulted in a greatly expanded tournament schedule that placed the United States firmly at the centre of the international golfing world.

A similar structure has developed in tennis. Despite the existence of a few professional players as far back as 1926, the sport was dominated by the national tournaments of the major tennis playing nations, all controlled by amateur bodies, and the institution of an annual internations amateur competition — the Davis Cup — in 1900. In the 1950s a more concerted effort to establish tennis as a professional sport was mounted by the American Jack Kramer (himself a former champion player), who recruited many of the leading amateur players of the time — predominantly Americans and Australians — to join his touring troupe playing exhibition matches around the world. The continuing drift of the best amateur players into the professional ranks affected the stature of major tournaments such as Wimbledon and the US Open, and placed increasing pressure on the International Tennis Federation to allow professionals to compete against amateurs as had been the case in golf for some time. This was achieved in 1968 resulting in the rapid total professionalisation of top level tennis. Spectator interest also benefited from a concomitant change in the previously elitist image of tennis in the United States, that helped transform it in the 1970s into a fashionable popular pastime. Similar to golf, entrepreneurial efforts in the United States have established an elaborate network of lucrative tournaments and exhibitions that attract professional competitors from all parts of the world. The international popularity of golf and tennis has stimulated the worldwide growth of professionalism in these sports with tournaments staged in Europe, Australia and Asia supplementing those in the United States, establishing a year round international calendar of professional events. Also, it is only in these two sports that women as participants have made any substantial inroads into the world of professional sport, with the establishment of a parallel international circuit of women's tournaments.

A number of the more populist sports, notably boxing and wrestling, have a long history of participants competing for prize money. This has generally been the result of entrepreneurial enterprise on a contest by contest basis. Historically, the greatest spectator interest has been in the heavy-weight division in which title holders have become international celebrities as well as earning substantial purses. Once again, American entrepreneurs have been at the forefront in promoting top-level boxing matches, and American fighters have dominated the heavier weight classes for most of the century. Even when the presence of a non-American participant in a championship bout makes it attractive to schedule a contest in another country, American based financial and promotional interests are often involved. Outside of the United States the fortunes of professional boxing as a commercially viable sport have risen and fallen together with the number of world ranked boxers emerging from any particular country. This is a general pattern repeated in many sports, particularly individual sports lacking the structure of competitive leagues that provide an inherent continuity for team games once they are securely established within a local or national culture.

Over the past twenty years or so, commercialisation and professionalisation of sport in Europe has advanced significantly. This has occurred in certain sports such as soccer, road cycling and alpine skiing that have always had a more extensive following in Europe than in North America. It has also occasionally become viable in some locally indigenous games previously played at an amateur or semi-professional level and also, in some countries in the internationally popular sports of basketball, baseball, ice hockey, tennis and golf. In most instances the entrepreneurial principles and organisational techniques pioneered in the United States have operated as prime examples and dominant commercial models.[47]

Sport and the socialist movement

The rise of modern competitive sport occurred at around the same time the politics of Europe were becoming increasingly polarised around the growing interest and support engendered by the theories and programmes of the socialist movement. The writings and political activities of Karl Marx, together with his long time associate Friedrich Engels, were at the forefront of a devastating critique directed against the exploitative and antihumanist characteristics they proposed lay at the root of the historical processes associated with industrialisation.

From the Marxist perspective the capitalist class not only determined the direction and organisation of economic production but also legitimated their social dominance through authoratitive control of the society's leading institutions—political, cultural and ideological. Therefore not only work but leisure in capitalist societies reflected a structure designed to maintain the existing class system and the economic exploitation of the many by the few.[48]

The leading socialist intellectuals and activists of the nineteenth century gave little consideration to the 'problem' of competitive sports. The bourgeois origins of modern sport, its affirmation of the Social Darwinist ethic of competitive struggle, its association with racialism and nationalism, the support provided by business, the military, education systems and the state placed it squarely in the category of 'capitalist culture', seducing the workers away from their real concerns and diverting them from the ranks of the socialist struggle. In the orthodox Marxist vision of the society that will replace capitalism,

> work and physical recreation will merge, or...work will be elevated to the plane of recreation by the removal of the yokes of specialisation and compulsion. But Marx evidently did not envisage recreation under communism as simply games—rather as a fusion of work-like activities with play. In this, he affirmed a principle criterion of playful activities, namely, that they were freely chosen and are pursued for their inherent pleasure rather than for practical results.[49]

However, the organisations committed to actively propelling capitalist societies towards some form of socialism were forced to confront the fact that the working class was demonstrating an enormous attraction for competitive sport both as participants and spectators. Furthermore, industrialists and businessmen in Europe, Britain, North America and Australia began to offer beneficient inducements to their workers in the form of patronising their participation in sports.[50]

In response to such endeavours, and as an acknowledgement by some segments within socialist and labour organisations that the issue of sport must be directly confronted, from the last decade of the nineteenth century onwards, most prominently in Western Europe but also in Britain and North America, emerged the Workers Sport Movement. Growing slowly but steadily before the First World War, socialist organisations and trade unions in a number of countries became directly involved in setting up and assisting workers' sports clubs through which, it was hoped, the opportunity for physical exercise and friendly competition would be provided within a framework that differed from, and was openly critical of 'capitalist sport'. The growth of commercial sport, still then in its infancy, was seen as the major target for socialist vilification.

While the socialist critique of commercial/professional sport ironically echoed that coming from the middle class proponents of amateurism, its rationale was based on a deep suspicion of the ideological implications of competitive, high-achievement sport of any sort which, it was considered, effectively operated as a diversionary tool of the bourgeoisie. The guiding aims and philosophy of the Workers Sport Movement sought to salvage sport through an emphasis on those aspects that were consistent with a socialist programme.

> Not only did workers' sport seek to remove the class line from participation, it also sought to substitute socialist for capitalist values in the process and thereby help to lay the groundwork for a uniquely working-class culture. Such thinking contributed to the tendency within the movement prior to 1914 to emphasize less competitive physical activities such as gymnastics, cycling, hiking and swimming.[51]

However, an important shift towards competitive sport took place within the movement between the two world wars. A much greater emphasis was placed on team sports, which, it is suggested, represented 'a response to grassroots pressure from working people'.[52]

This shift, not coincidentally, paralleled that which took place within the Soviet Union between the time of the Bolshevik revolution in 1917 and the early 1930s. Attempts by some groups inside the Soviet Communist Party during the early years following the revolution to transform sport from the bourgeois competitive model to one emphasising physical health, a relationship to nature and the outdoors and to the benefits of the needs of labour were soon abandoned as party policy. The ideological debates within the party were swept aside and competitive sports, which had existed in a relatively undeveloped form prior to the revolution, were given official support by the party because it was felt that such a policy would have a number of immediate pragmatic benefits. Riordan notes the urgent need of the Soviet Union in the 1930s to achieve the following goals: develop physical fitness in the military, stimulate general improvements in health, create broader-based identities within and between Republics, ethnic and religious groupings, divert attention both from the oppressiveness of bureaucratic domination in politics and work and from the relative lack of material benefits in comparison to the West. All of these were important priorities that the party felt could usefully be served through the encouragement of competitive sport.[53]

In the West, the Socialist Workers' Sports International gained significantly in strength with the switch to competitive sports, claiming a worldwide membership in 1931 of over two million, including

350 000 women.[54] During the decade of the 1930s, there was a 'workers' Wimbledon as well as three workers' Olympiads, the latter organised as a 'counter to the chauvinistic tendencies of the more well known modern Olympic games and as an expression of international working-class solidarity'.[55] However, the labour sports movement suspended its operations during the Second World War and did not re-emerge after the war. Wheeler has suggested a number of reasons for this. First, the class barriers that had inhibited workers' participation in 'bourgeois' sports clubs had, by the 1940s, virtually disappeared. Public funding and media coverage heavily favoured the established organisations so that 'only the most class conscious workers would forego the "advantages" of the bourgeois world for the frequently second rate status of workers' sports'. Mainstream clubs lured away many of the better worker athletes with attractive financial inducements. There were still competing factions within the labour movement pushing different directions for sports. Some argued that the workers' clubs were not sufficiently raising the political consciousness of members, while others — notably in the anglo-saxon countries — desired less emphasis on politics.[56]

But basically the problem lay with the Workers Sport Movement from the point it accepted competitive team sports, embracing the constellation of cultural values implicit in bourgeois sport — achievement, records, spectacles, victory as the central goal of participation — while remaining at a disadvantage in mobilising support in competing with the institutionalised amateur and professional sports organisations. The latter had a longer history, established financial and cultural resources, the backing of government, business and the media, and ostensibly no overt connection with any particular political party or ideology. The practical reality facing working class people interested in participating in or watching sport was simply that labour sports seemed to be an inferior imitation of 'non-political' sports so they 'might be excused for choosing the latter with its higher quality facilities, teams and spectacle'.[57]

From the end of the Second World War, in the 'socialist bloc' countries, support for competitive sports have become a significant component of official social and cultural policy. In 1952, the Soviet Union entered the Olympic Games for the first time since the Bolshevik revolution, signalling a desire to participate in international sporting competition. Many of the socialist countries have placed the promotion of a sporting culture at the forefront of their internal priorities, most notably East Germany which, on the basis of recent international successes in a number of sports, has been widely acclaimed as the achiever of a modern 'sporting miracle'.[58] Even China, which, during the dominance of Mao Tse Tung, committed itself to an official policy on physical culture 'comparable to the early Bolshevik programmes of the 1920s' has since 1976 enthusiastically embraced competitive sport

effectively discarding almost all of the ideological constraints previously imposed by Maoism.[59]

Thus, ultimately, the sports model constructed in Britain in the
nineteenth century has swept all before it and emerged as a truly
universal modern cultural form. As Riordan has observed with regard
to the confluence of sporting trends in the socialist countries and the
West,

> there are today features of organised sport strikingly common to
> both socialist and capitalist societies. There are, of course, the very
> sports themselves. Together with these sports goes an elaborate
> system of government sports departments, giant amphitheatres,
> officials, trainers, semi- and full-time professional players, sports
> journalists and so on — even gambling establishments (for horse-
> racing, for example). A similar sports ideology in East and West
> cultivates irrational loyalties and ascribes similar prominence to the
> winning of victories, the setting of records and the collecting of
> trophies. Indeed the 'citius, altius, fortius' design has nowhere such
> an elaborate supporting system as in the socialist countries for
> spotting, nurturing and rewarding sports talent, with the aim of
> establishing world sporting supremacy.[60]

One consistent theme that emerges from this survey of the birth and
growth of modern competitive sport is the increasing shift away from
the Victorian ideals of individual participation and self-cultivation
towards the public exhibition of high-achievement sport as both a
universal vehicle of mass entertainment and a symbolic representation
of international political/ideological struggle. With regard to both of
these aspects, and intrinsically involved in the overall direction sport
has taken over the past half century or so, has been the importance of
the role played by the media of mass communications — as economic
industries in their own right, as organs of political socialisation at the
service of powerful interest groups, and as central disseminators of
values supportive of the processes of modernisation as rationalised
social progress. It is on the increasing interpenetration of the organised
establishments of sport and the mass media that the remainder of this
work will concentrate.

Notes

1 John M. Hoberman, *Sport and Political Ideology*, Heinemann, London,
  1984, pp 100–1.
2 Andrew Strenk, 'What Price Victory? The World of International Sports
  and Politics', *Annals of the American Academy of Political and Social Science*,
  445, 1979, p.134.
3 Strenk, p.135.
4 Strenk, p.136.

5 Strenk, p.136.
6 Strenk, p.136.
7 Claudio Veliz, 'A World Made in England', *Quadrant*, 27(3), March, 1983, p.12.
8 Allen Guttman, *From Ritual to Record*, Columbia University Press, New York, 1978, pp 42–4.
9 Veliz, p.13.
10 Walter Camp and Lorin F. Deland, *Football*, cited by David Reisman and Reuel Denney, 'Football in America: A Study in Culture Diffusion', in Eric Dunning (ed.), *Sport: Readings From a Sociological Perspective*, Frank Cass & Co., London, 1971, p.156.
11 Rhea Foster Dulles, 'In Detestation of Idleness', in George H. Sage (ed.), *Sport and American Society*, 2nd edn, Addison-Wesley, Reading, Mass., 1974, p.76.
12 R. Terry Furst, 'Social Change and the Commercialization of Professional Sports', *International Review of Sport Sociology*, 6, 1971, pp 159–60.
13 Peter McIntosh suggests that Rousseau's 'naturalistic' educational theories of the mid-eighteenth century were extremely influential in forming modern social attitudes towards the positive benefits of sport, as for example,

The training of the body, though most neglected is . . . the most important part of education not only for making children healthy and robust, but even more for the moral effect, which is generally neglected altogether or sought by teaching the child a number of pedantic precepts that are only so many mis-spent words.

Quoted in Peter C. McIntosh, *Sport in Society*, C.A. Watts & Co., London, 1963, p.54.
14 John R. Betts, 'Mind and Body in Early American Thought', *Journal of American History*, 54(3), 1967, p.792.
15 Betts, pp 798–9.
16 Betts, p.805.
17 Thomas M. Kando, *Leisure and Popular Culture in Transition*, C. V. Mosby Co., St Louis, 1975, p.209.
18 Ian Tyrell, 'Money and Morality: The Professionalization of American Baseball', in Richard Cashman and Michael McKernan (eds), *Sport: Money, Morality and the Media*, New South Wales University Press, NSW, 1980, p.87.
19 Kando, p.209.
20 Tyrell, p.88.
21 Tyrell, p.89.
22 Tyrell, p.90.
23 Tyrell, p.90.
24 Tyrell, p.91.
25 Tyrell, p.92.
26 Tyrell, p.92.
27 Furst, p.157.
28 As Claude Levi Strauss has observed, modern games or sports have a structure that is diametrically opposed to that of ritual in tribal societies. Rituals commence with assymetry and inequality of the participants but

result in the union of all. The ritual *resolves* tensions that existed between, for example, the sacred and the profane, the dead and the living, the initiated and the uninitiated, so that at the end, all pass to the 'winning' side. Modern games, on the other hand appear to have a *disjunctive* effect; they end in the establishment of a difference between players or teams, where before the contest they are assumed to be equal. See Claude Levi Strauss, *The Savage Mind*, Weidenfeld & Nicholson, 1966, p.32.

29 Tyrell, p.99.

30 Thus, the 'mixed doubles' competition in tournament tennis stands out as one of the rare instances where this taboo is breached.

31 Tony Mason, 'Football and the Workers in England: 1889–1914', Cashman and McKernan (eds), p.250.

32 Dulles, p.71.

33 Heinz Meyer, 'Puritanism and Physical Training: Ideological and Political Accents in the Christian Interpretation of Sport', *International Review of Sports Sociology*, 8(1), 1973, p.40. Meyer also notes the work of Christian Graf von Krockow in which it is suggested that Puritanism with its 'anti-hierarchical impulse helped to realize the idea of equality and together with it to deepen a more inward motivation of performance—two essential characteristics of sport' (p.41).

34 Meyer, p.41.

35 Thus Pope Pius XII publicly pronounced:

Sport is an effective antidote against effeminacy and the leading of a comfortable life, it raises a sense of order, it cultivates self-control and self-command, and the despise of braggardism and faint-heartedness. You see, how far it goes beyond normal bodily strength, and how it leads up to moral strength and greatness ... Sport is a training in decency, courage, perserverence, energy and common brotherhood: all of them natural virtues that are, however, the firm ground of the supernatural virtues and prepare man to carry the heaviest burden of responsibility without breaking down.

Cited by Meyer, p.46.

36 It has been estimated that the value of such 'subsidies' to the major professional sports in the United States was close to $23 million dollars in 1970–71. See Benjamin A. Okner, 'Subsidies of Stadiums and Arenas', in Roger G. Noll (ed.), *Government and the Sports Business*, The Brookings Institution, Washington DC, 1974, p.345. For a discussion of the historical roots of the public subsidisation of sport in the United States, see, Robert Goldman and John Wilson, 'The Rationalization of Leisure', *Politics and Society* 7(2), 1977, pp 180–2.

37 This is discussed at greater length in Chapter 5.

38 Kando, p.215. See also, Veliz, pp 14–15.

39 It is not surprising considering that the athletes had to pay their own way, that only three non-European nations were represented, with a total of sixteen competitors (United States—14, Australia—1, Chile—1). Figures obtained from Erich Kamper, *Encyclopedia of the Olympic Games*, McGraw Hill, New York, 1972, pp 293–301.

40 Paul Weiss, quoted in Paul Kuntz, 'Paul Weiss on Sports as Performing Arts', *International Philosophical Quarterly*, 17, 1977, p.159.

41 *The Age*, 22 December, 1984.
42 *The Age*, 14 February, 1986.
43 For an extensive discussion of the early growth of sports professionalism in England, see Wray Vamplew, 'Playing for Pay: The Earnings of Professional Sportsmen in England 1870–1914', in Cashman and McKernan (eds), pp 104–30.
44 Detailed in Peter R. Shergold, 'The Growth of American Spectator Sport: A Technological Perspective', in Richard Cashman and Michael McKernan (eds), *Sport in History*, University of Queensland Press, St Lucia, 1979, pp 26–7.
45 Shergold, p.23.
46 This is not to say that American professional sports have been untouched by scandals and accusations of nefarious activities since this time. Allegations of underworld involvement, the fixing of results for gambling purposes and, more recently, extensive use of illegal drugs by players continue to crop up periodically. These have been the subject of official inquiries instigated by sporting, legislative and judicial bodies. If there is some foundation to the allegations, there are usually some efforts made to take some disciplinary action against offenders and to restore the 'clean' image to the sport.
47 Major exceptions are the various long distance road racing sports— automobile, motorcycle and bicycle—which have long held a strong fascination for Western Europeans. While all of these sports are also practiced in North America, Grand Prix motor racing and 'Tour de France' style of endurance cycling events would appear to be indigenously European contributions to the historical development of commercialised professional sport.
48 Although Marx did not directly confront competitive sport, his general view of popular culture within capitalism was pointedly dismissive, considering it contained nothing of positive value for the subjugated class. The outcome of the working-class's subservience to the dictates of capitalist economic organisation meant that,

> Through excessive exhaustion of their powers, brought about by lengthy, drawn-out, monotonous occupations, they are seduced into habits of intemperance, and made unfit for thinking or reflection. They can have no physical, intellectual or moral amusements other than of the worst sort.

(Karl Marx, *Grundrisse*, Penguin, London, 1973, p.714)
49 James Riordan, 'Sport and Communism—On the Example of the U.S.S.R.', in Jennifer Hargreaves (ed.), *Sport, Culture and Ideology*, Routledge, London, 1982, p.216.
50 See Robert F. Wheeler

> Increasingly sport was viewed as a way of combating worker militancy and ensuring 'industrial peace'. For example, one of the most famous British soccer clubs, West Ham United, was started in 1895 as the Thames Ironworks Football Club by the plant owner. The founding came shortly after a major strike and was part of a concerted programme to improve 'cooperation between workers and management'. An analogous set of circumstances seems to have been responsible for the establishment of a

baseball team in Patterson, New Jersey in 1896 by the prominent mill owner and Republican politician Garrett A. Hobart. And it was during this same decade that Andrew Carnegie took a leading role in establishing professional baseball and football teams near the Bessemer Steel Works in Braddock, Pennsylvania following a violent strike at this plant. A half century later an estimated 20 million employees in the United States were participating in industrial sports programs... In Germany, industrial sports reached their peak in the late 1920's under the coordination of an employers' organisation know as the DINTA.

'Organised Sport and Organised Labour: The Workers' Sports Movement', *Journal of Contemporary History*, 13, 1978, pp 194–5.

Also, in Australia in the 1920s and 1930s, numerous industrialists sponsored soccer teams then sought to have such contributions to the worker's 'welfare' taken into consideration in industrial disputes with unions or by the independent tribunals determining wage standards. Reported by Phil Mosely, 'Factory Football: Paternalism, Profits or Plain Exhaustion?' Paper presented to the Conference on the History of Sporting Traditions, Melbourne, 17–19 August, 1983.

51 Wheeler, p.196.
52 Wheeler, p.197.
53 Riordan, pp 224–5.
54 Wheeler, p.201.
55 Wheeler, p.200.
56 Wheeler, pp 203–5.
57 Wheeler, p.206.
58 For a detailed discussion of the rise of sport in East Germany see, Hoberman, pp 201–18.
59 Sport in China since 1949 is discussed in Hoberman, pp 219–31.
60 Riordan, p.227.

3
Sport as entertainment: The role of mass communications

The development of the commercial mass media

In earlier chapters it has been argued that the emergence and spread of modern competitive sport can best be understood in the broader context of the growth of urbanised, industrialised society. Similarly, the structural and ideological characteristics associated with this process have been equally influential in shaping the rise to prominence of another significant modern cultural institution — the technologies and organisations of mass communications.

The invention of the movable type printing press by Johann Gutenberg in 1440 is conventionally considered to be the major technological breakthrough facilitating the possibility of mass production of symbolic material, but, it was not until two centuries after this that the first daily newspapers appeared in Western Europe and North America. In Europe, from the time of their earliest appearance, newspapers have been closely connected to political interest groups, serving as a forum for the circulation and discussion of contemporary issues, ideas and viewpoints. Consequently, from the outset, newspapers attracted considerable attention from authorities fearful of their potential for disseminating troublesome and subversive material. The battle over the 'freedom of the press' was an important element — both practical and symbolic — in the ongoing struggle for political control waged between the landed aristocracy and the urban bourgeoisie in Britain and other parts of Europe from about the seventeenth century onwards.

The newspaper quickly established itself as an important vehicle for articulating grievances, presenting arguments for social and political change and mobilising interest groups into action. Consequently, governments and powerful groups in society endeavoured, through licensing, censorship, the laws of libel and sedition, to exert some control over the contents of newspapers and thereby prevent the public dissemination of viewpoints they considered critical or in any way threatening — categories both extremely broad and often subject to the vagaries of arbitrary and authoritarian interpretation.

However, in the United States, the positive involvement of the press in the colonial struggle for independence against Britain helped enshrine its absolute freedom from official authoritative interference. The United States became 'the first nation to detach its press from the official machinery of government' through the libertarian provisions of the first amendment to its constitution which stipulated that no law could be passed that might abrogate the absolute freedom of speech, of worship and of the press.[1]

> The absence of political constraints and the nearly universal sufferage fuelled the growth of the press; the federal structure ensured its localism. Localism became an abiding characteristic of the US media; the detachment of the press from government and then from close party involvement led also to dependence on advertising. News and advertising grew together — as two parts of a sandwich whose filling was entertainment.[2]

Thus, writing in 1835, Alexis de Toqueville astutely contrasted the American Press with that of his native France.

> In France little space is given over to trade advertisements, and even news items are few; the vital part of the newspaper is that devoted to political discussion. In America three-quarters of the bulky newspaper put before you will be full of advertisements and the rest will usually contain political news or just anecdotes...
> In France the hallmark of the spirit of journalism is a violent but lofty and often eloquent way of arguing about great interests of state... the hallmark of the American journalist is a direct and coarse attack, without any subtleties, on the passions of his readers; he disregards principles to seize on people, following them into their private lives and laying bare their weaknesses and their vices.[3]

It was America then, that was at the forefront of the development of an alternative to the partisan political newspaper. The commercial newspaper emerged as a business in its own right concerned with expanding its readership to the urban, working class among whom, understandably, the general level of literacy and formal education was not extensive. In order to attract such readers, vocabularly and sentence structure was simplified, items kept short and breezy, increasing emphasis placed on local personalities, issues, gossip and entertainment combined with a few brief descriptive articles on the broader political, economic and cultural affairs of the nation.

More importantly, the sale of advertising space in a newspaper could become the primary source of financial return for the publishers thereby subsidising the direct cost per copy charged to the reader. The greater the circulation of the paper the more advertisers were prepared to pay for space to reach potential customers, which in turn gave greater flexibility to newspaper publishers to reduce the purchase price. In large competitive markets such as New York, by 1833, the price of a daily newspaper was as low as one cent, yet the publishers could still operate profitably from advertising income, provided readership continued to expand.

A similar trend developed in Britain in the latter half of the nineteenth century. The last vestiges of governmental control over newspaper production were removed in the 1850s with the repeal of laws relating to advertising duties (1853) and stamp duty on each copy sold (1855).[4] This led to an intense competition between the more established, generally conservative newspapers and somewhat ironically, to the virtual eradication of the radical, working class press that had vehemently opposed and often evaded the taxes. Also, the repeal of the advertising duty tax increased the volume of advertising attracted by the more popular newspapers which allowed them to reduce their price to as low as a penny per copy, thereby giving them an important competitive edge in the market place. Consequently, in the twenty-five year period from 1856, sales of daily newspapers in Britain increased by more than 600 per cent as compared with a 70 per cent increase over the previous twenty years.[5]

Although a number of the larger newspapers maintained strong partisan ties with various political factions and parties, the growing dominance of advertising as the basis of financially profitable newspaper publishing directed the British Press into a broadly populist mode with a format, style and content not dissimilar from their American forerunners. To a large extent, and taking into account the segmenting of the market place through a broad division between 'quality' and 'populist' newspapers, the business rationales underlying the operation of the daily press that were first developed in America and Britain in the nineteenth century established both the principles of journalistic style and the range of content for the successful commercial newspaper. Both have changed very little to this day. As Jeremy Tunstall succinctly observes:

> The news-entertainment-advertising medium of the newspaper had a distinct technology and raw materials; it had a peculiar double system of finance — public sales and advertising; it evolved an elaborate division of labour — printers, journalists, commercial management. All of these were developed in ways which fitted with

American (and British) circumstances, and were then copied, often in countries where quite different sets of circumstances obtained.[6]

So, the technology of printing became a vehicle for the production of another form of consumer commodity—the daily newspaper—to be manufactured and marketed in accordance with those entrepreneurial principles of organisation and distribution that worked most effectively in a capitalist economy. The direct link between the continued financial success of mass circulation newspapers and the consistent growth of advertising revenues tended to align the interests of the proprietors of commercial newspapers more closely to those of the owners of capital, rather than to the sellers of labour. This communality was further strengthened as newspaper publishing itself became 'big business'. In those societies in which industrialisation advanced most rapidly, and in which 'free enterprise' remained the dominant politico-economic orthodoxy, the structural trends that developed in the newspaper business paralleled closely those of many other industries. The process was typified by fierce competition for circulation, the swallowing-up of the smaller, less successful papers by the larger organisations and the establishment of chains or networks under the control of the most successful entrepreneurs within the industry.

Following the economic 'laws' of capitalist mass production, the aim was to compete against other suppliers to produce a cost-efficient commodity attractive to a broad target market. In the newspaper business this translated into the development of a number of specialised sections and features of direct interest to particular sectors of the potential market, such as business, real estate, fashion (directed mainly towards women) and entertainment/leisure.

The period of the latter part of the nineteenth and the early decades of the twentieth century was one of significant growth and expansion for both the commercial daily newspaper and entrepreneurially based forms of popular entertainment. The newspaper served as an extremely effective vehicle for the marketing of the latter. In addition to the direct purchase of advertising space by the producers and distributors of the various forms of popular entertainment, the more circulation oriented newspapers assessed the positive benefits of devoting increasing amounts of copy to 'news' items, critical appraisals, features, biographies and gossip that informed readers on almost every aspect of available commercial entertainment. Such welcome 'free' publicity greatly assisted the entrepreneurial development of first vaudeville, music hall and variety theatre, and later the Hollywood film, the popular music industry and spectator sports. The commercial newspaper thus operated as a promoter, an adjunct and itself a significant component of a modern social phenomenon broadly identified as 'mass culture'.

Mass communication, leisure and commercialised culture

As evidenced by the history of the 'rational recreation' movement in nineteenth century Britain, despite the respect accorded to the principles of liberalism and individualism, there were strong pressures from sections of the middle-class to direct the populace as a whole — and in particular the working class — into gainfully filling their non-working hours with leisure pursuits that were 'uplifting', 'educational' and of 'cultural value'. For the more committed, this meant inculcating into the 'lower orders' a reverant appreciation for the carefully nurtured heritage of Western culture that had been preserved and patronised over the centuries by aristocratic and religious elites.

But a position widely held within intellectual and political circles was that this rarified cultural world of theatre, art, literature and music would lose its integrity and its creative dynamism if it was to be made accessible to the 'rude mechanicals' who had neither the temperament nor the social background to appreciate its 'true worth'. Such views were particularly strongly felt by those who found many aspects of both political democracy and industrial capitalism a threat to 'civilised' values. Many still refused to accept the irreversibility of recent political demise of the 'natural', aristocratic order, an example of the type of social structure they believed provided a necessary prerequisite for the operation and maintenance of any worthwhile expressive culture. Such a position was further reinforced when the majority of the working-class preferred to decline the entreaties of 'rational recreation' for the earthier pleasures of communal ale house, brassy music hall, vaudeville theatre and the local sports field. Similarly, the general growth of literacy throughout the population did not translate into an immediate and insatiable rush to absorb the 'classics' of Western literature — although certainly some working people sought them out, read them and found them edifying — but rather stimulated an explosion in the publication of crudely written romance, adventure and fantasy. The working class in general stubbornly showed a marked preference for genres and styles that ranked fairly low on the institutionalised cultural scale of literary and creative merit. At the same time, the economic rationalisation of popular entertainment by leisure entrepreneurs and pioneers of the new media technologies was primarily being directed towards maximisation of profit through the application of already established commodity production techniques of standardisation, centralisation of production, aggressive marketing, controlling costs of labour and equipment, increasing avenues for distribution and the amalgamation of competitive enterprises in order to develop more effective economies of scale.

The economic success of the cheap commercial newspapers, 'pulp' literature and later other commercially based entertainment forms amplified the already established tendency by intellectual observers to debate, from various theoretical and political perspectives the supposed division between 'high' and 'mass' culture (or popular culture as it has more recently been relabelled) and in particular, the social and artistic value of the latter. To many of the cultural critics, the rationalised materialism of industrial society was breaking down intermediary social groupings — regional, ethnic, religious, status and class — undermining particularistic group values and aesthetics with the resultant formation of a new entity identified as 'mass society' with its concommitant 'mass culture'. This 'mass culture' was continually portrayed as a corrupt and degraded derivative of the established 'high culture' forms of literature, art and theatre. Considered synthetic and exploitative, 'mass culture' was negatively contrasted with the 'authentic' alternatives of, on the one hand, 'high culture' as the refined expression of talented, independent creators, and, on the other, with 'folk culture', as the organically rooted examples of narrative, music, dance and ritual growing naturally out of the life and experience of pre-industrial rural communities.

While it has its origins as far back as the sixteenth century, the framework for the debate over the social, political and cultural effects of the rise of 'mass culture' intensified with the expansion of the newer communication technologies and remained the central paradigm for most critical discussions of modern culture until well into the 1960s.[7]

Without entering into a detailed exposition of the various arguments in the debate, it does seem indisputable that with the general increase in material wealth and the consolidation of a new industrial order came a general reconstruction of the relationship between work and leisure. The 'folk culture' identified with rural society as an expression of religio-cultic communalism had little relevance to the everyday lives of the new generations of urbanised factory workers. The conditions of wage-labour provided the wage-earner and salaried worker a daily portion of discretionary time which, by the end of the nineteenth century, gradually increased as political pressures achieved a reduction in the hours employers could reasonably expect employees to work each week in exchange for their 'living wage'.

Thus, what came to be perceived as 'mass culture' was constituted from the wide variety of commercialised performances, activities and artifacts increasingly presented to the public as attractive leisure or entertainment pursuits to be purchased from any money left available beyond that required by each individual family unit for their obligatory survival needs. The most successful entrepreneurs of commercial entertainment quickly became attuned to 'public taste' and in a market-place in which numerous alternatives were being offered, sought to attract and nurture within their organisations, those with the creative, administrative, technical and marketing skills most suited to the presentation of 'entertainment' that would return an attractive rate of profit.

In style and content, the entertainment forms being developed drew from the broader cultural experiences and recognisable performance styles most familiar to their potential audience. Many of the creative and performing talents who achieved the greatest commercial success came from the same working and lower middle class material and cultural environments as the people they entertained. For both performer and audience their relationship to the 'great tradition' of the literary, artistic and performing arts was, in the main, to an alien and inaccessible culture; one expressed through forms and styles that were intellectually intimidating, nurtured by a numerically small supporting community of creators and appreciators, and identified with the materially and educationally privileged classes in society.

Within the range of commercial entertainments provided for them, the paying customers of popular culture clearly made discriminatory choices. But the basis for such preferences did not often coincide with the aesthetic, moral and intellectual criteria applied by an institutionalised body of literary and cultural critics who authoritatively guarded a cultural status hierarchy primarily concerned with those contributions they considered representative of 'high culture' or 'the arts'.

The new media technologies of the twentieth century proved to be eminently suited to the further expansion of the popular entertainments. The novelty and creative potential of film introduced a medium that could draw upon and expand the narrative conventions of the novel and the theatre. But the organisation of the American film industry as an entrepreneurial venture in cheap mass entertainment, the structure of which was definitively formed by a claque of predominantly immigrant sales and advertising men 'of a basically promotional disposition'[8] ensured that it set its course in the direction of primarily seeking to maximise the financial return on production costs. This could be most effectively accomplished through ensuring a steady output of material consciously tailored to attract the largest and broadest possible audience. The early establishment of the Hollywood studio system institutionalised the commercial basis of the film industry and the outstanding financial returns from this policy ensured the continued preference for 'entertainment value' — a convenient euphemism for the broadly popular — in production decisions over 'art' — meaning 'intellectual', 'high culture' or minority tastes.

In this, the early Hollywood tycoons were merely extending the marketing principles previously established in the domains of the travelling circus, vaudeville and variety shows. They soon became aware that the new film technology might be applied to the creation of a standardised easily distributable product that could be displayed concurrently in thousands of theatres to aggregate audiences numbering in the millions. Thus the mass communication technologies could be exploited to enormously expand the audiences for professionally produced entertainment and thereby to create the conditions for universalised forms of cultural experience significantly different from either 'high culture' or the traditionally localised 'folk culture'.

The forms of presentation and distribution of the vast body of content making up 'mass' or 'popular' culture were further extended with the development of technologies for sound recording and re-production, and for the transmission of sound and visual material directly into domestic receiving apparatus. The future characteristics of both radio and television were largely predetermined by the general assumption that the most rational and appropriate social application of their technological possibilities was as a means for the centralised distribution of professionally produced programme material to a mass of receivers. As some critical observers have pointed out, this is by no means the only arrangement by which the potentialities of these media technologies might be utilised. But the political decisions surrounding the introduction of radio and television transmission services were limited by the premise that these were essentially organs of 'mass communication'. Once this was accepted the question of what type of arrangement was most appropriate depended, in the main, on the particular society's broader political and economic structure. Basically, the decisions to be made concerned the nature and extent of central-ised political control over the organisation and/or content of radio and television transmission services; the economic basis upon which the cost of operating such services would be financed; the number of stations or channels that would be permitted to operate; the mechan-isms for monitoring and regulating the content of the transmissions; and the broader responsibilities of television services to cater to certain social, political and cultural 'needs' of the 'communities' to which they transmitted.

Effectively the resultant decisions on these questions produced three major models for the societal organisation of radio and television services. In the United States the constitutional protection of the rights of the individual to freedom of speech and of the press which, as noted above, assisted the development of the commercial newspaper, also ensured minimal state interference in the process whereby privately owned organisations came to own and operate subsequent organs of mass communication. It was left to a Federal regulatory agency to administer the orderly allocation of transmission wavelengths. Licences were issued, first for radio and later television, to a number of individual or corporate applicants in each city, town and rural region. The licensee was legally entitled, within established guidelines, to beam a broadcast signal encoded with programme material into a specified area of the country. It was accepted that, as was the case with newspapers, those granted radio and television licences could most effectively finance their operations through interspersing within their transmission commercial messages paid for by advertisers seeking to reach potential customers for their goods and services. Therefore the costs of production and purchase of programme material and the other technical and organisational expenses incurred in the running of a broadcasting enterprise become directly linked to the sale of advertising time. In such a system, both the rates charged to the purchasers of advertising time and the level of profitability achieved by the broadcasting organisation are then broadly determined by total audience size as assessed in periodic 'ratings' surveys. Initially, the only major regulatory restrictions on the material broadcast required some sensitivity to established community norms with regard to language and sexual content and specified a 'fairness' doctrine to be applied to material connected with candidates campaigning for electoral office. Other than these, the content broadcast was effectively constrained only by other relevant legal statutes relating to libel, sedition, incitement to riot, racial equality, and so on.

Such a system was designed in principle to encourage a certain level of pluralism and community responsibility. However, it also institutionalised the commercial market principles in American broadcasting that led to the economic rationalisation of programme production — particularly with regard to television given its more potent marketing potential for advertisers and broader entertainment appeal to audiences. This resulted, at least for the first thirty years of operation, in the establishment of three major commercial networks that dominated American television broadcasting, each with hundreds of affiliated local stations throughout the country, transmitting, from centralised sources, a standardised range of programmes and competing for nationwide aggregate audiences to sell to large national advertisers.

As the United States has remained, throughout this century, a major world economic and political power, it is not surprising that the basic elements of American commercial broadcasting have been widely reproduced in other societies, most notably in a number of Western industrialised countries, but also in many developing countries of Latin America, Asia and Africa. With regard to the latter this has often been connected to a high level of economic dependence on the United States, as well as, in some cases, political control in these countries remaining in the hands of small elites sympathetic to America's international role in championing the principles of 'free enterprise' (not to mention a reliance on American support against internal political movements dedicated to 'radical' or 'social' reform).[9]

A second type of broadcasting model emanated from Britain. This evolved with the establishment of the BBC in 1926 as a government funded monopoly to control both the production and transmission of all radio broadcasting in Britain. The cost of such a service was to be financed through the sale of licenses legally required by all households with a receiving device. The British conceived of broadcasting as a form of national 'public service'. Within certain guidelines laid down by the government, the BBC was to be a department of the civil service but nominally independent of political interference, with its own chairman and administrative structure and a budget allocation to employ the required personnel to produce and distribute programme material. As Raymond Williams comments in his analysis of this peculiarly British approach to the question surrounding the appropriate application of broadcasting technology,

> a dominant version of the national culture had already been established, in an unusually compact ruling-class, so that public service could be effectively understood and administered as service according to the values of an existing public definition, with an effective paternalist definition of both service and responsibility . . . The flexibility which was latent in this kind of solution, though continually a matter of dispute, permitted the emergence of an independent corporate broadcasting policy, in which the independence was at once real, especially in relation to political parties and temporary administrations, and qualified, by its definition in terms of pre-existing cultural hegemony.[10]

The BBC's radio monopoly was extended to television when domestic services were introduced into Britain in 1946. The principle of direct state regulation and production of radio and television has been adopted by a number of Western European states. Such an arrangement can be expanded to allow for the establishment of a number of alternative transmission channels catering to different cultural and regional interests, while all still remain under the umbrella of the government administered service.

In countries where there exists a reasonably stable and securely legitimated liberal-democratic political culture, the American and British approaches to the organisation of radio and television broadcasting have invariably served as influential working guides. In certain instances, notably Australia and Canada, broadcasting policy legislation was introduced to permit both privately owned commercial stations and publicly funded national corporations to operate side by side. In fact in Britain itself, in response to extensive public pressure on the government, the BBC's monopoly over broadcasting was broken in 1955 with the granting of the first commercial television licences.

A third model of broadcasting tends to operate where effective political power is concentrated in a party or clique identifying itself with statist ideologies of both the Left and Right. In such circumstances all forms of public communication, particularly the organs of the mass media, are placed strictly within control of such groups or nominally at the service of 'the state' — which in most cases amounts to the same thing.

However, notwithstanding the considerable variations in the extent to which political power is exercised to limit the overall autonomy in the operation of mass communications systems, there has been an almost universal tendency to employ these technologies for the provision of public entertainment, however this term may be defined within a particular culture. Mass communication systems also operate as a source of general information, a forum for discussion or debate of social and political issues, an avenue for the dissemination of political propaganda and as an adjunct to formal educational training. But, in the main, they are considered, both by those who produce the transmitted material, and by the majority of their audience, as a major source for diversion and relaxing entertainment with which to fill some portion of discretionary leisure time available. As such they have operated as an important institutional focus for the extensive growth of a wide range of popular performance forms such as music, variety, dance, fictional narratives of all types, and, most pertinently, the sporting contest.

The interpenetration of sport and the mass media has been greatly facilitated by the modern construction of the high-level sporting contest as essentially an expressive performance form and therefore an appropriate vehicle for popular entertainment. The conceptualisation of sport as performance links modern sport once again to the Games of the Ancient Greeks. For in the Classical Games, the arts of poetry and music were included alongside the athletic contests, and exceptional performances in each treated with equal respect.

> Pindar devoted Pythian Odes to the winners in chariot races, horse races, wrestling matches, foot races, but without any incongruity the XII Pythian lauds, as no less worthy of the gods and noble ancestors Midas of Acragas, winner in the flutepaying match, 490 B.C.[11]

The connection was certainly familiar to Baron de Coubertin whose vision of a regular international sporting festival also included a place for artists, musicians and poets.[12]

However, for modern sport, the relationship to performance is significant not so much in the sense that it might best be considered one of 'the arts'—although this has been a matter of some intellectual discourse[13]—but rather the extent to which its attractiveness to spectators has influenced the development of sport as an important sector of the modern culture industry. Over recent decades, the latter has, from an economic and organisational standpoint, come to incorporate the marketing of all aspects of what is conventionally designated as both popular and high culture.[14] In a recent paper that offers an approach to understanding modern cultural forms and practices that convincingly goes beyond the sterile confines of the longstanding 'high' versus 'mass' cultural paradigm, Langer forcefully concludes:

> Certainly the myth that 'high culture' is not 'commercial' must be abandoned. So too must the notion that the experience of 'high

culture' is necessarily more informed and self directed than the experience of 'mass culture'... 'High' and 'mass' culture thus exist within a constellation of 'packaged experience' which includes cuisines, therapies and travel. From this perspective, we have not two opposing 'cultures' but 'up' and 'down market' commodities in a 'cultural supermarket'.[15]

Thus, both the line of development of sport in this century and its relationship to mass communications may best be understood in the broader context of the general industrialisation of culture, promoted and packaged by interested parties as a consumer commodity competing in a market against similar products.

Sport and mass communications before television

The reporting of sports events in daily newspapers began to appear intermittently in the early part of the eighteenth century with a predilection towards the sporting interests of the leisured class — notably horse-racing, prize fighting, boat racing, fishing, hunting, golf and cricket. The *Boston Gazette* of 5 May, 1733 is credited with carrying the first sports story — on a prize fight — in an American newspaper, but this was copied directly from a London daily.[16] Consistent with the earlier growth of a general interest in sport in Britain, the appearance of books, magazines and newspaper reports on sporting topics in this country antedated their American counterparts. By the early 1800s, London magazines such as *Bell's Life* and the *Weekly Despatch* had developed a solid readership both at home and abroad by concentrating heavily on articles and stories about the sports mainly associated with the leisure pursuits of the rural gentry.

> *Bell's Life*, often cited as the 'Bible', was the authority for devotees of the turf, the ring, the hunt and angling... Pierce Egan's *Boxiana* and other works were popular reading for ring enthusiasts. The *London Sporting Magazine* and the *English Sporting Magazine* were drawn upon for material or served as a model for American publishers.[17]

But the Americans very quickly produced their own indigenous journals on sports beginning with *The American Farmer* that first appeared in 1819 providing its readers with 'the results of hunting, fishing, shooting and bicycling matches as well as essays on the philosophy of sports'.[18] The keen interest in horse racing in the Atlantic states and the American south stimulated the publication in 1829 of the *American Turf Register and Sporting Magazine* and, two years later, the emergence of *The Spirit of the Times* 'which was destined to become the leading sporting journal of the middle years of the nineteenth century'.[19]

The numerous sports journals and magazines that proliferated in the nineteenth century, in both Europe and America, helped to form the sporting subcultures that grew up around particular games and competitions. Apart from describing events and providing results, they created a sense of cultural continuity — keeping records, lionising outstanding performers, developing the mythologies of 'golden eras' and in general operating as publicists, literary chroniclers and philosophers for the new codified games.

But the inclusion of sports results into the routine format of daily news was greatly facilitated by the development of the wire telegraph in the middle of the nineteenth century. The telegraph made possible the establishment of centralised news agencies such as American Associated Press and Reuters that provided subscribing newspapers with a daily selection of reports gathered by journalists employed directly by the agencies. Their services increasingly incorporated sporting information thereby expanding the geographical limitation of localised sports cultures by bringing to keen followers of any particular sport or contest, through their local newspaper, results and descriptions of what had taken place a considerable distance away within a few hours of its completion.

Both the sources and distribution of sporting news were further expanded in 1866 with the laying of a telegraph cable across the Atlantic. The importance of sports news to the competitive commercial considerations involved in attracting and expanding newspaper readership is evidenced by the considerable sums papers were prepared to pay correspondents and the wire services for the rapid transmission of such information. Thus:

> by 1867 the *New York Herald* only twice paid eight hundred pounds for dispatches: the first, to record the King of Prussia's speech after war with Austria: the second, to provide readers with a blow-by-blow description of the boxing match between Mace and Goss. The *Herald's* priorities were generally accepted. When in 1888, William I lay dead in Berlin, the *New York Sun's* principal European correspondent, Arthur Brisbane, was concerned not with the future of the continent but with the aftermath of the Sullivan/ Mitchell fight in Chantilly.[20]

In the 1880s came the beginning of the regular sporting section within the daily newspaper and the emergence of specialist sport journalists. There can be no doubt that the regular and detailed coverage of sporting events in the daily newspaper amplified an already broadening public interest in the major sporting leagues and consequently contributed towards providing such competitions with the cultural legitimacy that further propelled sport into the mainstream of popular culture.

Newspaper attention, much more than specialist sporting journals, broke down the localism and class exclusivity previously associated with certain sports, transforming games such as cricket, baseball and soccer into truly national (and even international) spectator pastimes. The established leagues and competitions benefited, as evidenced by the steady growth in spectator attendance that developed concurrently in a number of countries between the 1880s and the 1930s. This, in turn, justified more prominent newspaper coverage. It allowed the press a direct involvement in the promotion of sporting events by focusing attention on peak events in the sporting calendar which helped build up an atmosphere of excitement and societal significance for a 'cup final' or a 'world series'. Local newspaper coverage often fuelled an atmosphere of intense partisanship for the 'home team' in inter-city or inter-community competitions.

Sports journalists frequently wrote their stories from the point of view of unabashed 'sports fans' consciously seeking to boost the popularity of the sport, and in particular the fortunes of the local team or the status of certain 'star' performers. In this manner, the expansion of sports journalism invariably assisted the entrepreneurial promotion of top level spectator sport—both amateur and professional. Most astute team owners, managers, officials and the athletes themselves nurtured close friendships with selected reporters, eager to co-operate in providing them with 'inside' stories, interviews, leads and angles, well aware of the generous benefits to gate receipts that accrued from the free publicity they received from the newspapers' decision to treat sport as 'news'.

As with other more specialist fields of journalism, there emerged a number of writers of considerable literary skill who brought to the genre of sports reporting a thoughtful, articulate and broadly philosophical approach, rooted both in the classical tradition and the nineteenth century ideals that saw sport as potentially ennobling to the human spirit and an expression of 'civilised progress'. Certainly, much of this kind of writing was concentrated upon sports such as cricket, golf, athletics, the turf, hunting and fishing and, in America, baseball, many of which had long associations with the leisured lifestyles of the socially privileged. Such writings helped to develop a formal aesthetic of appreciation, articulating many of the idealist beliefs of the participatory amateur value system that associated sport with self cultivation, social harmony, human achievement and the significance of 'good sportsmanship' to any 'civilised' culture.

However, only rarely has the writing about sport in the daily press reached these levels of literary or philosophical sophistication. It would not be overly critical to say that, in the main, most of it has been fairly mundane and descriptive with a heavy emphasis on results, individual performances and records. More importantly, rarely have newspaper journalists been critical of sport as a social institution. There has been some newspaper discussion of the contemporary trends towards increasing professionalisation and commercialisation of certain sports such as tennis and, more recently in Australia, cricket, but overall after some initial soul searching, these are invariably seen to be ultimately 'good for the game'. Excessive violence, both on the field and among spectators, and drug-taking by competitors are fairly universally condemned by the press, but generally in terms that carefully avoid linking any of these to broader social issues nor to any critique of the dominant values and ethics institutionally entrenched within the sporting culture. A recent assessment of contemporary sports journalism in Australian newspapers might serve as a harsh, but not inaccurate, summary of the somewhat dismal general history of the genre, applicable almost anywhere in the world. 'The press engages in crude sensationalism, often the promotion of rabid partisanship, over-emphasises violence and exaggerates the qualities and talents of the players . . .'[21] Certainly, up to the advent of the later media forms, and since that time, the attention paid by the daily press to the world of sport, and the extent to which it emphasised those aspects described above have served to assist the successful development of high-performance sport as a commercially saleable spectacle.

If there was, and continues to be, a certain ambiguity in the extent to which the content of daily newspapers might be considered 'entertainment', then this has been far less problematic for both film and radio, both of which emerged as popular communication forms in the first decades of the twentieth century. Film's intrinsic ability to represent action and movement proved enormously attractive and apart from the telling of fictional, acted stories it developed a documentary side very early, manifested in its most commercial form by the newsreel. Cinema programmes began to include a weekly summary of filmed news together with their feature film. Newsreel segments covering recent sporting events proved to be extremely popular. The already fine line between documentation and entertainment was soon blurred as many of the first 'news' films of sporting contests, while presented to the public as a true record, were in actuality later reconstructions of the events set up especially for the newsreel cameras, sometimes featuring the sportsmen involved, but on occasion using hired actors to play their parts.

While over the years one could compile a substantial list of feature films that have used sport or particular sporting heroes as the central theme, in the main, the producers of commercial cinema discovered that such movies had somewhat limited audience appeal. Consequently, sport has not figured as prominently in cinematic features as one might have expected. The number produced has declined considerably since the 1940s when the subject of sport began to develop a widespread reputation in Hollywood as 'box office poison'.[22]

The electronic media of radio, and later television, proved to be far more suitable than film for the secondary transmission of sport to the mass public. The cinema lacked immediacy and authenticity of experience, both of which are distinctive characteristics of radio and television. The technology of distribution brought the content of radio and television directly to the audience via a small, portable receiving device that could be located almost anywhere. For the sports fan, a radio transmission describing, as it was happening, an ongoing sports event taking place a considerable distance away was a positive substitute for the experience of attending in person. Sport thus played a prominent part in radio programming from the beginning of regular domestic transmissions in the 1920s.

In the early years, technical limitations sometimes inhibited direct live coverage, but the absence of visual clues for radio audiences suggested the possibility for presenting 'simulated' or 'synthetic' sports commentary. This technique was occasionally employed in the United States, but also independently developed in a sophisticated and ingenious manner in Australia. In the early 1930s, ABC radio introduced 'synthetic' broadcasts to Australian listeners of test cricket matches being played in England. 'Commentators' in the Australian studios 'described' the game from a continuous stream of cablegrams that provided them with the bare essentials of what was happening on the field in England. Although listeners were informed that such broadcasts were simulations, the verbal commentary was augmented by appropriate sound effects of crowd noises and bat striking the ball to provide a more convincing sense of 'reality'. Like the 'reconstructed' prize fights of the early newsreels, the simulated radio broadcasts reflect the value priorities of the mass media with regard to resolving any intrinsic conflict between the principles of journalistic veracity and keeping the audience entertained. Thus as one writer has noted

> Synthetic cricket distorted the game in a number of ways. Not only were fictitious happenings invented to cover a break in the cables, the commentary even falsified the game itself on some occasions ... Radio also made cricket appear to be a faster-moving, more exciting game than it actually was ... [23]

But live radio broadcasts of sports events signified the beginnings of an important economic relationship that was to develop between the mass media and organised sporting bodies. Unlike the newspaper reporting of sport, live radio descriptions incorporated the legal issues of proprietorship and copyright.

The successful growth of spectator sport was premised on a set of well established entrepreneurial principles that applied throughout the 'entertainment' industry. As determined by the organisers, a price, or a range of prices was fixed, the payment of which entitled any member of the public to be admitted to a venue in which the performance or event would take place. The venue, be it a circus, vaudeville house, concert hall, theatre, cinema or stadium, was physically constructed in a manner that limited the potential audience to a finite number of paying customers who, from variably privileged vantage points— depending on the price they were prepared to pay—could experience that performance or event. Through the construction of some form of physical barrier or boundary, those unwilling to pay the cost of admission or unable to gain entry to the venue, because all the legally sanctioned audience space was already committed, were excluded. Until well into the twentieth century sports venues differed significantly from other entertainment structures in that most sports required fairly large playing areas and took place in the open. The factor encouraged the establishment of enclosed arenas that prevented non-paying spectators obtaining a free view of the contest.

The bodies administering the various sports, whether amateur or professional, claimed legal ownership of the events under their jurisdiction and, as they charged admission to the public, the matter of licensing radio broadcasters to transmit live descriptions and the question of payments for such rights emerged as issues for consideration. In the early years of radio broadcasting, most sports bodies considered it advantageous to provide free access to the event to any broadcasting organisation and often were even prepared to pay the broadcasters for providing live transmissions. Despite strongly voiced fears by some sports administrators that allowing radio broadcasts would lead to a catastrophic decline in spectator attendance, the early experiences did not convincingly validate such fears.[24] An established view began to emerge that the increased publicity and extended audience offered by radio exposure was of some benefit in broadening public interest and awareness of the sport and would contribute to an increase in the sale of admission tickets for future events.

However, it began to become increasingly apparent that sport was a form of commercial performance that provided radio with considerable programming content. Thus, for example, in the early 1930s, a number of commerical radio stations in Australia went as far as to position commentators in vantage points outside but overlooking suburban racecources and proceeded to broadcast descriptions of the events to their listeners without paying the organisations involved for the rights.[25] As sports broadcasts of major events proved attractive to large audiences, which ultimately benefited broadcasters both economically (for commercial stations), and in terms of their corporate image for providing service and entertainment to the public, the relationship turned more and more into a complementary business arrangement between competing branches of the popular culture industry. Again it was in North America where both sports and broadcasting had a well developed and unambiguously commercial basis that the formal components of the financial accommodation between sport and the electronic media began to take shape. Thus, already by the 1930s,

> networks and stations were paying for sports broadcast rights. Large sums of money were involved; moreover, profits from radio rights were evident by 1938. This development marked a reversal or roles between the networks (from benefactors to client) and sport owners (from client to supplier or benefactor).[26]

However, once the basis of the relationship between sport and the electronic media was forged it was subject to significant change with regard to the relative strengths and bargaining power of the two institutions, particularly upon the successful development of a far more potent and comprehensive form of electronic communication — television. The required technology for the simultaneous transmission of pictures and sound, without wires and cables between transmitter and receiver, was available from the mid-1920s. Experimental services applying this new form of communication were already in operation, both in Europe and the United States by the 1930s, but the introduction of television as a medium of mass entertainment was postponed until after the end of the Second World War.

The pattern of development in television followed closely that of radio. Most of the leading manufacturing, distribution and transmission organisations that had emerged with the development of radio as a domestic medium saw television as a natural direction in which to extend their interests, financial investment and accumulated expertise. Similarly, as noted above, the general policies decided upon by state authorities to regulate domestic radio services in the most part determined the manner in which they approached the critical questions surrounding the later introduction of television services. Invariably, the principles, guidelines and even the regulatory bodies set up to administer the orderly functioning of radio services were extended and adapted to include television.

Initially no one seemed very clear as to what exactly television was going to do. As Raymond Williams has pointed out, like radio before it, television was a system *'primarily devised for transmission and reception as abstract process[es,] with little or no definition of preceding content.'*[27]

Within a few years television showed itself to be a medium capable of usurping and absorbing many of the informational, and entertainment functions previously the domain of the daily press and radio. In its role as a provider of cultural experience and entertainment, television quickly challenged the entrepreneurial and market structure of currently dominant commercial forms notably cinema, dramatic and variety theatre, and a number of other spectator-based leisure pursuits. As another rising branch of the popular entertainment industry it was obvious by the late 1940s to the administrators and controllers of spectator sport — both amateur and professional — that it was necessary and desirable to come to a satisfactory accommodation with television. It is to the progressive development of this relationship over the next forty years that we must now turn.

Notes

1 Jeremy Tunstall, *The Media Are American,*‛ Constable, London, 1977, p. 23.
2 Tunstall, p. 23.
3 From Alexis de Tocqueville, *Democracy in America*, first published in 1835, quoted in Tunstall, p. 24.
4 James Curran, 'Capitalism and Control of the Press, 1800–1975', in James Curran, Michael Gurevitch and Janet Woollacott (eds), *Mass Communication and Society*, Edward Arnold, London, 1977, p. 212.
5 Raymond Williams, *The Long Revolution*, Penguin, Harmondsworth, 1965, p. 216.
6 Tunstall, pp. 23–4.
7 The various intellectual positions in the long standing debate over 'mass culture' are well articulated and discussed in the following works: Leo Lowenthal, *Literature, Popular Culture and Society*, Pacific Books, Palo Alto, Calif., 1968; Bernard Rosenberg and D.M. White (eds), *Mass Culture: The Popular Arts in America*, Free Press, New York, 1957; Herbert J. Gans, *Popular Culture and High Culture*, Basic Books, New York, 1974.
8 Tunstall, p. 80.
9 For an extensive discussion of these processes see, Tunstall; O. Boyd Barrett, 'Media Imperialism', in Curran, Gurevitch and Woollacott (eds), pp. 116–41; Herbert I. Schiller, *Mass Communications and American Empire*, Augustus M. Kelley, New York, 1969.
10 Raymond Williams, *Television: Technology and Cultural Form*, Fontana, London, 1974, pp 33–4.
11 Paul G. Kuntz, 'Paul Weiss on Sports as Performing Arts', *International Philosophical Quarterly*, 17, 1977, p. 164.
12 Arts festivals and competitions, for which medals were awarded to entrants in a variety of fields including town planning, architectural designs, sculpture, painting, literature, drama and music, were included as adjuncts to the sporting contests at a number of the modern Olympiads, but the practice was discontinued after 1948. See Erich Kamper, *Encyclopedia of the Olympic Games*, McGraw Hill, New York, 1972, pp 285–92.
13 See, for example, the discussion in Kuntz, that draws on the work of philosopher Paul Weiss. Kuntz presents a case for the structural similarities between sport and theatre.

Many points of resemblance must be noted between a game and a stage play. Neither is 'the world of everyday, but we also know it is no fiction, no semblance, no mere make-believe. We are affected by it, cheered or sobered by it. We learn much from it . . . we give ourselves up to it.' Both a game and a stage play create tension, which is maintained or suspended, heightened and finally resolved. Conflicts impend and conflicts rage, within a connected scheme. Sometimes there is a climax, but sometimes anti climax (pp 151–2).

14 Despite the continuing employment, both in the literature and in public discussion, of the distinction between 'real art' and 'mass entertainment', a convincing case has been made that similar patterns of commercialisation and commodification operate in almost all areas of modern culture, see Beryl Langer, 'The Culture Industry: High Culture as Mass Culture', Paper presented to SAANZ Conference, Brisbane, 1985.
15 Langer, pp 20–1.
16 Susan L. Greendorfer, 'Sport and Mass Media', in Günther R. F. Lüschen and George H. Sage (eds), *Handbook of Social Science of Sport*, Stipes Publishing Co., Champaign, Ill., 1981, p. 162.
17 John R. Betts, 'Sporting Journalism in Nineteenth-Century America', *American Quarterly*, 5(1), 1953, p. 40.
18 Greendorfer, p. 162.
19 Betts, pp 40–1.
20 Peter R. Shergold, 'The Growth of American Spectator Sport: A Technological Perspective', in Richard Cashman and Michael McKernan (eds), *Sport in History*, University of Queensland Press, St Lucia, 1979, p. 30.
21 Colin Tatz, 'The Corruption of Sport', *Current Affairs Bulletin*, September, 1982, p. 9.
22 Robert Cantwell, 'Sport Was Box-Office Poison', in John T. Talamani and Charles H. Page (eds), *Sport and Society: An Anthology*, Little Brown & Co., Boston, 1973, pp 440–54.
23 See Richard Cashman, *'Ave a Go Yer Mug!*, Collins, Sydney, 1984, pp 102–3. For a discussion of similar 're-creations' of baseball games on American radio, which continued into the 1950s see Benjamin G. Rader, *In Its Own Image*, The Free Press, New York, 1984, pp 27–8.
24 Cashman, p. 94.
25 K. S. Inglis, *This is the ABC: The Australian Broadcasting Commission 1932–1983*, Melbourne University Press, Melbourne 1983, p. 36.
26 Greendorfer, p. 167.
27 Williams, 1974, p. 25.

4
Television and sport: A match made in heaven

The economic nexus

The earlier success of sports broadcasting on radio, the generalised belief that television was a communication form extending the capacities of radio, and the fact that many of the television services in both Britain and the United States were operated by organisations that had already established themselves in the earlier broadcast medium, stimulated the early development of sport as a staple form of television programming. Already, by the mid-1930s, the BBC's infant television service was regularly covering cricket matches and the FA Cup Final was first telecast in 1939.[1]

Similarly, in the United States, in May 1939, at a time when there were only a few hundred television sets capable of receiving their transmission, NBC, the American broadcasting subsidiary of the giant RCA corporation and an early entrant into commercial television, attempted a live coverage of a local college baseball game in New York. Of course these early ventures into sports television were severely hampered by limited technology and inexperience. A *New York Times* reporter wrote of the single camera telecast that, 'The players were best described by observers as appearing "like white flies" running across the screen'. But, only a few months later, a second, apparently more satisfactory, sports telecast — this time of a professional baseball game — was achieved using two cameras. By September of the same year, after watching a telecast of a college football game, *The Times*' critic had been won over to such an extent he proposed that, 'Viewing the game on the screen (as perhaps some 2,000 people did) was more rewarding than seeing it at the stadium'![2]

Such an observation points to one of the primary dilemmas faced by sports administrators and commercial entrepreneurs with regard to the most advantageous approach to take on the question of allowing television access to 'their' particular sport. On the one hand, the economic and organisational infrastructure of any high-level, competitive sport had developed as part of an ongoing subculture that included those who administered and scheduled sporting fixtures or competitions, the participants, who, as individuals or members of clubs or leagues exhibited their skills, and regular supporters of the sport who for a variety of reasons, were prepared to pay entrance money to experience the contests. In the main, all of the participants in the subculture shared a general loyalty to sport itself as a worthwhile social pursuit, although given the structural determinants of sporting involvement and the bewildering variety of formalised sports, the typical pattern for many 'fans' was that they tended to develop a special interest in one or a few sports while remaining relatively indifferent or perhaps even hostile to others. Within each sport, most of those actively involved with the subculture wished to see their particular sport grow in stature. They were keen to see more people playing, more competitions at more levels, more clubs, broader based participation — the sport should strive to become popular in other parts of the country or the world — and more spectators attracted to contests. As was the case with newspapers and radio, exposure of the sport through television was perceived as an attractive and potentially effective means of arousing interest and support within the general populace and thereby assisting in such proselytising endeavours.

However, on the other hand, there were also a number of apprehensions expressed with regard to opening up the sport to television coverage. Most obvious of course, from the point of view of the administrators, was the fear that television — even more than radio — would fracture the established economic relationships by directly affecting the number of paying attendances. Would there be an adequate trade-off between the sums that television would pay for the rights to telecast the sport and the probable decline in gate takings? To allay such anxieties, a number of sports sought to ensure that live television coverage would not take place in the geographical vicinity from which most of the paying spectators to an event were drawn. So television broadcasts would be welcome only if directed towards viewers who were not potential paying attenders. Through relays and networking those too far away to attend could watch on television, but those living within reasonable commuting distance would have to pay the entrance price if they wanted to see the event. In some cases, notably in the United States, this 'area black-out' principle had operated for radio broadcasts, but was seen as an even more critical safeguard with respect to television.

A further concern expressed was with the potential effect that the widespread televising of top-level sport would have on the 'grass-roots' participants at a local and minor-league level. For most sports — particularly team games — depended on the broad based localised competitions that provided the training grounds for potential recruits to the 'big leagues'. While these lower-level competitions were amateur or semi-professional, they still drew paying spectators and relied heavily on the modest returns from the gate receipts to pay costs and overheads and thereby keep the competitions operating. It was feared that the televising of 'big league' contests, taking place elsewhere at the same time as minor competitions (generally on a Saturday or Sunday), might draw away a significant number of regular spectators who would be attracted by the opportunity of seeing the highly skilled professionals on television rather than supporting the lesser able locals. Financially the smaller leagues would be harder hit by the decline in income and, furthermore, the attraction of the 'big league' games on television might also diminish the pool of young players who made up local teams, thereby seducing potential participants into watching the champions on television rather than playing the sport themselves.

The situation was somewhat different for well established amateur sports. In athletics, swimming and even tennis, the interest of television was almost exclusively in the highest levels of competition, for example, the annual national championships. A respectable number of paying spectators was almost assured at such events and the income to the sport from the sale of television rights together with the broad exposure that television provided was eagerly welcomed. Also, in the United States, inter-collegiate competitions in a number of sports, that were nominally amateur, but traditionally drew spectator crowds and brought into the participating universities substantial direct and indirect income from the sale of season's tickets to local supporters and alumni, welcomed the support of further income from television for the rights to show their games.

For the newly emerging television services of the late 1940s and early 1950s, sports programming appeared a 'natural'. If, as Raymond Williams notes, for television, 'the technology of transmission and reception developed before the content', this also meant that in the early years, there was 'the familiar parasitism on existing events'.[3] Both news and sports had been a staple programming format of radio broadcasting. The technology of television, it was conceived, would essentially provide 'radio with pictures' and therefore merely require the extension of many of the journalistic forms originally developed in the print and radio media. The economics of programme production also made the televising of live sport an attractive proposition.

> What television could do relatively cheaply was to transmit something that was in any case happening or had happened. In news, sport, and other similar areas it could provide a service of transmission at comparatively low cost. But in every kind of new work,

which it had to produce, it became a very expensive medium, within the broadcasting model.[4]

Within the commercial American model of television services, the early aim of the broadcasters was to establish the appeal of the medium to transmit programme material attractive to mass audiences and thus to stimulate the sale of receivers. As with newspapers and commercial radio, the major source of income and potential profit for television stations and networks came from their ability to deliver guaranteed audiences to advertisers. The televising of sport provided a form of programming that assisted the broadcasters in achieving both of these aims. Coverage of a wide variety of sports became incorporated into American television programming schedules in the decade between the end of the Second World War and the mid-1950s, the period during which the home television receiver moved from an exotic, futuristic toy to an obligatory domestic appliance. Only five thousand television receivers were sold in the United States in 1946 but this had increased to more than 7 000 000 in 1950. By 1956 more than three-quarters of the country's homes had a television set and by 1960 only five per cent of homes were without one.[5] The significance of sports for this phenomenal rate of penetration should not be underestimated. A number of television network executives have attested to its importance. It has even been suggested that the 'televising of major league baseball, boxing, and college football in the nineteen-forties was a key element in launching the television industry'.[6]

The validity of such an assessment is not limited to the United States. In Australia, the introduction of television services in 1956 was timed to coincide with the country's hosting of the XV1th Olympiad in Melbourne. This spectacular, and widely publicised, event greatly assisted the rapid sale of receivers and provided a powerful promotional device for the fledgling industry.

In Great Britain, where television transmission, at least until the mid-1950s, remained the sole prerogative of the non-commercial and publicly financed BBC, sporting programmes also emerged as a central component in their programming schedules. As the spiritual home of modern competitive sport, and, given the class differentiated, but well established, support by the British of a number of spectator sports — soccer, rugby, cricket, horse-racing, equestrian competition — the BBC interpreted the televising of many of these competitions as one of its statutory obligations within its charter to provide a service broadly incorporating as many elements as possible of what constituted the 'national culture'. As one of the leading trustees of the nation's cultural treasures, the BBC firmly aligned itself with the paternalistic populism perhaps most effectively articulated by T. S. Eliot, who, in seeking to define the culture's 'essence', fondly included '. . . Derby

Day, Henley Regatta, Cowes, the twelfth of August, a cup final, the dog races, the pin table, the dart board . . .'[7]

By the early 1950s, the American and British television models, having been the first to develop and build upon the earlier international dominance established by both countries in the field of entertainment media—technology, organisation and content—were providing the basic frameworks for the newly emerging television services of Europe and Latin America. With the sizeable costs of television programme development, services in most countries, to a greater or lesser extent, relied on purchasing programme material from either the United States or Great Britain, and sometimes from both. This included sports programming, particularly in sports such as soccer and baseball which had large followings in many of these countries. Also, given the tendency to follow the programming models of the television pioneers, the advantages of producing television sports programmes already mentioned, as well as the considerable popularity of local sports competitions, it is not surprising that sports became firmly entrenched as an obligatory televisual form within almost all national services—be they commercial, government funded corporations or state-controlled bodies.

The development of televisual sporting forms

For television, there were a number of problems associated with the development of sporting telecasts. Sports events took place in arenas and stadiums physically separated and at variable distances from television studios and transmission facilities. As such they came under the category of an 'outside broadcast' similar to the coverage of public events such as spectacles and ceremonies or the live transmission of other entertainment forms such as a circus or a theatre performance. This required the development of reliable links via cables or through-the-air relay of sound and picture from the source through the production and transmission facilities to the television receivers. These problems required the development of a mobile unit—usually a large van incorporating the necessary equipment—that could be transported relatively easily to the site of the broadcast and act as an operations base for the technicians and production personnel. In the early years, outside broadcast equipment was crude and the various links in the chain were notoriously unreliable resulting in the frequent breakdown of transmissions.

Television camera equipment, apart from being large, cumbersome and generally immobile during operation, had been developed primarily for use in studios, shooting across relatively short distances. The focal lengths of lenses were fixed within a narrow range. In a studio, two or more cameras could be used, and by the director switching from one to another, different angles or distances kept in frame or focus. Lenses on the cameras not 'on air' could be changed or rotated or the camera position moved while a different camera carried the live picture. This was laborious and complex but manageable within a studio setting. However, such problems were magnified for any outside broadcast — particularly of a sports event.

In a large arena, there was the problem of where to place the cameras for the most desired televisual vantage points. Often special scaffolds had to be built to gain height. Being out in the open the camera positions became susceptible to inclement weather such as winds and rain, both of which constituted some danger to equipment and personnel.

Apart from being bulky, cameras were expensive and given other commitments by the television station, the number available for sports telecasts was generally limited to two or three. Furthermore, unlike a studio broadcast in which camera positions and movement could be rehearsed prior to the telecast, in a sporting event the movements of players and ball were not so predictable and often difficult to follow with only a few stationary cameras of fixed focal length.

The picture received in the home occupied a screen no larger than sixty-five centimetres in diameter and this created further difficulties. In team games played in large arenas the camera could only take in a small portion of the playing field keeping in viewable shot only a few of the participants at one time. In ball games, the ball moved around the playing field at great speed, often high in the air where the camera might lose it against the crowd or the sky.

From the outset, the form of the sporting telecast was mediated to television viewers not merely through the limitations and restrictions on possible camera perspectives, but via the central role of the commentator or commentary team. Media sports commentary first emerged in radio where, of necessity, the commentators provided a detailed description, analysis and evaluation of the ongoing action which was mixed with other sound sources — the reaction of the crowd and the sounds intrinsic to the contest on the field — to create an atmospheric narrative construction of the event. It is of some interest and significance that even when the possibility of adding visuals to sound became a reality, the role of the sports commentator did not diminish but rather, if anything, developed itself into an essential component, a fundamental anchorage around which the form of the sporting telecast was built. It may be argued, particularly in the early years, that the technical limitations of the visual coverage outlined above necessitated the presence of the commentator. As the *New York Times'* report on NBC's first baseball telecast in 1939 suggested, 'Those who watched the game ... agreed that the commentator "saved the day", otherwise there would be no way to follow the play or to tell where the ball went ... '[8] But despite the enormous technical improvements in sports television from this pioneering effort, the assumption that viewers at home require a continual verbal commentary on what they are seeing and hearing has rarely, if ever, been questioned.[9]

This alerts us to the critical constructive role inherent in television's presentation of events in the 'real world' and to an examination of the ways in which the televisual construction of home viewers' experience differs significantly from that of the spectator in attendance. The problem lies in the differing interpretations of the role that television plays, or should play, with regard to the representation of 'reality'. From the outset, the content of television has been constituted from a patchwork of reportage and documentation that is essentially journalistic together with the artful construction of various entertainment forms, some drawn from pre-existing models—the novel, theatre, cinema—and others—the situation comedy, the variety and talk shows—developed to suit the medium itself. The evolution of sports television has been, to put it at its simplest, a movement from a type of journalistic reportage towards a form of pre-structured, but still open-ended, live dramatic spectacle.

Sports contests are pre-scheduled well in advance with regard to time and place. As such they have a number of characteristics in common with similar events taking place in society that are monitored through television's journalistic role and reported as news—elections, important meetings, conferences, the routine activities associated with prominent societal institutions. As with the others mentioned, the exact outcome of sports contests is uncertain and the journalistic role of television is to monitor and report on the critical aspects and vicissitudes of the event that lead to and explain the particular outcome that emerges.

However, sports differ significantly from many other events in that they are performances played out for paying spectators like the theatre or the cinema, but more loosely structured in sequence and not fixed in terms of outcome. By their nature they fall somewhere between the two categories of television outlined above. Thus, the live televising of sport enormously expands the potential audience of the performance while at the same time reporting and following the various elements within the specific contest that lead to the particular and unique outcome. The open-endedness of the result directs television to the appeal of the live coverage as this allows the medium to provide instant access to a process that is unfolding as the viewer watches and thus taps the central monitoring and information functions that, from the outset, made the technological capabilities of television so attractive.

But on the other hand, sports contests are played out over a number of hours, in a variety of weather conditions and between opponents of varying strengths and abilities. Even if, on form, the contestants are evenly matched, the particular outcome of any sporting confrontation is difficult to predict. On the day, any contest may emerge as extremely one-sided with little doubt quite early as to the eventual winner. Adverse weather conditions may turn a skilful team game into a tedious scramble unattractive to spectators and provide little opportunity for the application of the techniques and strategies typically associated with the sport in more favourable conditions. Also a number of popular sports incorporate in their structure short bursts of action and activity irregularly punctuated by breaks, pauses, regrouping, time-outs and other delays.

Such characteristics create problems and difficulties for television, particularly commercial television. Anyone attending a sports event has already travelled some distance from their home, paid an admission price and may have a particularly strong personal commitment to the sport, a particular team or individual. Any regular sports follower learns to expect poor games, weak contests and to experience unpleasant weather conditions. Television stations include sports within a continuous programme schedule hoping to attract viewers, most of whom are at home, have alternative stations and programmes they could watch or the choice of not watching television at that time. They have paid no admission and from their point of view access to a sporting telecast involves no direct expense.

In scheduling live sport, television stations were taking a calculated gamble. First, they calculated on a sizeable population of sports fans who would relish the opportunity to view the telecast of an event they were unable or unwilling to attend. Thus, they sought to present a sporting telecast that would be attractive to those used to experiencing the game in person. Second, they set out to create a form of programming that was less likely to alienate and even attract viewers marginally or not at all interested in sport, thus building popularity for sports television as a distinctive genre of home entertainment.

This required applying the technology and personnel available to construct a televisual experience of broad appeal using the raw material of the sporting contest as the base, but working on and refining such material to minimise the likelihood of succumbing to television's greatest sin—losing the viewers' interest.

The result, as one observer has recently noted, is that live televised sport is constructed of three embedded layers of 'events' that are taking place simultaneously.

> They are (1) the *game event*, defined as the action on the field plus directly related activities taking place on the sidelines, (2) the *stadium event*, defined as the total sequence of activities occurring in the stadium, both perceived and participated in by the fans and including the game event, and (3) the *medium event*, defined as the total telecast of which coverage of the game event is part.[10]

The medium event incorporates the game and stadium events but supplements these with the commentary, interviews, graphics and other visual inserts, advertising material from sponsors and station promotions. Over the years, the development of new technology, such as video tape, slow motion replay, computerised information banks to generate statistics, the increasing capacity to incorporate material from other sources outside the stadium, has shaped the form of the medium event in a manner primarily determined by the dictates of 'good television'—a media creation that is qualitatively removed from the experience of sports by the spectators in attendance.

Deconstructing the forms of sports television

Overall, the quantity and range of sports programming is indicative of the prominent position that television assigns to sport in general and to particular sporting subcultures. The amount of sport on television varies considerably from country to country. Even within the same country, the quantity produced varies from year to year. Predictably the United States is one of the leading producers of sports television. While, as noted, sport has been a staple programming form from the time of television's inception, its prominence in the schedules accelerated rapidly from the early 1960s. Between 1960 and 1972 there was a 65 per cent increase in sports telecasts.[11] By the mid-1970s, the major television networks in North America produced twelve hundred to fifteen hundred hours of sport annually—about twenty-five hours per week which represented approximately 15 per cent of total programming time.[12] Similarly, in Britain, sport in recent years has represented about 15 per cent of all output on BBC 1 and BBC 2, and overall, it is reported that in 1982 British television broadcast some two thousand five hundred hours of sport.[13] Available figures for the late 1970s indicate that in few countries throughout the developed world do the television services devote less than 5 per cent of their broadcast time to sport. Some provide considerably more, notably Canada (8.5 per cent), Australia (8.4 per cent), Yugoslavia (8.1 per cent), Czechoslovakia (8.6 per cent) and Switzerland (16 per cent).[14] Furthermore, trends indicate that sports programming is on the increase facilitated greatly by recently developed, more comprehensive and cost efficient, transmission technologies.[15]

Over the past thirty-five years, we can identify the evolution of a number of different forms within which television has and continues to present sports to the viewing public. These are:

1 preview programmes—discussion and prognostication about up coming events;

2 complete coverage—presented live or shown at a later time;

3 selected highlights and post mortems—an edited version of one or more games, often interspersed with other related material such as analysis of games, interviews, viewer competitions, etc.;

4 news item—short segments within the newscast or as a special

category of news focusing on results of particular contests recently completed or previews of forthcoming games;

5 magazine programmes — compilation of short pieces on a variety of sports;

6 documentary programmes focusing on historical events, outstanding individuals or teams, particular competitions.

Sports also occasionally appear on television as a leading theme in movies, drama, situation comedy or with the appearance of well known sports 'personalities' on general talk or magazine programmes. The latter are sometimes deliberately arranged to publicise future sports events contracted to the station or network. Sports also receive extensive in-house publicity through the regular station promotions that have become an almost universal component of programming strategies over recent years.

Such a broad range of programmes incorporating sport directs us to the central role that television has come to play as the self-appointed guardian and interpreter of the sporting culture. The commitments of time and resources television assigns to sports are significantly more substantial than to almost any other area of contemporary life, with the possible exception of news and current affairs. The breadth of television's coverage makes it possible for an individual who regularly watches sports programming to be confronted by a seemingly endless stream of material concerned with what is currently happening in the 'sports world' without the necessity of moving very far from their living room. Not only the myriad of sports events themselves, but the personal background of the participants, the coaches, the administrators, the relationship between sport and other institutions — all are the standard subject matter of an ever expanding battery of television sports experts who write, direct, produce, comment upon, criticise, pontificate and propagandise about the 'world of sports'.

The characteristics of this 'world' can best be examined if we analyse the leading television sporting programmes themselves and look more closely at the ways in which they are constructed. By doing so we should be able to provide some insight into the strategies and processes that television employs in appropriating and representing this world, primarily, it is argued, in order to satisfy the dictates of television as an industry and an entertainment form.

The sporting narrative

In documenting events in the world, television invariably presents them to viewers in the form of a coherent narrative or story. Daily newscasts, current affairs programmes, documentaries are the standardised forms developed by television within which such stories are constructed and presented. A number of administrative, technical and creative personnel combine their particular skills and employ established structures to create televisual stories that provide viewers with consistent accounts of a broad variety of contemporary actions and events in the world. While attempts are sometimes made to distinguish between descriptive and explanatory narratives, Will Wright argues strongly that this is misleading. Drawing from the philospher Arthur Danto's examination of the narrative he maintains:

> Narrative in itself is a *form* of explanation, a selection and an arrangement of events that make their successive occurrence understandable... Any successful narrative description will necessarily include assumptions, made by the author or narrator, as to why particular events were chosen, why others were left out, and why the chosen events, arranged in this way, comprise a satisfactory description. These assumptions amount to an explanation of the events, in the sense that they provide reasons why the final events follow from, are the result of, the earlier events.[16]

The sporting narrative is exactly this kind of explanation. Given the cultural legitimacy accorded to the 'universal sports model' outlined in earlier chapters, the essential narrative and dramatic structure of all sporting contests has become very much the same. Any sporting event is a contest between protagonists (or teams of protagonists) who compete according to a set of rules administered by authoritative adjudicator(s), so that ultimately a result emerges. From such a simple and seemingly limited structure, television using its technical and creative resources, proceeds to construct a style of sporting drama best suited to one of the primary dictates of the medium—the accumulation of audiences. Furthermore, through the variety of televisual forms listed above the same raw material can be reworked to achieve a satisfactory narrative appropriate to a broad range of programming needs, potential audiences and commercial strategies.

The most inclusive narrative form is the complete live telecast of the sporting event. Until the introduction of videotape into television production, in the 1950s, this was, of necessity, the most widely employed form of sports television, and despite the subsequent development of others, remains the type that attracts consistently large viewing audiences. The strength of its appeal lies in providing the television audience with an ostensibly complete and immediate experience of the sporting event.

The duration of the live telecast will of course depend on the sport that is being covered. Most team contests are played out over a period of two to four hours, and at least until the last fifteen years or so, invariably scheduled on a Saturday or Sunday afternoon. A fixed time period and regular starting time is most desirable from the point of television programming schedules. While there is some flexibility for special events, television — particularly commercial television — attempts to operate with continuous programming throughout its transmission day, divided into blocks of between half an hour and two hours in length, with programme changes on the half hour or hour. So as not to play havoc with regular schedules, programmes longer than two hours need to be some multiple of thirty minutes. From experience as to the approximate length of particular sports events, television programmers determine the time block required to incorporate the entire game event and the production crew prepare an appropriate amount of supplementary televisual material to fill the designated timeslot.

While there is some variation in the manner in which different television services throughout the world cover live sport, it is possible to present a detailed analysis of the 'typical' contemporary telecast, breaking it down into its constituent parts. For analytical purposes, it is useful to first divide the telecast into its visual and audio components and further look closely at the constituents of each and the manner in which they are combined and overlaid.

The *visual components* consist of the following:

1 Pre-prepared material on tape or film. This may include a title sequence at the beginning and a credit sequence at the end. Previously filmed interviews, background material, archival footage and viewer competitions may also be incorporated.

2 Graphics. Some pre-prepared (titles, credits, names of participants, statistics) and superimposed at the appropriate points in the telecast, and others — generally scores and more detailed statistics relating to the particular contest in progress — compiled and generated throughout. Special symbols, explanatory diagrams, analysis of particular plays, promotional material for future telecasts, play-outs and play-ins at commercial breaks may also form part of the telecast.

3 Action of the contest. This includes the play of the game as well as breaks built into the structure of the sport where play stops temporarily — when a ball goes out of bounds, a score has been effected, a point decided, preparation and post-action time. Some sports consist of almost continuous action — for example soccer and basketball — while in others there are short bursts of action punctuated by constant breaks. American football, baseball, cricket and tennis are good examples of the latter type. In analysing six telecasts of American football games, Brien Williams calculated that live play action constituted about 10 per cent of the total telecast time of about three hours. A detailed breakdown by Michael Real of the 1974 Super Bowl telecast which included pre-game and post-game material, indicated that only 3 per cent of the time was taken up with live visuals of the game.[17] Close analyses of tennis telecasts have also shown that over a three hour contest the time that the ball is actually in play constitutes only a surprisingly small proportion of the overall telecast time. What

has developed in sports television over the years, pioneered by American network productions, has been the tendency to include a steadily increasing proportion of ancilliary material to break up the continuous and fairly restricted — from the point of view of television producers — visual field available within even a multi-camera coverage of the on-field contest alone.

4 Slow-motion replays. The facility of videotape freed the sports telecast from limiting itself to a 'real-time' transmission of events as they occurred. First, a sports event could be recorded and transmitted — in whole or as an edited version — at a time more convenient to audiences in different time zones or more advantageous to television stations from the point of programming strategies and/or the maximisation of advertising revenues. A further attraction emerged in the capacity to insert into a live telecast, slow-motion segments of exciting or significant passages of play. This presented to the television audience a privileged cognitive and aesthetic experience of the sports contest qualitatively different from that of the paying spectator. Given that the action in many sports is extremely rapid, that the size of many stadiums makes it difficult for all patrons to have a good view of all the action on the field and that sports fans tend to savour the few brief and explosive moments of skill, daring, tragedy, conflict and exhiliration, the slow-motion replay represented a revolutionary innovation in the evolution of sports television. Technical improvements have enhanced the clarity of the slow-motion replay and it has become almost a mandatory component of television sports coverage throughout the world.[18] Apart from providing the viewers with the opportunity to closely analyse the form and style of skilled action, it is used to evaluate the validity of critical decisions by officials adjudicating the contest. The tape can be stopped at any point to present a still-frame image for even closer analysis if desired. Through the use of multiple videotaping facilities, slow-motion replays can be recalled within a few seconds of the action occurring and can be shown from one or more camera positions not originally used by the director in a live action transmission of the same passage of play.

5 Spontaneous or pre-arranged live coverage of non-action elements of the game or stadium event. These include shots of the crowd responding to what is going on, or of unscheduled disruptions or disturbances among the spectators or on the field. Cameras will be trained on off-field personnel — particularly coaches and managers — to yield 'reaction shots' that can be included at critical points in the game. Interviews with participants, coaches, managers, former players, celebrities attending the contest, are sometimes pre-arranged and shown during half-time breaks or other appropriate times when action on the field is temporarily suspended. Television directors will sometimes note the location in the stadium of wives, children, parents, business associates of leading participants and include close-up camera

shots of them at opportune moments. Before, during and after the contest, the commentary team may also appear on camera. Access to the dressing rooms is also sometimes available to the television crew although usually restricted to before and/or after the game.

6 Commercials. Where appropriate, these are inserted throughout the telecast almost always when there are breaks in the action on the field. Pull-through messages or logos paid for by sponsors may also be superimposed over action sequences.

The *audio component* of the live sporting telecast is also constituted by combining a number of separate sources. These consist of the following:

1 Audio soundtracks associated with pre-prepared material. Commercials, station promotions, interviews, background pieces etc.

2 Music. This may be used to accompany titles and credits, with play-in and play-out segments at commercial breaks and as background to pre-prepared pieces.

3 The 'international sound'. This is the term employed within television for the 'natural' sound emanating from the stadium event itself. By placing a number of microphones around the playing arena (sometimes even implanting them in the playing field itself), and at various points in the crowd, balancing and mixing these sources together, an audio track is created to provide the home viewer with some sense of the sounds and noises experienced by the spectator in the stadium.

4 Commentary. The most prominent portion of the audio track is assigned to the sports commentator, or as is most generally the case, to the 'commentary team'. While the very early sports telecasts relied on one commentator, and on occasions this is still the case, it is a well established norm in lengthy live telecasts to have two or more commentators sharing the load. A commentary team generally consists of an 'anchor-person', who is usually a television professional — in the early days invariably a graduate from radio sportscasting — assisted by one or more 'experts' employed for their inside knowledge of the game. The latter role has become a natural career path for reasonably articulate and/or 'colourful' former sports persons or coaches. Apart from the regular team, 'guest' commentators are sometimes employed, often individuals still active in the sport but not participating in the particular contest being telecast.

There is perhaps nothing that better illustrates the mediational role of television than the curious phenomenom of the television sports commentary. Instead of providing the viewer with a 'direct' access to the event through visual images of the contest mixed with the international sound, the commentary team attempt to present a coherent exposition, analysis, evaluation and assessment of the on-going game and stadium events, as well as locating a particular game in the broader context of a historically developed subculture that draws upon previous performances of present day participants, as well as the noteworthy champions and 'legendary' contests of previous eras. Thus, in the manner that the television newsreader or the narrator of a documentary presents a comprehensive and consistent story that coherently binds together the somewhat disparate and unanchored visual images being presented, similarly, the role of the sports commentator is to act as an authoritative guide to the 'reading' of the sports contest for the benefit of the television audience.

The participants in the commentary team are assigned specific tasks. Some describe the action, others are called upon to make assessments or evaluations on strategy, tactics or technical aspects of the game. In some cases, individuals are employed to comment on extra-game aspects relating to the crowd, the venue, the atmosphere of the occasion, etc. The central commentary team may be supplemented by roving specialists assigned to carry out interviews with leading participants — coaches, managers, star players — report on injuries during the game, or even to call on comments from celebrities or ordinary spectators in the crowd.

All members of the commentary team are in audio contact with the director of the telecast and when speaking on air are expected to refer their comments to the visual pictures that the television viewer is watching at the time. At times members of the team, through on air comments, may also alert the director to certain events going on so that cameras can be assigned to focus on these. The director, in turn, can inform commentators off-air of the visuals coming up such as the insertion of slow-motion replays, interviews, superimposed statistics and advertising breaks.

To a large extent, it is through the verbal commentary that the television sporting narrative is constructed. The visual aspects of the telecast operate as a sign system for the elaboration of particular verbal codes. The three major elements intertwined within the sports commentary may be identified as the descriptive, the evaluative and the dramatic.

a) The descriptive component consists of an ongoing verbal account of the action of the game. This is articulated within a specialised code that is heavily reliant upon a specific terminology or jargon developed within sport generally, as well as the sub-code appropriate to the particular sport. While the general characteristics of such codes remain essentially the same over time, specific nomenclature is constantly evolving and changing as a result of the continuing interaction between participants, ex-participants (a number of whom move into roles of sports journalists or television commentator), professional reporters — in both print and electronic media — and the broad subculture of fans and supporters of the sport. This specialised vocabulary is often so highly developed it can make television commentary almost incomprehensible to the uninitiated. Aside from the technical jargon developed to describe skills, strategies, tactics and styles of play, the commentary is liberally peppered with historical references to players from previous eras, details of memorable past contests, significant milestones, records, current gossip about players, coaches, administrators and so on.

b) However, incorporated alongside the descriptive element is an ongoing causal account of why the contest is developing in this particular way. The commentators and 'experts' are continually presenting evaluations and interpretations of the actions of the participants that direct the viewer to an 'official' or 'preferred' reading of what is unfolding in front of their eyes. Such evaluations are sometimes qualitative and impressionistic, but, certainly in recent times increasingly reliant on the incredible volume of quantitative statistics generated and transformed into tables, charts and diagrams superimposed over the picture on the television screen. Much of this involves the toting up of raw figures over a seemingly endless number of categories, sometimes the use of averages or means and, on occasions, the construction of special statistical indices. The latter represent attempts to apply modern rationalistic assessment techniques to sporting performance. The aura of science is invoked through the conspicuous application of its most popularly recognised manifestations — quantification and rank ordering — to legitimate the commentators' collective 'reading' of the contest. Even when not drawing on quantitative statistics, the commentators are constantly evaluating the particular efforts of players ('a great shot', 'a woeful attempt', 'a half-hearted pass'). Comments of this type consistently evoke an expected standard of skill as determined by 'the experts'. There also tends to be an ongoing interpretation revolving around the 'momentum', the 'balance' of the contest and the identification of 'critical points'.

Television's heavy use of the close-up shot directs the commentators to frequently allude to the hypothesised psychological or 'mental' states of the participants. Commentators will explain that the action of a particular player is due to 'nerves', 'lack of concentration', 'mental lapses', or perhaps the dreaded 'lack of desire'. They read deeply into the faces of the competitors and freely interpret the significance of what they see within a culturally standardised populist model of motivational psychology.

Other evaluative elements in the commentary include an assessment of the previous form of the participants, predictions as to the outcome, the possible influence of external forces — weather conditions, type of ground or surface — and the effects of tactics and strategy. The last is linked to the construction of an elaborate mythology revolving around the role of 'the coach' in team sports as the 'master-mind' of events on the field, the ideological connotations of which will be further explored below.

c) There is the repertoire of dramatic elements employed within television commentary. Binary oppositions, an essential element of any contest and therefore built into the very structure of sport, facilitate the perceived need of television to present a dramatic story. One of the principle tasks assigned to sports commentators is to help ensure that the contest does not come across to viewers as 'bad television', this being a 'story' that is flat, boring, colourless and uneventful. Despite the image of sport as natural drama, often particular contests do not turn out that way. Weather conditions, poor form, obvious differentials in levels of skill between opponents and numerous other factors frequently intervene to drain a game of much of its drama. During an interview with an Australian former test cricketer he candidly admitted that despite his personal affection for and involvement with the game, only three of the twenty-three international tests he played could be classified as exciting, the remainder being 'dull and boring'.[19] In such circumstances, the television commentator's job is to look for other aspects upon which to focus the viewer's attention.

When questioned about this aspect, a leading Australian football commentator, himself a former player stated:

> Well, that is where the entertainment part of it comes in. You don't drop off it because it's unentertaining or because it's a bad game. Your job is to try to make it look or sound a bit more exciting than it really is, because that is when you lose customers. That's not false at all. That's showbiz.[20]

Commentators therefore come armed with a number of appropriate dramatic oppositions which they can draw upon, both in advance and throughout the telecast, to characterise the competing individuals or groups. The following are frequently employed:

strength *vs* skill
favourite *vs* outsider
youth (enthusiasm, vitality) *vs* age (experience, craftiness)
natural ability *vs* dogged determination
temperament/volatility *vs* coolness/rationality
innovation/unpredictability *vs* mechanistic discipline/rigidity
friendship/affection *vs* hatred/'traditional' rivalry

Pre-established culturally shared stereotypes can assist the commentators in assigning particular sporting characteristics to individuals or teams in a manner consistent with popularly held conceptions of national character. Thus, in tennis for example, Bjorn Borg's 'personality' on the tennis court fitted admirably with generally held notions of Swedes as cool, rational and emotionally controlled. Throughout his playing career he was invariably identified by television commentators as the 'cool Swede' and labelled the 'Ice-Borg'. This provided useful dramatic coding for his clashes with his more volatile American opponents Jimmy Connors and John McEnroe.

While such broad characterisations may often be reasonably accurate, they may also, when applied to whole groups of participants in
international team sports, operate as artificial dramatic props that
merely act as crude reaffirmations of ethnocentric and ideological
values about other societies and political systems. A number of studies
analysing British television coverage of international soccer games
testify to this tendency. In an article on the 1978 World Cup coverage,
the writer notes:

> Schematically, the signifying map of the World Cup is one which
> on the one hand opposes Europe to South America and on the other
> hand associates one half of Europe (the Southern half) with the
> majority of countries of South America. The division within Europe
> can be described as Nordic versus Latin, while that within South
> America opposes the Spanish-speaking nations of the continent
> (which in Northern European eyes represent an intensified degree
> of Latinity) to Portugese-speaking and multi-racial Brazil. The
> motivating signifiers of these divisions are hair and skin colour,
> onto which are overlaid imputed differences of national 'tempera-
> ment' and style of play. Thus, on a crude example, 'Latin' is
> associated with 'fiery', while 'Nordic' is supposedly 'cool'. But the
> 'cool' of the Nordic fair-haired Dutch, expressed in their controlled
> possessionplay, is shared by the 'tropical' Brazilians (often of African
> or Amerindian descent) in implicit contrast to the hot headed
> Italians or Argentinians.[21]

A reference to 'traditional' rivalry between contestants or teams is
also a useful device employed by commentators to create a sense of
dramatic anticipation over the impending 'clash'. A recently reported
study indicates that there is a sound commercial basis for promoting
such an emphasis. In a cleverly constructed experiment, American
researchers presented sixty subjects with one of three versions of the
same tennis match, the commentary for which had been specially
produced to create a variation in a perceived affective relationship
between the two players ('unspecified', 'amity', 'enmity'). Upon analysis of questionnaires filled in by the subjects after viewing the match,
the researchers reported that, as a group, those who watched the
version in which the commentary suggested the two players vehemently
hated each other found the experience more enjoyable, interesting,
exciting as well as more involving than subjects in the other two
groups.[22]

In addition to the variety of oppositional codings, the dramatic
elements of the televised contest are further heightened by continual
references to the closeness of the scores; the number of times the lead
has changed; the possibility of a tight finish regardless of the actual
situation of the game ('anything can happen in modern football')
through references to extraordinary finishes and sudden turns of
fortune in some past contest.

While some would argue that most viewers are astute enough to be conscious and sceptical of the dramatising techniques of television sports commentary, there is research evidence to suggest that it is quite powerful in structuring the audiences' interpretations of the visuals they are watching. Subjects in an experimental situation were presented with two segments of a televised ice-hockey game, one of which a group of pre-experimental observers had rated as 'normal play' and the other as 'rough play'. Each of these televised segments was then overlaid with a commentary stressing the opposite to the visual material and then shown to different groups of subjects, while two other groups were shown the same visual sections with no commentary whatsoever. The 139 subjects, distributed across the four experimental conditions, then answered a questionnaire on their perception of the experience. The results were reported as follows:

> In the normal-action condition, the commentary stressing the roughness of play made the normal play appear rough; actually it made it appear rougher than the rough play. In the rough-action condition, on the other hand, the commentary that did not emphasize roughness made rugged play appear less rugged. The other measures of perception of play show very similar effects. There can be no doubt, then, that commentary can substantially alter perception of play.[23]

A further study focused directly on the subject of dramatic commentary in American television's coverage of professional football employing a content analysis technique to examine six games televised during the 1976 season. While the researchers' definition of 'dramatic' was somewhat broader than the one used here, a detailed sentence by sentence analysis of the audio commentary revealed about 72 per cent classified as 'descriptive', 27 per cent as 'dramatic' and 1 per cent as 'humorous'. In interpreting these figures the authors' conclude that,

> the finding that more than one-fourth of the commentary in televised professional football is 'dramatic' would appear to be rather significant. This certainly supports the contention that the role of the contemporary sportscaster involves more than reporting the action. He has the additional duty of complementing the drama on the field and presumably, of generating involvement and excitement for the television spectator.[24]

One other point should be made at this stage on the role of commentary. There is significant variation in the commentary style associated with particular sports. The degree of intrusiveness of the commentary, the tone of voice, vocabulary employed, intonation and accent of the commentators tend to operate as broad class signifiers. For example, compared to most other sports, tennis has been traditionally associated with the middle and upper-middle classes, played in well appointed private clubs. The style of television commentary accompanying tennis tends to reflect these social origins. At Wimbledon, the tone of the television commentators is hushed and reverent; they remain silent during the points, as the spectators are expected to do, so that for long periods the only sounds heard by the television viewer are the players moving about the court accompanied by the back and forth pinging of ball against racquet. In sharp contrast, the television commentary accompanying the various codes of football — sports strongly identified with the working and lower-middle classes — tends to be loud, continuous and overly descriptive.

Of course, all of the visual and audio elements outlined above are not incorporated into all live sporting telecasts. The amount of money, time, personnel, equipment and facilities available to television services will vary and the budget allotted to sporting telecasts will be determined on the basis of executive decisions that take into account the amount paid for the rights and the position of sports within their organisation's overall programming policies and strategies. As already mentioned, live sport is a relatively cheap form of programming and it is possible to mount a sporting telecast that consists of two or three cameras to film the action, one or two commentators in a booth and an outside broadcast van to house the few technical personnel required to edit the camera shots and mix in the commentary. Apart from the occasional slow-motion replay, the telecast may focus exclusively on the game-event itself.

However, as professional sport has become increasingly international over the past decades, so have the examples of sports television produced by the wealthier and technologically more sophisticated services — those of the North American commerical networks, Western Europe and to a lesser extent Australia — become the leading models of media professionalism throughout the world-wide industry. Their styles and techniques are perceived within the industry as 'state of the art'. As technical and on-air personnel from various countries are often involved in covering major international sporting events there are numerous opportunities for observing, interacting with and learning from the production techniques of the large American and British networks.

Also, local television services and stations in most countries import sports programmes produced by the Americans and/or British and the styles and techniques used in these are seen by their regular viewing audiences. If such telecasts become popular there are professional pressures for local production to imitate and incorporate such structure and techniques — particularly where there is commercial competition for domestic audiences.

However, there do appear to be significant differences between the two leading styles of sports television represented, on the one hand by the American commerical networks and, on the other by British television, in particular the BBC. The underlying basis of these differences can best be conceptualised by the somewhat artificial, but still meaningful, distinction between an emphasis on commercial *entertainment* values best represented by the American networks and *journalistic* values emphasising accuracy and 'objective' reporting of events that has become the established ethos within the BBC and a significant element of its institutional self-image. Thus, in Australia, a recent interview with a leading sports producer for the ABC, the government financed non-commercial national network closely modelled in many ways on the BBC, alluded to the recent change in emphasis within his own organisation with regard to television sport:

Murray Ashford: That is a problem in England ... They have a very old fashioned idea over there that if the sport was good enough before television came along there is no reason to alter anything, all you do is just carry on and put the camera in front of it.

Interviewer: Do you think that this is true across the board in Britain?

M.A.: Yes, indeed. Very much so.

Int: They won't interfere with it at all?

M.A.: They won't interfere with it very much. I don't know if you've ever seen their golf compared with our golf. It isn't structured for television. They will take two, three golfers hitting off from the tee and walking up the fairway for five minutes. We try not to show the golfers walking up the fairway. I model my coverages on the Americans, who while their chaps are walking up, there is someone else who is contending for first or second place, let's see how he's getting on. And when he has hit, someone in the other group is ready to hit his second and so on.

And further in the same interview:

M.A.: ...We are not just reporting ... that's where we have drifted more to the American style of things than the Brit's. I think the Brit's still think that if they are watching sport it is a reportage job. And I don't think this is good enough these days ... things are going snap, snap, snap, snap on television these days, in all departments not only sports ...

Int: So it's not a documentary as such where you are documenting what is going on out there?

M.A.: No, it's a form of entertainment.

Int: You've got to break it up to make it a television event?

M.A.: Yes ...

Int: You don't see any signs of this sort of thing with the British?

M.A.: Not a thing.[25]

Within the Australian television industry, and elsewhere, British television is greatly admired for its technical quality and high production standards. However, particularly with regard to the BBC, this is only seen to be possible because guaranteed government funding minimises the necessity to be commercially competitive and they are able to maintain production quality regardless of projected audience size. Thus, a sports producer at the commercial Nine network in Australia voiced strong admiration for the quality of British material saying:

> They're class, they really are—the quality of the production ...they go out and they shoot stuff on *film*. Now that's unheard of, to go out and shoot sport on film... they go out there with six film cameras—the rallies they cover—beautifully put together, edited beautifully, good documentary stuff, good picture quality and all that sort of stuff.

But when asked if he considered the British material better sports television he adamantly stated, 'No, because I think that when you talk about better, I think better is commercial...'[26] This position is certainly reinforced by the manner in which the Nine network produces its own sports programmes, notably their cricket coverage, which we will deal with at greater length below. Their orientation towards the American entertainment model is such that they often supplement sports material originating from Britain with their own inserts and graphics.

The other networks in Australia, both commerical and non-commercial, aim for a mix somewhere in between the British and American styles. Thus, when the Ten network covered the Los Angeles Olympics, buying the visuals and international sound from the American ABC network, one of the Australian producers co-mented:

> We argued a lot with the Americans to keep their razzamataz out of the coverage a lot so that we could do a fairly straight visual coverage, and we used the technology more to personalise the coverage than to show how fantastic our technology was... We didn't use a lot of the ABC graphics which they had in their coverage and we didn't use any, or very many of their 'close-up and personal' things... And the Americans used the policy that they have to keep changing things every few minutes...they need to change the perspective of what they're looking at at least every four or five minutes because they think that's the attention span of their average viewer. I give the viewer a bit more credibility than that—in Australia, any way.[27]

This is not to say that British television stands at the most transparent end of the spectrum. A comparative analysis of British and West German visual styles in the televising of soccer found that the tempo of alternation from one camera shot to another was far more rapid in the former than the latter. In three 1974 World Cup games for which German television supplied the pictures, the average shot length was fifteen and a half seconds while on the BBC's *Match of the Day*, a weekly edited review of soccer in Britain, the average shot length was eight and a half seconds. While, ideally an unedited British game should have been used as a comparison, the researcher suggests that after looking at all British soccer coverage on both the BBC and the commerical ITV over a period of three weeks, it was his impression that the distinction would still hold. Furthermore, after watching a recording of a complete game televised by the BBC in 1960, the developmental direction of the British style of coverage — more rapid tempo of alternation of shots, a higher proportion of close-up shots in the coverage — is further reinforced. In the 1960 telecast:

> Virtually no cuts are evident except after the scoring of a goal, and even those are few. Average length of shot is more than a minute. The camera follows play in a 'transparent' style, adjusting by pan and tilt to the movement of the ball. On the evidence of what is shown on British television when home teams go into Europe, most countries remain closer to this model than to the highly fragmented, sophisticated British style of today.[28]

The contrast between the 1960 British telecast and a 'high-tech' form of 'snap, snap' television typified by contemporary American network coverage of sports can best be illustrated through a detailed analysis of a number of recent sports programmes monitored from Australia's Nine network. As noted above, in the Australian context Nine's approach to sport appears to be based heavily on the American style and has been applied in a revolutionary way to its televising of cricket, the rights to which were obtained after a protracted and bitter struggle with the Australian and international cricketing authorities in the late 1970s. Apart from the cricket, Nine, in recent years, has greatly expanded its sports repertoire, through its purchase of satellite distributed programming from the United States and Europe. This includes a substantial number of the major international tennis, golf and motor-racing events, and selected games from the American major league baseball and football offerings.[29] In some cases, notably their tennis coverage, the Australian network contracts its own commentary team but uses the visuals and international sound provided by the host country. The American team sports are presented with the original commentary intact, almost exactly as seen by the domestic audiences in the United States, apart from a local studio presenter who intro-duces the telecast and may appear briefly at half-time and at the conclusion of the game-event.

The manner in which the contemporary American style of sports television is constructed emerges as we analyse the visual structure of the sports narrative as represented by a few recent examples. Four telecasts have been used in the analysis. In three (tennis, baseball and American football), the pictures originate from one of the United States' networks, while the fourth, being one of Nine's live cricket telecasts, provides us with an example of the Australian network's own sports production style.

A thirty minute section of each telecast was chosen, avoiding any period in which unusually long breaks in action of the game occur (half-time, weather delays or other unscheduled interruptions to play).

The visual content of each thirty minute section was then divided into its component segments. An *action* segment is one in which the pictures focus on some aspect of the contest on the field. This is not only when the ball is 'in play' but also the natural breaks between points or plays. It includes occasional shots of officials and off-field personnel. The *slow-motion* segments are self-explanatory and are generally inserted at points where play has temporarily stopped. *Other* segments include statistics and graphics (not superimposed), play-outs and play-ins to commercials, shots of commentators or 'expert' analysts, crowd shots and any other visual material extraneous to the game. The fourth category takes in the *commercial breaks* which appeared in all of the monitored telecasts, although the length of each commercial break varies depending on the type of sport being shown. In tennis, the commercials are usually inserted after odd games when the players change ends and customarily take a ninety second break in play. It is significant that this aspect of tennis has only become institutionalised since television became involved to ensure the standardised regular break essential to commercial stations. Previously, particularly early in a match, players would merely change ends at the appropriate games and play would continue when both indicated they were ready to proceed. In baseball, longer, but less frequent, breaks are available at the end of each innings or if there is a change in pitching, while American football is structured to allow numerous fairly regular breaks of about a minute in length. Within the live cricket telecasts, a brief thirty second spot can be inserted after each over with other less predictable stoppages in play (the fall of a wicket) providing occasional opportunities for lengthier commercial breaks.

A breakdown of the four telecasts provided in Table 4.1 indicates that a thirty minute section of each game was made up of between twenty-three and fifty-six segments, the smaller figure occurring in the tennis telecasts while the higher figure applies to the Australian cricket coverage. The two major American sports fall somewhere in between, with the pattern of the baseball coverage being closer to that of tennis, while American football telecasts revealed a structure closely comparable to Nine's cricket coverage.

For both the cricket and American football, the action segments are relatively short (the average length being forty-five and fifty-two seconds respectively) and in total take up about two-thirds of the

Table 4.1 Comparative analysis of visual components of live telecast of four sports[a] (Thirty minute segments of each telecast sampled)

	No. of segs	Tennis[b] % of time	Av. length (secs)	Range (secs)	No. of segs	Baseball[c] % of time	Av. length (secs)	Range (secs)	No. of segs	Football[d] % of time	Av. length (secs)	Range (secs)	No. of segs	Cricket[e] % of time	Av. length (secs)	Range (secs)
Action	12	80.8	120.0	21.6 → 290.1	15	70.0	83.9	18.6 → 176.3	23	66.0	51.6	6.1 → 131.6	28	69.5	44.7	6.0 → 141.9
Slow motion	7	5.2	13.4	8.9 → 24.2	11	9.0	15.0	4.1 → 27.4	15	11.0	13.2	9.5 → 19.2	17	11.2	11.9	8.9 → 25.6
Other	–	–			3	1.0			8	5.5			2	2.3		
Commercials	4	14.0			3	20.0			5	17.5			9	17.0		
Total	23	100.0			32	100.0			51	100.0			56	100.0		

a) All shown on Nine network in Australia. United States originating material shown live by satellite or slightly delayed.
b) Semi-final, 1985 Masters Championship played in New York, 12 January 1985; Jimmy Connors *vs* Ivan Lendl (NBC with Nine Australia commentary).
c) Final game, 1984 World Series. Detroit *vs* San Diego (NBC visual and commentary).
d) Super Bowl, 1985 broadcast live on 20 January 1985. San Francisco *vs* Miami (ABC (USA) visual and commentary).
e) Preliminary game, World Series Cup 1985 played in Sydney, 17 January 1985. West Indies *vs* Sri Lanka (Nine Australia visual and commentary).

sampled time of each. The longest action segment within each was a little over two minutes. Both also contained a substantial number of slow-motion segments — on the average one every two minutes — and these occupied more than 10 per cent of the overall time. The football telecast included a slightly higher proportion of 'other' visuals than the cricket. It should be noted that the particular cricket game monitored was played in Australia between two visiting teams and attended by a relatively small crowd. Interestingly there were no crowd shots in the thirty minute segment analysed, although these are a regular feature of most cricket telecasts, particularly those in which the Australian team is involved.

While the proportion of live action in both the baseball and cricket coverage was almost identical, the average length of each segment in the baseball was almost twice that of the cricket. Tennis emerged as by far the 'sparsest' telecast consisting entirely of action (81 per cent) with relatively few slow-motion replays (5 per cent) and no other extraneous segments apart from commercials. Furthermore, the average time of an action segment in the tennis was almost three times that in the cricket telecast and one particular action segment within the monitored period ran unbroken for almost five minutes.

However, even within any one segment of action the television viewer's perspective cannot be compared to that of a live spectator observing the game from a fixed position in the arena. Over the past fifteen years the tendency has been to consistently increase the number of cameras covering the event — particularly in arena team sports — to facilitate an extensive variety of angles, perspectives and close-ups so that the visual image appearing on the television screen can be alternated rapidly. To best illustrate the effects of these developments, a ten-minute section of each of the four telecasts has been further analysed in terms of the shot components appearing on the screen and the results are indicated in Table 4.2.

The primary visual perspective used in television sports coverage is the *medium shot*. In team sports played on large arenas, *wide shots* are shown, but used very sparingly. In individual sports played over a small area, such as tennis, the primary medium shot is able to take in most of the relevant action without much camera alternation or movement, although alternative perspectives, such as those obtained from ground level cameras are sometimes employed. However, in team sports the tendency has become to situate a number of cameras in the stands to cover the primary shots, sometimes supplemented by mobile cameras along the sidelines for close-ups. With a large number of cameras employed, cuts from one to the other are generally preferred to pans or zooms in and out from the same camera, although there are occasional examples of the latter. The major types of image alternation are accomplished by switching between medium shots from different camera positions or from a medium shot to a close-up. While the medium shot in team sports generally takes in a group of perhaps

Table 4.2 Comparative shot analysis of four live sports telecasts (Ten minute sample from each telecast) Tennis (US), Baseball (US), Football (US), Cricket (Australia)

Sport:	Time (secs)				No. of shots				Av. time per shot (secs)				% of time				% of shots				Time: longest (secs)				Time: shortest (secs)			
	T	B	F	C	T	B	F	C	T	B	F	C	T	B	F	C	T	B	F	C	T	B	F	C	T	B	F	C
Medium shot/ wide shot	326.0	395.4	214.6	251.2	21	42	17	64	15.5	9.4	12.6	3.9	54.0	65.6	35.7	41.7	34.4	57.5	27.0	55.2	33.8	27.9	27.2	17.1	3.6	1.5	1.9	1.3
Close-up	206.3	133.8	223.3	169.6	32	18	29	25	6.5	7.4	7.7	6.8	34.1	22.2	37.1	28.1	52.5	24.7	46.0	21.6	22.2	51.2	17.5	19.0	1.3	1.9	1.5	2.0
Slow motion	34.5	50.5	128.4	82.5	3	4	9	13	11.5	12.6	14.3	6.3	5.7	8.4	21.3	13.7	4.9	5.5	14.3	11.2	12.6	15.5	22.6	13.3	10.1	10.0	9.5	1.8
Crowd	–	22.6	6.0	–	–	9	2	–	–	2.5	3.0	–	–	3.8	1.0	–	–	12.3	3.2	–	–	3.5	3.5	–	–	1.7	2.5	–
Other	37.5	–	29.5	99.7	5	–	6	14	7.5	–	4.9	7.1	6.2	–	5.4	16.5	8.2	–	9.5	12.0	14.3	–	12.1	14.4	3.9	–	0.2	1.3
Total	604.3	602.3	601.8	603.0	61	73	63	116	9.9	8.3	9.6	5.2	100.0	100.0	100.0	100.0	100.0	100.0	100.0	100.0	33.8	51.2	27.2	19.0	1.3	1.5	0.2	1.3

up to half a dozen or so players, the *close-up* focuses in on one person — sometimes very tightly as in a head and shoulder shot — and punctuates the visual narrative by singling out individual performers prominent in a particular passage of play. It is also employed as a 'reaction shot', not only of competitors but also of coaches, managers, team mates and even spectators. The other kinds of shots used have already been detailed in the previous discussion of Table 4.1 above.

For the sampled ten minutes of each telecast, Table 4.2 indicates that the number of shots employed ranged between sixty-one for tennis to 116 for cricket, the number used in the latter being substantially higher than in any of the other three. Tennis, being the only individual sport, also understandably had the highest proportion of close-up shots (52.5 per cent), but despite this it was the American football coverage that devoted the greatest proportion of overall time to close-ups (37 per cent). In general, the football telecast seemed to be shot extremely tightly with many of the medium shots showing a group of players only from the waist up. In fact football was the only one of the four in which more time was devoted to close-ups than to any other kind of shot — somewhat surprising considering there are twenty-two players on the field at any time. The baseball telecast contained both the highest proportion of medium or wide shots (57.5 per cent) and the proportion of the overall time taken up by these shots was the highest (65.6 per cent) of the four. While visually more than half the cricket telecast consisted of medium or wide shots (55.2 per cent), the average length of each shot was extremely brief (less than four seconds), indicative of the extent to which the Australian telecast alternates images even more rapidly than any of the American examples. This is further reinforced when we compare the average overall shot lengths. In the portion of the cricket telecast sampled this was a brief 5.2 seconds compared with a slightly higher 8.3 seconds for the baseball, 9.6 seconds for the football and 9.9 seconds for the tennis.[30]

Perhaps more illustrative of the overall tendency towards fragmentation of viewpoint is that the longest shot of any kind over all four telecasts lasted 51.2 seconds and this was a close-up of a baseball pitcher warming up before an innings, while graphics listing the team line-up were superimposed over the picture. Overall, rarely did any shot exceed twenty-five seconds in length — in the cricket the longest was only nineteen seconds.

The multiplicity of viewing perspectives provided by the television coverage is further increased in that the slow-motion replays are often from one or more camera positions different from that shown in the live segments.

The analysis undertaken above sensitises us to the extent to which the sporting event is transformed through the dictates of what is considered to be 'good television' into a form of rapidly alternating images and visual perspectives that has much in common with the

editing style of many other contemporary commercial television programmes. In a recent article analysing one of Nine's cricket telecasts,
the writer noted that the average shot length in a randomly chosen five
minute section from a popular adventure series and from a newscast
were 5.85 seconds and 6.8 seconds respectively, almost identical to
that of the sports programme, 'despite the enormous production
differences'. He goes on the suggest:

> The similarity of average shot length across these different genres of
> TV is significant because it denies the common professional's claim
> that the nature of the reality they are shooting dictates the way they
> shoot it, and supports the academic's contention that the prime
> determinant is the nature of the TV discourse.[31]

The broader social and political connotations of the transformation
of sport into a form of television discourse will be explored in
subsequent chapters. The primary point to be made at this stage is
that the overriding concern of television professionals, and of the
organisations for whom they are employed, is the construction of
programming material that can be presented within the style and
structure the industry considers attractive television. The raw material
of a high-level sporting contest intrinsically provides television with
dramatic elements that demonstrably attract large audiences. However, the commercial and organisational prerogatives directed towards
the accumulation of audiences together with the powerful, socially
constructed value system within the industry that positively reinforces
professional work that is most successful in achieving this, dictates the
direction within which this form of programming is most likely to
develop. In the form described and discussed above, it encourages, as
it has in the area of news and current affairs, an overwhelming concern
with 'entertainment values' defined in terms of the application of
available technological facilities to the production side together with
the creative restructuring of the content in a manner that achieves the
greatest possible emphasis on colour, excitement, conflict and audience anticipation. It seeks to establish, through these means, television's version of the sporting contest as both a unique and satisfying
experience for the potential sports spectator and, beyond this, as a
general form of entertainment more attractive to potential television
audiences than other available alternatives.

Edited sports telecasts

Even greater control of the event is facilitated for television through
the editing of sports contests into packages of highlights and magazine
style programmes. In these formats all of the televisual elements
available in a live coverage are employed with the added advantage of

Television's impetus towards continuously alternating the images presented to viewers is illustrated in the above sequence drawn from the Nine network's cricket coverage. In following the course of one ball bowled, seven separate shots (plus superimposed informational graphics) are employed within one 16-second segment.

In arena team sports, apart from the occasional 'establishment' shot (1), only a small section of the play is framed for the viewer (2). Typical of American football coverage is the extensive use of the tight group and individual close-up (3, 4, 7, 8). The sport's 'stop-start' structure permits numerous replays and time for detailed analysis by 'expert' commentators (5, 6). © 1985 ABC Inc.

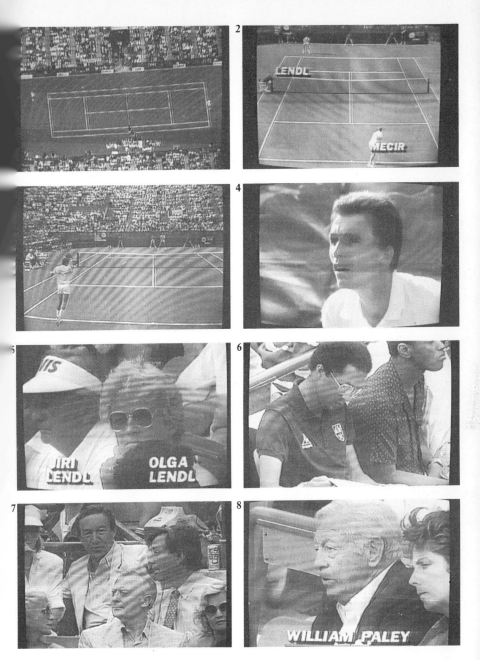

Shots 2–4 almost exhaust the possible camera perspectives in tennis coverage. These are supplemented by the occasional wide-shot, overhead (1) and audience shots. The CBS coverage of the 1986 US Open heavily featured the 'celebrity' shot (5–8) and managed to incorporate about twenty (including Arthur Ashe, Edward Woodward and William Paley - the 'founder' of CBS) within one half-hour segment.

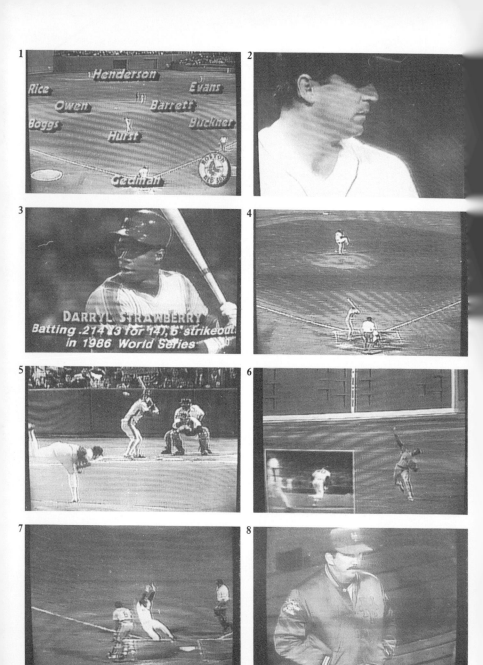

Again, with the exception of the 'establishment' shot early in the telecast (1), television's baseball coverage incorporates mostly medium shots (4, 5, 7) and close-ups (2, 3, 8). As, similar to cricket, simultaneous action occupies distant points of the arena, the viewer is supplied with a technologically fragmented perspective via the superimposed insert (6).

eliminating from the presentation much of the material that, from the point of view of the producers, does not represent good television entertainment. The focus of highlights programmes are high action, individual and team skills, excitement and the scoring of 'goals', certainly all facets of a contest of interest to most sports spectators. But, by editing down a contest from a couple of hours to fifteen or twenty minutes, the 'natural' rhythm and structure intrinsic to the game is fractured, real time is telescoped and the television viewers' experience of the contest even further distanced from that of the paying spectator at the arena.

Editing sports allows television to tailor a programme in terms of length and structure almost entirely to its own needs. The insertion of secondary material such as slow-motion replays can be achieved without danger of missing ongoing action, required commercial breaks taken into account and a variety of forms of post-hoc analysis included so that a coherent narrative structure is created — one that presents an authoritative and consistent 'reading' of the event.

Again this type of programming can vary significantly in style and content. The earliest type represented a television version of the print journalists' accounts of a contest or a series of contests — an extended version of the sports report within a television newscast. Highlights programmes would focus on all the games played within a particular sports competition or league and often emerged as a substitute for live coverage, when this was not possible, or to supplement the coverage of one game in a competitive league with reports of other games. A general form of a sports 'post-mortem' programme might include brief coverage of a variety of sporting competitions mixed with 'expert' analysis, interviews, viewer competitions and general information about the sports world. In the main, this type of programme is directed towards those who are already close followers of particular sports or sport in general. Such programmes were often developed independently by local stations being extremely cheap to produce and primarily directed towards local and regional audiences. They rely heavily on the local sports subcultures for the recruitment of on-air personnel who make up 'expert' panels to analyse the events and add local colour.

While highlights programmes focusing on one particular sport or sports competition are prevalent — usually restricted to the one or two major spectator sports most prominent in the local or national sporting culture — there has been a discernible trend towards more slickly produced magazine style programmes that would have potential audience appeal beyond the hardened local sports fans.

Two programmes that pioneered this style of sports programming were the BBC's *Grandstand* and the American ABC networks' *Wide World of Sport*. Both were scheduled on Saturday afternoon, consisting of brief segments covering a variety of different sports each week. The

American version first went to air in the early 1970s, each week mixing live coverages of two or three different sports contests being played in various places—both within the United States and other parts of the world—tied together by a studio 'anchorman'. Rather than following through a single contest, sections of each—perhaps ten minutes in length—would be serially presented continuously throughout the running time of the programme. The underlying strategy of such a structure is to maximise the potential audience for the show as a whole, while not alienating viewers who might be bored by lengthy concentration on one particular sport or the other. The emphasis is on visually exciting sports not traditionally covered by television on a regular basis such as skiing, high diving, surfing, water sports, gymnastics, ice skating, many of which could potentially attract an audience that included a respectable proportion of women of all ages and young children, groups that television programmers were aware were strongly underrepresented in rating figures for most television sports programmes. The television ratings indicated that the television sports audience was heavily skewed towards males aged between fifteen and forty-nine. Furthermore, rating surveys indicated that early Saturday afternoon was one of television ratings 'wastelands' despite evidence that many people are at home with their families at this time. The strategy from the point of view of the television programmer was to develop a format that would be most effective in drawing in a demographically diverse range of viewers who were not only generally not watching television at this time but who rarely watched sport on television at any time.

The American show ran up to two hours on some weeks and the British programme filled a longer timeslot with a slightly different format, mixing pre-edited highlight packages in a variety of sports with some live coverages, sports updates, interviews and background pieces. Both programmes proved successful and stimulated the development of an Australian version, also called *Wide World of Sport*, on the Nine network which was originally put to air in 1981. Drawing upon the availability of their satellite transmitted material, the programme evolved a format that consisted of brief edited segments constructed from overseas material, together with periodic crosses to local live events padded out with pre-recorded interviews and studio patter by the two co-hosts, one a former Australian cricket champion, Ian Chappell, and the other, a Sydney radio journalist and 'personality', Mike Gibson. The essence of this type of programme is variety and high production values. It runs for four hours but moves along at a rapid pace with few segments longer than eight minutes and with some pieces running only two or three minutes. The production style is slick and youthful, incorporating 'state-of-the-art' graphics, tight editing and a significant use of contemporary music to create atmosphere and maintain the pace. Again, the style appears to owe a great deal to the up-market approach associated with similar American network productions. The programme's producer attested to this when asked about his personal influences and reference standards:

> The American shows. Watching *Entertainment This Week* and watching *Eye on Hollywood* and those sort of shows that have the pace, the variety. I mean you just sit there glued to them ... they tease you all the way through as I try to do, and you know if you don't like what's happening then there's something always coming up and there's very slick production.

In order to achieve the show's aims, certain sports material is considered inappropriate for inclusion. The criteria determining which sports are suitable was explained as follows:

> I don't like sports that take a long time to tell the story. For instance, basketball—you could never put it on because it's a continuous scoring game, you could never edit it down to an eight minute package ... So that the sport has to lend itself to being packaged in that sort of format—it has to be broken down. Things like ice-skating is good because you can run three minutes of it. See, that's the thing—in the old days they'd run ten minutes of ice-skating, you know, three different routines. Now, we never run ice-skating back to back ... you just run a little of it and run something else in the same segment ... If you run ten minutes of ice-skating and if they don't like ice-skating you're gone, you're finished. It gets boring. Any sport gets boring if you run too much of it or you run a risk that somebody who doesn't like it will leave, so you have to keep that montage and variety happening.[32]

The search for variety and the necessity of filling a four hour timeslot almost every week means that, as with news and current affairs, the eccentric, the weird and the oddball item are eagerly sought after. The boundary defining where sport begins and ends tends to become blurred around the edges. Thus, as one of the on-air presenters of Nine's *Wide World of Sport* put it:

> I regard sport as just about everything you do from Friday night to Monday morning when you've gotta go back to work again. I mean I sit down with my mates and have a game of cards. That's sport to me—not very athletic but it's still a game.[33]

Defined in televisual terms the world of sport comes to include almost any event that is competitive no matter how far removed it may be from traditional notions of sport.

> We've had Japanese ballroom dancing—a great reaction, one of the most hilarious things you've ever seen—it only went for a minute and a half. Ralph the diving pig—those sort of things—anything that was a well put together story ... anything that is a competitive

situation. Sport is classified in the dictionary as diversion, a pastime, and that'll do. There are some pretty oddball sorts of things on the show but it's entertainment.[34]

Inevitably, when talking with people in the television industry—particularly commercial television—any criticism of programming content and style is met with the rationale of 'entertainment', the meaning of which seems to reside exclusively in the magnitude of the viewing audience that chooses to watch. Sport becomes a vehicle for 'entertainment', which is in turn a euphemism for accumulating audiences to sell to advertisers. The magazine style sports programme reflects the general trend in many areas of 'non-fiction' television towards this style of programme. The content matter is largely immaterial, it is the format that sells. The magazine style promises that there will be something for everyone and that none of it will go on for very long. This is sensible television programming from the point of view of commercial television executives. As Mike Gibson explained:

It seems to us that if they're going to watch gymnastics, and maybe some of the guys don't like that, if you tell them 'Coming up next there's a boxing match'—okay, you say, 'Well I'll hang around for that'. You watch the boxing. By the same token if it's good and he gets his ten minutes, he's going to watch more. You know, he's going to hang around. You can never cut anything too short in my opinion... I mean there's nothing better than leaving people wanting more. A fella' sees a good fight and says 'Gee, that was good', and you say 'Well, if you liked that one, we've got a better one next week'—he's going to come back... I mean it's just selling something—we're selling sport.[35]

Notes

1 William O. Johnson, Jr, *Super Spectator and the Electric Lilliputians*, Little Brown & Co., Boston, 1971, p. 45; Stephen Wagg, *The Football World: A Contemporary Social History*, Harvester Press, Brighton, UK, 1984, p. 42.
2 Richard Harmond, 'Sugar Daddy or Ogre? The Impact of Commercial Television on Professional Sports', in F. J. Coppa (ed.), *Screen and Society*, Nelson Hill, Chicago, 1979, pp 82–3.
3 Raymond Williams, *Television: Technology and Cultural Form*, Fontana, London, 1974, p. 29.
4 Williams, p. 30.
5 Harmond, p. 84; Susan L. Greendorfer, 'Sport and Mass Media', in Günther R. F. Lüschen and George H. Sage (eds), *Handbook of Social Science of Sport*, Stipes Publishing Co., Champaign, Ill., 1981, pp 167–8.
6 Quoted by Harmond, p. 83.
7 T. S. Eliot, *Notes Towards a Definition of Culture*, Faber, London, 1948, p. 31.
8 Harmond, p. 83.

9 The US network NBC televised a football game without any commentary in January 1981. Apparently the response from the public—after more than thirty-five years of 'naturalising' the concept of sports commentary on television—was not positive and the experiment has not been repeated.
10 Brien R. Williams, 'The Structure of Televised Football', *Journal of Communication*, 27(3), 1977, p. 135.
11 Barry D. McPherson, 'Sport Consumption and the Economics of Consumerism', in Donald W. Ball and John W. Loy (eds), *Sport and Social Order*, Addison-Wesley, Reading, Mass., 1975, p. 243.
12 These figures are reported in John W. Loy, Barry D. McPherson and Gerald Kenyon, *Sport and Social Systems*, Addison-Wesley, Reading, Mass., 1978, p. 305. By 1980, the US networks totalled 1300 hours of sports programming and in 1983, the figure was 1446 hours.

These figures do not take into account the recent rapid growth of cable networks, pay television and satellite distributed independent stations in North America, a number of which include a substantial quantity of sport in their programming schedules. ESPN, a specialist sports cable network, commenced operation in 1979, broadcasting sport twenty-four hours a day, seven days a week—a total of some nine thousand hours per year. By 1982, the service had already signed up more than ten million subscribers and forecast up to thirty million by the 'mid-eighties' according to Rex Moorfoot, *Television in the Eighties: The Total Equation*, BBC, London, 1982, p. 69.
13 Moorfoot, p. 67; *Rydges in Marketing*, August, 1982.
14 Statistics calculated from the somewhat incomplete data on worldwide television programming in *Unesco Statistical Yearbook*, 1982. Prominent omissions from the table provided are West Germany and the USSR.
15 For example, in Australia, the number of hours of sport on television in 1981 increased by 37 per cent from the previous year as reported by Brian Stoddart, 'Sport, Television and Sponsorship in Australia, 1975–83', Paper presented to the Conference on the History of Sporting Traditions, Melbourne, August, 1983, p. 1. The writer reports a projection that by 1990, Australian television will be broadcasting a mind-boggling 10 000 hours of sport per year.
16 Will Wright, *Six Guns and Society*, University of California Press, Berkeley and Los Angeles, 1975, p. 125.
17 Brien Williams, p. 134; Michael Real, 'Super Bowl: Mythic Spectacle', *Journal of Communication*, 25(1), 1975, p. 32.
18 The slow-motion replay has become so much an essential component of televised sport it is incorporated into the coverage of even such leisurely paced sports as snooker, lawn bowls and even bocce.
19 Personal interview with Ross Edwards, Sydney, 19 November 1984.
20 Personal interview with Lou Richards, Melbourne, 25 November 1984.
21 Geoffrey Nowell-Smith, 'Television—Football—The World', *Screen*, 19(4), 1978/9, p. 55. See also Andrew Tudor's discussion of British television's coverage of the 1974 World Cup in *Football on Television*, British Film Institute, London, 1975, pp 60–5; Justin Wren-Lewis and Allan Clarke, 'The World Cup—A Political Football', *Theory, Culture and Society*, 1(3), 1983, pp 123–32 on the 1982 tournament in Spain.
22 Jennings Bryant, Dan Brown, Paul W. Comisky, and Dolf Zillmann,

'Sports and Spectators: Commentary and Appreciation', *Journal of Communication*, 32(1), 1982, pp 109–19.
23 Paul Comisky, Jennings Bryant and Dolf Zillman, 'Commentary as a Substitute for Action', *Journal of Communication*, 27(3), 1977, p. 152.
24 Jennings Bryant, Paul Comisky and Dolf Zillmann, 'Drama in Sports Commentary', *Journal of Communication*, 27(3), 1977, p. 144.
25 Personal interview with J. Murray Ashford (who began his television career in Britain and has been a producer/director of sports programmes for the ABC in Australia for some twenty years), Melbourne, 9 November 1984.
26 Personal interview with Saul Shtein who at the time was the producer for the Australian Nine network of *Wide World of Sports*, Sydney, 19 November 1984.
27 Personal interview with Bob Kemp who, at the time, held the position of Producer, Special Projects, Network Ten, and who was closely involved with Ten's mammoth coverage of the Los Angeles Olympics — Melbourne, 23 November 1984.
28 Charles Barr, 'Comparing Styles: England v. West Germany', in *Football on Television*, British Film Institute, London, 1975, p. 50.
29 Although the Nine network in Australia introduced American football to local television and continued showing it for some five years, in 1985, the rights were secured by the Ten network. Late in 1985 an exhibition game between two minor American college teams was played at VFL park — the 'home' of Australian rules football — and televised live on the Ten network.
30 The reliability of such statistics might be questioned given the limited sample, but, at least for the cricket telecast, the figures are consistent with those reported in a previously published study by John Fiske, 'Cricket/T.V./Culture', *Metro*, 62, 1983, pp 21–6. Fiske's analysis of four random sections of one of Nine's cricket telecasts yielded an average of around six seconds per shot.
31 Fiske, p. 22.
32 This and the previous quote are from a personal interview with Saul Shtein in Sydney, 19 November 1984.
33 Personal interview with Mike Gibson, at the time co-presenter of *Wide World of Sport* on the Nine network — Sydney, 19 November 1984.
34 From the interview with Saul Shtein.
35 From the interview with Mike Gibson.

5
Sport's political culture and the politics of televised sport

Values, ideology and sport

The material in the previous chapter analysed the way in which television operates as a primary instrument in the production and dissemination of sport as modern popular culture. Before attempting to assess the broader political and ideological implications of television's virtual colonisation of sport — in particular high performance sport — it is first necessary to consider a few of the thorny and complex questions surrounding the broader relationship between sport and politics.

The central values of participatory amateur sport which must be considered the primal modern sporting form were most clearly articulated and propagated by its influential supporters within the British bourgeoisie of the Victorian era. Thus the bald principles of rule-bound competition, in which individuals or small groups strive against each other for success and victory in a specified form of physical exercise, understandably represent a symbolic displacement of the values central to political and economic liberalism. As the new legal and political structures sought to sweep away the hereditary bases of power and privilege associated with the long standing aristocratic domination of society, and to establish in their place a form of social organisation that recognised and rewarded entrepreneurial enterprise and productivity, so the rules and principles applied to sports sought to ensure that the skills and abilities required to achieve success in 'the game' would be based firmly on similar meritocratic assumptions.

Ideally the outcome of any sporting encounter should be determined solely by the relative effort, application and energy exerted by the competing participants.

Thus, the process of formulating rules and conditions for modern competitive sports provided their founders with the opportunity to construct a set of circumstances metaphorically equivalent to the ideal market situation so beloved by liberal economic theorists. Wherever possible, all relevant conditions of competition would be standardised to eliminate chance and therefore to minimise the likelihood of the result reflecting inequitable cicumstances outside the narrow range of factors deemed to be directly relevant to the game itself. In sport, far more effectively than in real life, where the historical weight of proprietorship of land and capital accumulation, the legal right to bequeath land and property, and a less than perfect free market system contribute to the entrenchment of a hierarchical class structure, each event begins with a clean score sheet and each result, ideally, should be determined by the particular performances of the competitors in an equitably regulated contest. With each new confrontation or sporting season, the participating teams or individuals begin once again from a position of formal equality. So that in sport, the 'result' signifying success and failure, victory and defeat, champion and also-ran can be arrived at more 'rationally', meaning that, within the narrow confines of the competitive task, such designations have a greater 'scientific' validity than those that operate in the wider social and material world. Of course they are also susceptible to rapid temporal alternation — heroic champion today, vanquished and forgotten tomorrow — or next season.

Furthermore, the process of restructuring and formalising a variety of localised games and rituals established a non-instrumental region of social life that emphasised the practice of skills which were refinements or extensions of human physical capacities and psycho-motor co-ordinations widely shared, easily learned at a young age and universally distributed (accessibility and cultural tradition notwithstanding) across class, national and ethnic groupings in society.

However, the manner in which the bourgeois founders of sport conceived the 'game' should be played, how the individual should approach the challenge of sporting competition, was heavily influenced by a set of values and norms socially connotative of 'civilised behaviour', as well as a relationship to leisure long associated with the traditional European leisure class — the hereditary aristrocracy. This is clearly evident in the idealised code of the 'gentleman's' approach to sport that emphasises the qualities of self-discipline, the satisfaction of competing well regardless of outcome, the importance of respect for both opponents and the rules of the game and, most importantly, the conception of sport as a pastime for amateurs. The emphasis on participation above victory acknowledges that sport represents a peculiar instance of the suspension of the established social hierarchy and, while it might be somewhat distasteful, defeat at the hands of social inferiors is always a distinct possibility that follows from the universalistic principles underlying 'fair competition'. However, this should not be interpreted to bear any significance on the relative position individuals might occupy within the 'real' social order.

As Pierre Bourdieu has pointed out, there is a coherent political philosophy underlying this perspective.

The theory of amateurism is in fact one dimension of an aristocratic philosophy of sport as a disinterested practice, a finality without an end, analogous to artistic practice, but even more suitable than art... for affirming the manly virtues of future leaders: sport is conceived as a training in courage and manliness, 'forming the character' and inculcating the 'will to win' which is the mark of the true leader, but a will to win within the rules. This is 'fair play', conceived as an aristocratic disposition utterly opposed to the plebeian pursuit of victory at all costs.[1]

However, beyond the idealised values associated with both classical liberalism and aristocratic nobility of character as represented by the notions of equal competition, rational rules and an adherence to the spirit of 'fair play', lurks a deeper, and perhaps more politically significant, current that links sport with the cult of virility referred to by Bourdieu. Within the broader nineteenth century political context of intense national rivalries, a concern with forging national loyalties superseding those of traditional village, regional and religious identifications and a public obsession with military preparedness, sport opened an important pathway to the socio-political task of building strong bodies. Further, it offered a controlled training ground in which reasonably contained physical aggression could be ritualistically unleashed by young males and legitimately admired by spectators. It is in these aspects that the English version of competitive sport appropriates and absorbs many of the political connotations openly acknowledged by the European gymnastics movements of the nineteenth century.

As outlined in Chapter 2, the German Turner Movement's philosophy subsumed the physical training of the body within a fully articulated political philosophy — significantly a cultic, racial nationalism. Given such a background, it comes as no surprise that in more recent times the Turner Movement eagerly embraced Nazism. In his recent book devoted to the historical relationship between sport and political ideology, Hoberman observes, 'the three fundamental themes of Nazi physical culture — the feeling of racial superiority, the health of the *Volk*, and military education — are all present in Jahn', the movement's founder and guiding philosopher.[2] In both the Turner movement and the imitative Sokol organisation established in neighbouring Bohemia, sport, not in the form of competitive achievement, but rather as a political aesthetic of group virility through gymnastic training and display was embraced for the primary purposes of creating a collective sense of political power, psychological unity and active commitment to nationalistic goals.

The European approach to gymnastics emphasised neither individual physical skills nor the specialisation of function within a small group endeavour that were central features of the British competitive sport philosophy. Rather, mass syncronisation of physical routines, it was considered, would encourage the participants to subjugate their individual egos by submerging their identities into a mystical experience of the collective 'essence' of race and nation. The criteria of accomplishment adopted in this version of sport emphasised the attainment of a maximum level of co-ordinated precision in carrying out the choreographed exercise routines, the aesthetic and symbolic impact of massed displays by hardened, lithe male bodies 'whose contours were made particularly visible by the uniform Jahn invented for the gymnasts',[3] and the level of collective commitment engendered among participants and spectators for the achievement of national political goals. The Turner and Sokol movements reflected the European propensity to invest sport with deeply political connotations. As one observer has recently noted, this deliberate association of sport and political ideology represents an important legacy that manifests itself in the policies and attitudes to sport found in many of the present day European state socialist societies.[4]

But, as two British sociologists have recently pointed out, a strong emphasis on 'manliness' is also present in the English inspired version of competitive sport.

> This draws on many of the general themes of 'masculinity' within our culture — toughness, physical strength and capability, achievement, as the demonstration of virility, the importance of aggressive competitiveness. These qualities mark out the 'natural' character of the male. In doing so, they also construct by implication, the character of femininity, and the suspicion of the 'non-sporting' male as a real or potential deviant from masculinity.

The same authors continue:

> This conception of 'manliness' also draws some of its strength from a different class tradition of masculinity — a proletarian one. Here, life and work are acknowledged to be hard, a man ('the bread-winner') has to compete, strive and survive. He has to accept the severity of life, strive to overcome it, without complaint and without giving up. He must produce a 'workmanlike' performance, take pride in his honest endeavour. These two different traditions, arising out of different material circumstances, meet and are merged in the notion of 'manliness'. This form of construction of

sexual identities is one of the most powerful ways in which 'cross-class' unities are composed. But they are always composed 'structured in dominance' — they take on the character of dominant rather than subordinate conceptions.[5]

In the British version, competitive sport would improve physical health and develop character traits consistent with a dominant bourgeois imagery of the appropriate personal qualities required to succeed in a *laissez-faire* capitalist society with growing imperialist ambitions. Striving, self-discipline, respect for the 'rules of the game', leadership, tactical and strategic innovation — qualities it was implied that would be absorbed through competition on the sporting field — could then be positively applied in the individual's struggle to achieve status and success in the meritocratic competition of life for occupational and material advancement. But, at a higher level, the communality of sporting experiences would help to forge a sense of common cultural identity thereby consolidating the overall strength and character of the nation in its struggle for military and economic supremacy against international rivals.

Thus, in both the British and European models, an important rationale for the promotion of sport by authoritative groups derived from similar socio-political programmes that sought to incorporate large heterogeneous populations into a strong and unified national entity.

But while the oppositional structure inherent in competitive sport encourages certain individualistic goals, it also allows participation and identification to encompass social groupings other than the national collectivity. The establishment of competitive leagues in team sports helped solidify religious, community, city-wide and regional identifications. In the late nineteenth and early twentieth century, the sponsoring of sports teams by industrial, educational and military institutions was thought to be of benefit because it strengthened the individual's identification with the organisation. Thus, collective identification through competitive sport may, in certain circumstances, reflect broader societal divisions such as religion, class and nation, while in other circumstances, cut across them.

But significantly, while macro-political elements played an important part in the rise of both the British and European approaches to modern sport, in the former these were not overtly acknowledged. Indeed, one of the endlessly repeated central axioms of the competitive sport movement was, and continues to be (at least in the West), a vociferous, although at times a conveniently flexible, insistence on the importance of keeping sport separate from party, class or national issues.

Of course, that such influences were never really absent from competitive sport is evidenced by the decision of the Olympic movement, from its very beginnings, 'to introduce national flags and hymns into the victory ceremonies and to designate competitors according to their country' thereby immediately promoting 'politics and nationalism during the games'.[6] The elements of competition when linked to quantitive measures of comparative achievement make sport an ideal arena for symbolically signifying the relative strength and 'success' of entire nations and political ideologies.

As the earliest organised and most prestigious focal point of international sporting competition, the modern Olympic Games, far from the idealised imagery of a periodic 'festival of universal peace', have been punctuated by an almost continuous history of political turmoil and symbolic power politics. The ominous political symbolism surrounding the Nazi Olympics of 1936; the entry into Olympic competition of the Communist countries led by the Soviet Union in 1952; the 'Black Power' salutes made by two medal winning American athletes in 1968; the Munich massacre of 1972; the banning of South Africa from participation; the long string of politically motivated boycotts at recent Olympiads; the carefully engineered rise to sporting prominence of East Germany; all have emphasised the extent to which top-level sport is closely intertwined with both domestic politics and international power struggles.

The relationship between the Olympics and international politics has been a multi-faceted one. First, the symbolism of national success in sport against 'the best' competition is temptingly available as a visible index of societal strength through the conscious reification of imagery that equates physical prowess with a superior bio-cultural identity. Whether this is popularly believed to be causally related to communality of ethnic or racial attributes or, as in more recent times, to the underlying validity of a particular political philosophy, or as a sign of the innate 'character' of a small, materially impoverished or oppressed collectivity, success at the Games can be tapped as a positive vehicle for group aggrandisement. As Ball has observed,

> Given the popularity of sport in general, and the Olympics in particular, this makes such performances readily meaningful to relevant constituencies, both domestic and foreign. The Olympics provide a useful arena for the production and distribution of the symbols of successful international status-contesting. They become a stage where is played the drama of the politics of symbolic conflict.[7]

Thus, despite the pious declarations regularly forthcoming from the Olympic movement, tables of comparative national medal rankings have always been part of the Games' mystique, voraciously reported and analysed by the media and generally interpreted as a crude rank ordering of national and/or ideological strength. In recent years more complex statistical analyses weighted by factors such as population size have been produced. These have actually demonstrated the relatively superior achievements of some of the smaller nations. However, in an article based on a detailed factor-analysis of long term performances at the Olympics up until 1964, the writer concludes

> that the key to understanding national Olympic team scores is resources: possession and mobilization ability. Overall, Game success is related to the possession of resources, both human and economic, and the centralized forms of political decision-making and authority which maximize their allocation.[8]

These findings were reinforced by a later study extending the data up to 1972.[9] Thus, as some of the recent Neo-Marxist critiques have pointed out,[10] sport has been subsumed as another arena of material production in which the rational application of resources, techniques and management are deployed towards quantifiable goals, and not surprisingly, the results reproduce the international hierarchy by which 'underdeveloped countries remain underdeveloped in sports as in economy. Though it has been argued that the object is to "play" the game, rather than win it, somehow it is always the rich countries which win as well'.[11]

Second, political ends may be served by a country merely hosting the Olympics. The Nazi regime sought to make the efficient staging of the 1936 Games, and the competitive advantages to the home country, an international showcase for legitimating its underlying political philosophy. In more recent times, the international attention and economic stimulation to building, service, and tourism industries, not to mention the supposed boost to 'national morale' have been important motives for strong lobbying efforts from political and business groups in countries such as Mexico and South Korea to win the honour of hosting an Olympics.

Third, the assured media attention the Games now receive have made them the occasion for calculated political agitation, totally external to the sporting competition organised by activists representing particular group grievances or interests. In recent years this has included the local student demonstrations that surrounded the 1968 Olympics in Mexico City, the focus drawn to the rising militancy of American blacks by the members of the United States Olympic team at the same Games and the horrific events that followed the Palestinian terrorists' capture of Israeli competitors inside the Olympic village in Munich in 1972.

But the connection between sport and macro-level politics is not confined to the Olympic Games. As international competitions and tournaments have proliferated across scores of different sports — professional as well as amateur — there are numerous occasions each year for bouts of international muscle-flexing. Almost all national governments — irrespective of their particular political persuasion — have become increasingly sensitive to the political and economic benefits that may be harvested from the collective euphoria that accompanies success in some field of sporting endeavour. What research and observational evidence is available indicates that they are not misguided in such perceptions.

A useful illustration is the prominent role played by soccer in Latin America where, in the midst of widespread poverty, it has established itself as a highly professionalised sport with a huge spectator following drawn from all levels of society. Soccer is also one of the few sports in which Latin American countries have consistently succeeded at the international level with Brazil, Uruguay and Argentina winning between them nine of the fifteen recognised world championships played since 1924. Correspondingly, as one writer has recently observed, in Latin America, soccer:

> is almost a religion, a collective gathering where symbolic dialogue reinforces the values of society and a way of life. The soccer pitch transcends a playing field and serves as a proving ground of socio-cultural heritage and nationalistic pride.[12]

Focusing on Uruguay, the same author examined the long term relationship between the country's fluctuating fortune as a world soccer power between the years 1900 and 1979, and a number of objective measures of its political and socio-economic stability over the same period. By constructing a graph that plots the path taken by these three sets of variables he illustrates that they have followed a remarkably similar pattern (see Figure 5.1).[13]

In neighbouring Brazil, also over the past half century a leading international soccer power, the populace's passionate identification with their national team's on-field fortunes is so intense that flags in Rio de Janeiro and Sao Paulo were lowered to half-mast when the country was eliminated in the early rounds of the 1966 World Cup tournament. But perhaps more telling is a reported study that,

> In the weeks that the Corinthians (the most popular team in the city) win, production in Sao Paulo rises 12.3 per cent. In the weeks in which the Corinthians lose, the number of accidents at work increases by 15.3 per cent.[14]

Perhaps the most extreme incident tragically symbolising soccer's psycho-political significance in Latin America was the outbreak of military hostilities between El Salvador and Honduras in 1969, immediately following a disputed result in a World Cup elimination game between national teams representing the two countries. The war lasted seven days and the dead numbered more than 2000.

It is in economically impoverished and middle-level industrialised countries that international sporting successes frequently arouse an extremely high level of nationalistic fervour sometimes approaching a form of collective emotional hysteria. It is as if such occasions provide

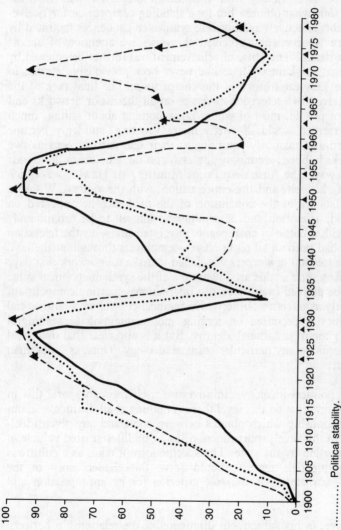

Figure 5.1 Uruguayan sociocultural and sport reflections 1900–80

.... Political stability.

——— Socioeconomic stability as determined by data gathered from government documents, the Bank of London, the Inter-American Development Bank and The World Bank.

– ▲ – Sport indicator as determined by world championship soccer status.

Source: March, L. Krotee, 'The Rise and Demise of Sport: A Reflection of Uruguayan Society', *Annals of AAPSS*, 445, September 1979, p. 152.

a form of psychic group compensation for a sense of relative power-lessness and dependency in world affairs — a symbolic outburst re-affirming their national virility.

Thus, for example, in Australia, which in recent years has suffered a general decline in its proudly held self-image as a successful sporting power, the 1983 victory over the United States for the Americas Cup — a somewhat obscure but long standing competition for twelve-metre yachts effectively restricted to syndicated challenges mounted by millionaire 'sportsmen' — received the obsessive attention of almost the entire nation. The sense of achievement was further heightened by the fact that the United States had never been previously defeated in the entire 132-year history of the competition. The final race of the series received live television coverage on all the major networks and millions of people, most of whom knew nothing about sailing, much less the rarified world of twelve-metre yachting, suddenly became rabid partisans anxiously squinting at their television screens as two small flecks bobbed, seemingly aimlessly, on the blue ocean thousands of miles away. The Australian Prime Minister, Mr Hawke, was quick to identify himself, and the entire nation, with the victory. Within a couple of hours of the conclusion of the final race he appeared on nation-wide television and, after allowing himself to be ceremonially doused with a bottle of champagne, suggested that — as the television coverage had been an all night affair — employers throughout the land should be tolerant of workers who failed to make it into work that day.

Occasions such as this are illustrative of the symbolic political value that can be derived from success in international sporting competition, particularly as effective authoritative political control over large social collectivities is premised on forging and maintaining a meaningful sense of a common national identity. But it is also clear that this trend is not specific to any particular political ideology. Thus, as Hoberman points out,

> if any political ideology can advertise itself through sport, this in itself shows that on this level there is nothing at all distinctive about the relationship which obtains between sport and any given ideol-ogy. On this level, sport functions as an undifferentiated vehicle of self-assertion by the state. The specific form it takes as a culture is inconsequential; that it should serve the greater glory of the state — any state — is the sole criterion for its appropriation and use.[15]

However, in his subsequent discussion of the relationship between sport and the more influential political ideologies of this century, the same writer proposes that 'there is a fascist temperament which shows an affinity to athleticism and the sphere of the body itself which the Left has not shared'.[16] This is not to say that athleticism, or even competitive sport, is necessarily fascist, but rather, that an obsession with the virile body, masculine power, aggressive dominance and an emphasis on the 'irrational' bases of human psychology and motivation lie close to the core of the political anthropology defining the 'essence' of 'human nature' within fascism and associated right-wing ideologies. This in turn would seem to represent a reaction to the ideas and values emerging from the Enlightenment with its corresponding emphasis on intellectualism and rationality. It is evidenced in the consistent contempt heaped on intellectuals by prominent fascist leaders such as Hitler, Mussolini, and Oswald Mosely. These men consistently portrayed intellectuals as weak, puny physical specimens whose philosophical support for liberalism and socialism reflected their essential 'effeminacy'. As Hoberman explains, the 'dream of dynamic virility, prominently featuring the perfected body as a symbol of force, has been the theme of every fascist culture' and 'a sportive style featuring quasi-athletic self-dramatisation in the form of the self-inflicted ordeal became a special province of the fascist imagination'. It is in this sense, he suggests, 'that sport may be said to be "haunted" by fascism'.[17]

In contrast, that the political Left has always had enormous difficulties in coming to terms with competitive sport (as evidenced by the problems of the Workers Sport Movement, the continuing internal ideological debates concerning the role of sport in many socialist states, the condemnation of competitive sport by contemporary neo-Marxist writers) points to the fact that Marxism 'cannot accommodate some basic impulses of this [sportive] temperament without violating the norms of its own official anthropology'.[18]

Thus, when, for pragmatic reasons, socialist states have embraced competitive sport they have been forced to make tortuously qualified rationalisations in an attempt to separate their approach from that associated with any virility ethos. In this regard, official Soviet Union policy prohibits 'exhibitionist' sports such as body building—not in the form of training—but as 'contests and exhibitions that include posing and the judging of the body'.[19] In East Germany, the recent intensive application of resources towards sporting achievement is presented as the harnessing of scientific rationality towards a greater understanding of the bio-physical limits of the human body. Sporting performance is treated as a metaphorical equivalent of productive labour serving the latter as 'a symbolic expression of maximum effort'.[20] However, when the official Maoist policy on sport that sought 'the renunciation of aggression [*viz.* the ban on boxing], partisan frenzy, egotism, and virile pride, and the cultivation of a sportmanship which humbled and distressed the western mind', was completely overturned by the new Chinese hierarchy, it would seem accurate to conclude that 'the anticompetitive sport cultures of the 20th century were finally extinct'.[21]

So, despite a certain concordance between ideologies of the Right and the 'expressionism of the body', ultimately,

The crux of the problem is that 'sportive' or 'virile' temperaments occur within every political culture; and virtually every political culture rewards its successful sportsmen. For this reason, the notion that Communist athletes are distinguished by a uniform mentality of ideological origin can only derive from a cloud-cuckoo land of political psychology, particularly if they are contrasted with the 'bourgeois-democratic' athletes of equal uniformity... What we can say is that, while all cultures include such people, not all of them promulgate ideologies which encourage and incorporate as doctrine the characterological traits peculiar to the (idealized) sportive temperament: competetive aggressiveness, self-conscious physicality, ascetic indifference to pain, and an indifference to ethical concerns, or what the psychologist W. H. Sheldon once termed 'psychological callousness'.[22]

The social signifiers attached to physical strength, virility, aggressiveness and domination over rivals or opponents, as symbolic indexes of superior achievement and accompanying status claims, all of which are built into the structure of competitive sport, also clearly pre-date modern political philosophies. Historically, the possession of such characteristics has formed a central core of masculine gender identity as well as a consistent guide to the social status and power hierarchy of organised group life. They have been the revered attributes of the hero, particularly the warrior hero. Thus, in more recent times, where modern political orthodoxy has institutionalised a distinctive separation between political and military roles within the nation state, there has been a notable tendency for many national leaders, particularly, but not exclusively, those of the political Right, to seek to cultivate an image of virility and strength. This is expressed by exhibiting and publicising their personal sporting prowess or past exploits on a sporting field. In addition (or if the former is not credible), political leaders are often quick to publicly associate themselves with national sporting success by the techniques of posing for pictures with the winners, sending telegrams of congratulations and awarding state honours to sporting heroes. In such ways astute politicians seek to reinforce the legitimacy of their authority by drawing on the traditional popular mythology that connects leadership with physical strength, the power to command with muscular power. Thus, for Mussolini,

> Every kind of sport was said to be close to his heart, and especially those involving danger. His horse-riding became legendary, as did the speed at which he drove a car... Occasionally, he invited foreign journalists to see him fence, play tennis or ride, and told them he hoped they would report how fit and expert he was; sometimes their honesty as reporters was sorely taxed.[23]

At the opposite end of the political spectrum, East Germany's recent obsessive focus on producing high-level sporting performances has been partly attributed to the historical coincidence that Walter Ulbricht happened to be that country's political leader between 1945 and 1971. Ulbricht, who in his younger days was an avid sportsman and a member of a workers' gymnastic club in Leipzig, 'was genuinely interested in sport both personally and as a vehicle for demonstrating the political superiority of socialism'. It is reported that very soon after the establishment of the GDR in 1949, Ulbricht resolved 'to create an exemplary, performance-oriented sport culture that would serve as a model for other sectors of East German society'.[24]

But also within a liberal-democratic political framework, it is by no means uncommon for an elected leader to make political capital out of his own sporting exploits. A recent example was the American President John F. Kennedy, around whom was built a powerful mystique incorporating his large extended family, that was 'very much bound up with the youthful, aggressive and competitive participation in a wide variety of sports'. In numerous public speeches Kennedy urged upon Americans the benefits of physical exercise and sport, consistently attaching 'a positive political impression to the concept of vigor' exemplified in his own personal style and demonstrating 'to politicians who were to follow him that the construction of an image of virility through active involvement in sport could have a powerful impression upon the electorate'.[25] It is suggested here then, that such examples demonstrate not that sport has no particular politics but rather that the value emphases of vitality/virility and group solidarity invest sport with attributes available for the popular legitimation of all types of modern political systems. Each system is able to appropriate sport through a conscious inflection of these elements to make them consistent with the dominant group's broader ideological and administrative concerns. Thus, with team sports, it is possible to inflect emphasis upon outstanding contributions by individual players, highlighting the performances of 'stars' and reinforcing a meritocratic reward structure. On the other hand, as was the case in the early years of socialist sport, considerable effort was expended to identify the *team* as symbolic of a collective in which all contributions are both vital and of equal importance to group achievement. Players were warned to eschew displays of individual brilliance and coaches urged to develop playing styles that minimised reliance on the particular abilities of the more highly skilled team members. However, this policy has gradually been relaxed, the most obvious pragmatic reason being the notable lack of success in open competition against Western teams. There has also been an increasing pressure within the socialist bloc for the official sanctioning of the spectator entertainment role of sport in which the exhibition of individual skills is recognised as a vital component attracting crowds and stimulating their enjoyment of the contest. Thus, regardless of official political ideology, as Grouneau suggests 'the ideological foundations of organized competitive sport are characteristically *meritocratic* rather than *egalitarian*'.[26] Therefore the acceptance of high achievement competitive sport within modern state socialist societies reflects their pragmatic incorporation of meritocratic political values which are in essence more closely 'in tune with the mainstream values of the modern capitalist societies'[27] than with the tenets of classical Marxism.

Ultimately then, the neo-Marxist critics are correct when they suggest that underlying the widespread support of competitive sport in the modern world is a universalised acceptance of the value of *performance* in both senses of the word. First, performance as the application of rationalised control to the output of the human body, and second, the symbolic reification of high achievement in such endeavours through the transformation of such displays into a form of mass entertainment where, as Jurgen Habermas has suggested, it becomes part of show business with 'professionals on one side, consumers on the other'.[28]

So, despite the extensive polarisation characterising contemporary political ideologies and practices throughout the world, the modern culture of high achievement sport incorporates a set of transcendant values that lie at the pragmatic core of successful bureaucratic management by political cadres of modern organised group life. These include the importance of providing comprehensible public rituals symbolising and reinforcing communal and national identity within the populace; the promotion of an ethos of national virility, vitality and muscular capacity as a pathway to individual and collective achievement — both economic and social; a faith in the rational/scientific techniques for infinitely extending and improving the physical capabilities of the human body; and a meritocratically based hierarchy for evaluating 'productivity' and determining appropriate material and/or status rewards.

Television as a political force in society

As suggested in Chapter 3, the type of television system introduced into any society was heavily contingent on broader political considerations and these factors continue to ensure that television services are unlikely to function as institutions that present a threat to the operative principles underlying economic and political power. In the main, their primary roles are fairly carefully restricted to the provision of general information, popular entertainment programmes (however this may be defined in the particular culture) and public education in the broadest meaning of this term. Their direct involvment in the political process is fairly carefully circumscribed. This is secured first, through the extent of their formal separation and independence from political authority and second, through the economic basis of the financial support upon which they depend to continue to function.

However, because television has become the major source through which much of the population in many parts of the world perceive the broader canvas of the day-to-day workings of their own and other societies, the medium has become a significant component in the political process itself. Where television systems operate as the direct arm of a state ideology their general political function is relatively unproblematic, but much debate surrounds the question of the nature of the political role played by the commercial and national television services that predominate in most of the capitalist Western industrialised world as well as in a number of the developing countries. It is not within the scope of this book to enter into a detailed exposition of the numerous conflicting theories and arguments on this subject, but a few general comments are necessary. There would seem to be an incontrovertible logic to the position that where television services operate as a business in the commercial arena, their primary prerogative is to maximise profitability for their proprietors and/or shareholders. As this is achieved by accumulating large viewing audiences thereby attracting the greatest possible advertising revenue, as an organisation their interests are consistent with the society maintaining a stable political structure, a healthy economy—preferably one that is growing at a reasonable rate—and a minimal level of bureaucratic, regulatory and political interference into their operations. As business enterprises they function within the areas of communications, entertainment and leisure, competing against others involved in these sectors of the economy. The day-to-day running of their operations requires the co-ordination of managerial, administrative, marketing, technical and creative tasks for which they employ appropriately qualified personnel. Where some regulatory or political body is charged with the responsibility of granting licences to operate television services, there are inbuilt constraints on such agencies to ensure that the chances for the future economic survival of the organisation holding such a licence is reasonable. Because, in most places, the extent of direct competition has been quite carefully regulated, at least until recent policy changes in North America, the overall result has been that acquiring a licence to operate a commercial television station is, as one Australian media tycoon put it, equivalent to being granted a licence to print money. Thus, it is no surprise that the mass media in general, and commercial television in particular, avoids demonstrating any obvious bias against any significant political faction that might someday win government office through the established electoral process. But beyond this, as Murdock and Golding have stated,

Given the insistent pressure to maximise audiences and revenues, there is not surprisingly a consistent tendency for the commercial media to avoid the unpopular and tendentious and to draw instead on the values and assumptions which are most familiar and most widely legitimated, which always inevitably mean those which flow authoritatively downwards through the social structure.[29]

For slightly different reasons, the same argument applies to non-commercial, national or government run television services. As they are generally funded from taxation revenues and administered by civil servants, there are legal and moral pressures on them to remain even-handed with regards to partisan politics. Compared to commercial television's obsession with populist entertainment, their programming may reflect a greater propensity to cater to minority audiences, particularly those professing an intellectual or high-culture orientation, but their brief is in terms of providing a 'public service'. This is unlikely to find them seriously challenging the fundamental assumptions of the society's existing political and social structure.

Ultimately then, the primary political role of television as a communication technology in modern society, derives from the simple premise that it has proved incredibly successful in attracting large numbers of people to watch professionally produced television programmes rather than do something else. This fact became very obvious as soon as the basic technology was perfected. Consequently, there were, and continue to be, structural mechanisms designed to ensure that television operates as a centralised form of message dissemination that remains, at best, a means of expanding the economic and ideological control of the dominant groupings in any society and, at worst, in no way a serious threat to their continuing dominance.

In circumstances where television services are recognised as rightfully endowed with a formally recognised autonomy from direct political control, it has became necessary for the style of electoral politics and public debate to adapt to the dictates of the medium. This has resulted in the widely observed tendency of the shift towards 'personality politics' which 'works' better on television than the old style of focusing on policy issues and intellectual debate. The recognition of the mediating power of television to reach large audiences has resulted in the pragmatic necessity of groups seeking to socially disseminate messages to develop appropriate techniques for gaining access to television exposure.

The institutional autonomy of television is greatest in circumstances where it is most free to place its own organisational interests ahead of pressures from any other sources in order to determine both which groups gain access and the form in which this will reach the viewing audience. Where a free-enterprise capitalist economy operates, access to television is an important element in economic competition between rival enterprises. This is not only in terms of buying advertising time on commercial stations, but also in the area of cultural production where the publishing industry, cinema, theatre, music, sport, tourism and other sectors of the entertainment/leisure industry are in intense competition with each other as well as with rival enterprises in the same field, to maximise audiences/buyers for their particular product.

In these areas television's interests in attracting audiences through the presentation of programme material that is 'entertaining' naturally colludes with the interests of the culture industries. In the formats of talk shows, variety, music specials, the presentation of opera performances, drama, movies, sport as well as in news items and current affairs programmes, there lies both a basis for mutual economic gain and mutual self-promotion for those who earn their living from both television and the production and marketing of other cultural products.

It is for these reasons that the alliance between television and high-performance spectator sport first developed and has proved to be so successful. With respect to political values and ideology, the process of adapting and tailoring sport for television audiences has two related consequences. First, television acts as an extremely effective channel to further disseminate the political values that have developed within the sporting culture itself. Second, the nature of television's mediation between the sporting performance and the viewing audience contributes political connotations and perspectives reflecting the peculiar characteristics of that medium as a social and political force.

Television and the political culture of sport

Televised sport as secular ritual

By amplifying the social visibility of high-achievement sport, television most obviously has operated as a powerful vehicle for more widely disseminating sport's political culture. One useful framework for understanding both the popular appeal of spectator sport and the success of the electronic media in attracting large viewing audiences for sports programmes suggests that the social significance of certain types of sporting contests lies in their representing an accessible form of modern ritual that affectively produces, within the populace, a heightened sense of communality and collective identification.[30]

Any arrangement for the socio-political organisation of group life (particularly in the modern world where the nation-state has become the most universally legitimated political form), must confront, as one of its central problems, a means of forging a necessary balance between individualistic goals and subjective identification with the broader collectivity. This has become an increasingly more difficult task with the almost universal marginalisation of religious beliefs and rituals as the basis of a national culture and identity. These have been replaced by the impersonal values associated with rationalised science and technology. It would seem that certainly by the middle of the twentieth century, the value-principles of rationalisation, positivism and professionalism were firmly entrenched as virtually unchallengeable norms guiding social policy and individual behaviour within the political cultures of both capitalist liberal-democracies and state socialist societies. In each system, they were effectively reinforced through the powerful socialising institutions of formal education and occupational role. Yet a significant basis for the continuing intense ideological and political opposition between the two systems is that the same set of values are attached to totally conflicting assumptions with regard to the most appropriate and effective means of further advancing the positivist engine of social and material 'progress'.

Within liberal-democratic capitalism this consists of the firm belief that collective political authority can only be effective if it follows a 'natural', utilitarian view of human psychology, thereby ensuring that there are minimal constraints placed upon any person's freedom to pursue whatever individualistic goals they might desire. On the other hand, the guiding principles of Marxist-Leninism supposedly reflect a 'scientific proof' that the transition to the next stage of historically determined social development necessitates the construction of a social order ensuring that each individual will voluntarily seek to contribute their productive energies (with the initial and as yet unrelinquished organisational guidance of the Party/State) for the overall benefit of the collectivity.

What remains important is that in both systems, indeed in any nation state, there are strong pressures to establish a public consciousness of collective identification through the creation of secular public rituals celebrated by a set of ceremonial events that will symbolise the validity of the social order and reconfirm the collective identification of the populace to the principles upon which it is based. Prominent examples are ritual ceremonies celebrating the anniversary of national independence (or revolution), memorial days to commemorate those who died in the nation's service during wartime and ceremonies marking legitimate succession of leadership such as those surrounding the British coronation.[31] Such occasions inevitably receive heavy television coverage, extending their ritual power, previously dependent on one's physical presence at a collective rite, directly into the private home.[32]

It has been suggested that television has even further added to the officially designated ritual occasions, in their 'sanctification' of national sporting events. Thus, for example, the American Super Bowl, the British FA Cup Final, the VFL Grand Final in Australia have become firmly fixed in the respective national ceremonial calendars. Such events now occupy the obsessive attention of the mass media and therefore attract the collective involvement of a sizeable portion of the nation's population each year. It is significant that it is contests between teams rather than individuals that are most likely to have qualities that propel them to the status of televised rituals. As Richard Lipsky has pointed out, the characteristics of the team and the enterprise they are undertaking, provide a perfect symbolic representation of an ideal-model of balanced collective relationships consistent with the society's broader value system. Thus, for example in America,

the team symbolizes on many levels the hierarchy, specialization and division of labor associated with the organized world of work...Another essential characteristic of organization is skilled leadership—an ability to be expert in technical strategy as well as efficient in handling personnel. In almost every single article on a team in *Sports Illustrated* over a two-year period (1975–1977) there is the prominent mention of owners, general managers, and coaches, whose expertise and leadership qualities are seen as essential to team success.[33]

The symbolism of team sports can also remain compatible with both the ideological premises and the pragmatic experiences of life under state socialism. The relatively simple structure of team contests, the carefully controlled conditions, the easily comprehendable objective of victory and the definitive results and rewards are in stark contrast with the complex, confused and sometimes impenetrable qualities of modern life that the typical spectator experiences outside the sports arena. Thus, 'in contrast to the barrenness of what Habermas calls the "technical life-world", the symbolic-aesthetic appeals of sports are warmly personal and concrete'.[34]

But, in another way, the unpredictability of the outcome of the sporting event and the intrusion of the mystical and unexpected subvert the overwhelming pressure towards rational explanation that permeates most other areas of modern life.

The rationalization of the real world is ameliorated by an injection of charisma, magical performances, gifted leaders, and intense rituals—certainly an ironic dramatization of Weber's hypothesized prescription for the ills of industrialism.[35]

For these reasons, team sports, television and pragmatic politics serve broad mutually reinforcing needs and interests across a variety of political contexts.

Masculinity and sexual politics

The world of television sport, consistent with the world of high achievement sport is overwhelmingly masculine. The realm of sexual politics thus also becomes an important consideration. The ethos of virility and the concomitant implications for the reinforcement of what are considered traditionally male characteristics finds considerable support through the bias of television towards the coverage of all-male sporting events mediated by teams of all-male commentators and analysts. The continuity of many of the traditionalist values, particularly those intrinsic to the sporting culture, is maintained through the consistent recruitment of former players—over-represented by those who have retired from highly distinguished playing careers—into the ranks of media sports journalism. This creates almost a closed world in which the values and perspectives being disseminated through the media maintain a remarkable internal consistency over time and across different sports.

With regard to male contact sports in particular, but also in any contest featuring youthful male participants, the linguistic framework for the television commentary shows a close affinity to that of the military campaign. Thus, the likelihood of victory is seen to depend upon the extent to which the contestants' preparation for, and performance in, the contest reflect physical and mental toughness, the application of focused aggression and the deployment of pre-determined tactics and strategy ('the game-plan'). Particular acts of courage in the face of extreme risk of physical injury, or after suffering injury are universally applauded as representing 'what the game is all about'.

As already noted above, the close links between the military and sport are quite deeply rooted. Thus, for example, the style of coaching in team sports has traditionally followed the model which draws heavily on military authority, hierarchy and training methods. In the sporting world, the coach is perceived to occupy the role of commanding officer, entrusted with the preparation and training of the unit under his 'command' and ultimately responsible for their 'performance on the field'. Consequently there is rarely any question of the coach's legitimate right to absolute authority over the players. The players are expected to follow the coach's directives with regard to training, physical conditioning, diet, curfews and any other aspect of their off-field behaviour or lifestyle he considers relevant to their sporting performance. In the past a number of the more successful coaches developed well known reputations as strict disciplinarians who demanded total loyalty and obedience from their players, meting out swift and rough justice in response to any infraction against their arbitrary directives. It was considered legitimate, and in some quarters still is, for the coach to monitor and control the players' personal and social relationships, to dictate on moral and ethical questions, and even to determine codes of dress and physical appearance.

This paternalistic authoritarianism has become normatively institutionalised as the most appropriate and effective form of relationship suited to an older male supervising the endeavours of a sporting team made up of younger males. This is reflective of the typical style of power relations socially sanctioned in a number of similar settings, such as all-male educational institutions, disciplinary and corrective facilities and, of course, the military. In more recent times, particularly as a result of the increasing professionalisation of all sporting roles, this style of coach-player relationship is not as prevalent as it has been in the past. However, it still elicits considerable support from the television commentary box, where the more conservative (and, it is argued, more effective) traditionalist coaching style finds consistent and authoritative reinforcement.

So, by cocooning itself as an unshakeable bastion of support for the values of group masculinity, paternalistic authoritarianism and military-aggression, the domain of television sports programming provides a prominent forum for these patriarchial Victorian values that have continued to permeate the ideology and structure of modern sport. From the sporting cultures of the Ancient Greeks, through the folk games of the Mediaeval period, the playing fields of the British public schools to the modern institutional structure which has developed around amateur and professional sport, runs the common thread that 'real sport' is an activity that is 'by nature' a manifestation of the bio-social characteristics of the male gender, and should remain so. As the writers of a recent paper have noted, it was the influential nineteenth century combination of social Darwinism and the strict separation of sexual roles that operated as conventionally accepted norms adhered to by the dominant groups of those societies in which the definitive values underlying modern sport were cast. Thus, the Olympic movement's founder, Baron de Coubertin firmly believed,

> males were inherently superior to females and since this was biologically determined it was both 'natural' and immutable... In the modern as much as the ancient world, Olympic ideals not only involved but were predicated on the exclusion of women, for whom the Social Darwinist goals of fitness and efficiency were of a markedly different order. Social Darwinism maintained and strengthened earlier Victorian ideas of femininity in its insistence upon separate spheres of activity for men and women.[36]

The sphere for women was of course home and family and it clearly excluded participation in organised sport. Therefore,

> rigorous exercise, whether physical or intellectual, was deemed prejudicial to child-bearing and hence both unhealthy and unfeminine. One commentator asserted: 'It was of little use that the girl had played centre-forward at hockey, or had been a wrangler, if she could not nurse her baby or even produce one.' Such views owed much to the notion of finite energies: the belief that energy expended in one direction was inevitably at the expense of other functions.[37]

Despite the social power of such values, women gradually gained entry to the male bastion of competitive sport, but not without resistance and subject to a great many qualifications and exclusions. At any level of organised competition, only in a handful of sports are women permitted to compete directly against men.[38] Furthermore, beyond the age of puberty, women are totally excluded from participating in 'mixed' contact sports. Rarely are women involved in any contact sports, even where these might be restricted to female participation only. Where they do occur, their existence is either given no public recognition by the media, or when occasionally reported, it is invariably from an angle that reinforces the belief that this sort of activity is an abomination against nature. The male discomfort at such behaviour can only be accommodated through assuming either a total lack of femininity in the participants or treating it as some sort of sexual side-show put on for the purposes of male titillation. The latter seems to be the most preferred as typified by the exploitative voyeurism surrounding 'female mud-wrestling', which, in recent years, appears to have become a staple item included in television sports magazine programmes.

This is not to argue that television totally ignores 'legitimate' women's sport. It includes a considerable amount of women's tennis as well as athletics, swimming, skiing and other sports, particularly when these are part of prestigious international competitions such as the Olympics and World Championships. But where there are parallel contests for both men and women in the same sport, the male events invariably take programming priority and are clearly considered more important.

The exception occurs with those sports where 'aesthetic' elements are considered equal or more important than muscular power and stamina. Such competitive sports as gymnastics, synchronised swimming, ice-skating and ice-dancing, apart from requiring muscular control and dexterity present the female form in activities considered more appropriate to traditional stereotypes of feminine grace and other aspects of women's 'proper' sexual role. The style of both presentation and commentary employed within the television coverage of such competitions leans heavily on visual techniques and verbal styles deliberately aimed to aestheticise the viewers' perceptions of these sports. Again, this is inherently supportive of the conservative patriarchial perspectives in the currently disputed area of sexual politics, thus, television's apparent eagerness to present the 'image of the youthful, gracious, lithe, subtle female . . . floating graciously in the water or twirling ribbons to music does little to challenge male power'.[39]

The televisual politics of sport

As well as acting as a conduit for the political culture of sport in the ways suggested above, television contributes its own political inflections in a manner that, certainly in capitalist societies, undermines many of those elements in sport that have in the past allowed it to operate as a vehicle for community control, class identification and opposition to hegemonic bourgeois values.

First, as argued in the previous chapter, television is primarily responsible for the transformation of many of the traditional working-class sports from relatively small-time expressive pastimes played out by and for members of the local community, into glamorous highly paid forms of professional entertainment. This has meant that a few skilled individuals find they are able to attain undreamed of social mobility—to become both rich and famous. This process reinforces the myth of a classless society where material rewards are open to all through hard work, perseverance and enterprise. The structural factors and inequities of the system are masked by the attention and emphasis paid to the successes of the few. As Harry Edwards has pointed out with regard to American blacks, the few thousand who are able to succeed as sports professionals thereby create impossible role models for the millions of young blacks who will never be able to emulate their achievements.[40] An obsession with following this path also diverts them from pursuing education and training which might ultimately prove to be a more practical means of survival, as well as contributing nothing towards challenging the entrenched structural barriers that continue to block the attainment of meaningful social and economic equality for black Americans as a social group.

Of course, those who do succeed in sport are unlikely to publicly present views that challenge the system that has rewarded them so well. If anything they are more likely to be among its strongest defenders, concluding that their personal success proves 'anyone can make it if they try hard enough'. Even those who may have more critical views are placed in an iniquitous situation. As Edwards observes,

> the rare black athlete who does succeed, who is aware, and who has the interest of the black community at heart is compelled to take an explicit position against the prevailing emphasis upon sport in black society—an extremely awkward stand for him at best. He runs a tremendous risk—particularly in the eyes of a naive public—of appearing not only ungrateful and arrogant, but presumptuous; that is, 'I made it in sport, but most of you are wasting your time'. His alternative is to be transformed through impersonal institutional processes and, to some extent, by orchestrated design into a 'Judas Goat' who, by virtue of his very success and visibility, perpetuates the tragedy which finds millions of black youth misled into the futile pursuit of sports careers.[41]

Furthermore, many sports teams in organised competitions such as British soccer and Australian football were, for a long period of time, firmly rooted in local communities often serving as visible symbols of pride and class identity. The infusion of television money and lucrative professional salaries severed the ties between the communities and the players. The rationale for maintaining a sense of team loyalty quickly dissipated as players 'sold out' for better contracts and switched clubs with bewildering regularity. The new breed of sports administrators cared little for fan loyalty as sport became a vehicle for business enterprise and marketing.

The spectator following for team sports was built upon fostering a communally shared sense of loyalty, partisanship and personal identification. Television still seeks to mobilise this aspect in international competition as discussed above, but the television commentary on local or national team sports is now mediated by carefully non-partisan experts who direct the viewer towards the general appreciation of 'the skills of the game'.[42] While the partisanship of the crowd is employed to create a sense of colour and drama, the television experts address the viewer as a detached connoisseur, constantly diverting the focus from the team to the prominent individual performers. A great deal of television's coverage of sports is devoted to ranking the achievement of the players—within teams, across teams, over the season, across time. The television image always seeks to draw attention to individual 'stars'—to personalise, to separate and to rank. In this way television presents a 'reading' of the contest to the home viewer that is often at odds with the aims of sports coaches, the feelings of team members and the experiences of partisan supporters. Much of the time, all of these groups are concerned with the efforts and achievements of a collectivity.

This clash of priorities is often revealed in post-game interviews with coaches and players. Invariably the coach wishes to promote the qualities of co-operation and teamwork rather than single out individuals ('a champion team is always better than a team of champions'). But television prefers to foster the bourgeois values of objectivity, individualism and professionalism, while it underplays those of partisanship, community and loyalty to the group.

If rationality, positivism and professionalism are indeed at the core of the ethos of technocratic modernity then television is a committed disciple. Television's conventional approach to high-achievement sport is devoted to reinforcing these values. 'A true professional' is one of the highest accolades of praise bestowed upon any sporting performer. Such a person is one who is totally devoted to their work as represented by a single goal such as running the fastest, jumping the highest, tackling the hardest. Television 'experts' continually praise the qualities of extreme specialisation, psychological monomania, and masochistic self-punishment that are necessary to reach the highest level of success in sport. The real professional will do almost anything to win, including taking advantage of the rules (television commentators will praise a player who commits a 'professional foul' thereby preventing an opponent gaining an advantage), or exploiting any weakness in their opponent.

The ethos of professionalism eschews conventional questions of politics and morality. It is the ultimate application of technical rationality to a group goal that avoids the problem of value judgements about the ethical considerations of the goal itself. Thus, the ideology of professionalism has become a safe haven for the 'modern' individual. It enables one to avoid the difficult task of evaluating the validity claims of the multitude of religious, philosophical, mystical and political systems, all of which offer conflicting versions of truth, morality and the 'correct' pathway to psychological well-being and social harmony. Professionalism implies the valued contribution of the individual to the group effort. But the group here is not the social collective as a whole but a small segment with valued skills that achieves elite status and respect through the combined application of the abilities of those granted privileged entry to the profession. In television and high-achievement sport we have one group of 'professionals' whose job it is to effectively present to the public the work of another group of 'professionals'. Both groups have achieved a position entailing high status and material rewards as a result of their particular skills and understandably hold each other in considerable esteem.[43]

Television's commitment to a positivist view of human development is reflected first in its deference to the 'scientific' approach to the analysis of sporting performance. This is expressed in the form of presenting to the viewer a stream of statistics, rankings and charts for evaluating performances and an obsession with 'records'. Each instance of a new sporting record surpassing a previous one adds weight to the positivistic belief in the capacity for infinite improvement in human physical performance. This is further reinforced by much of the vocabulary of television sport commentary that promotes the image of the human body as a machine in which the psyche must be in total control of the body and expel the influence of any extraneous emotions, feelings and distractions except those devoted to improved performance. The aim, it is implied, must be to eliminate all human 'mistakes' or 'errors' from the individual's game. Part of the television commentator's role is to draw the attention of the viewers to such errors and even to emphasise the flaw by repeatedly showing the segment in which the 'mistake' occurred in slow-motion replay. American baseball even provides the category of 'error' in the post-game statistical summary in which the number committed is listed for each team along with runs and hits scored.

Sports commentary proliferates with mechanistic metaphors — a team is described as 'playing like a well oiled machine' or perhaps 'running out of steam'. The former champion tennis player Bjorn Borg was said to have the perfect sporting personality—emotionless, with the machine-like attribute of coolness, consistency and a low level of breakdown. Tennis commentators would observe that on the occasions he found himself in trouble against an opponent, he would 'slip into another gear' or 'move into overdrive'. So, from the point of view of the media at least, the ideal sports champion is someone with a technique of 'production' closely approximating that of a machine. If we logically extend this viewpoint it could be considered that television's model of the ultimate sporting 'professional' would not be too different from many employer's model of the ultimate industrial worker—the robot.

So, in the combination of visual images and verbal mediation typical of the way television presents sports, certainly in the Western world, there emerges a consistent emphasis on a particular constellation of social values. These include conflict and competitive achievement, hierarchy and ranking, individualism, specialisation, professionalism, positivism and the rational organisation of resources to produce the maximum output of human effort. Such a combination of values is eminently compatible with the organising principles underpinning modern technocratic capitalism, and with minor changes of emphasis, most of these values can be easily accommodated to by the political orthodoxies currently predominant in the state socialist societies.

Notes

1 Pierre Bourdieu, 'Sport and Social Class', *Social Science Information*, 17(6), 1978, pp 824–5.

2 John M. Hoberman, *Sport and Political Ideology*, Heinemann, London, 1984, p. 163.

3 Quoted from George L. Mosse, *The Nationalization of the Masses*, New York, New American Library, 1975, in Hoberman, p. 101.

4 Andrew Strenk, 'What Price Victory? The World of International Sports and Politics', *Annals of AAPSS*, 445, 1979, p. 136.

5 Alan Clarke and John Clarke, 'Highlights and Action Replays—Ideology, Sport and the Media', in Jennifer Hargreaves (ed.), *Sport, Culture and Ideology*, Routledge, London, 1982, pp 82–3.

6 Strenk, p. 139.

7 Donald W. Ball, 'Olympic Games Competition: Structural Correlates of National Success', *International Journal of Comparative Sociology*, 13, 1972, p. 188.

8 Ball, p. 198. Significantly, the points' scoring system for comparing national achievements at the Olympics was first devised by the American press representatives covering the 1908 Games. See Benjamin G. Rader, *In Its Own Image*, The Free Press, New York, 1984, p. 158.

9 Ned Levine, 'Why Do Countries Win Olympic Medals? Some Structural Correlates of Olympic Games Success: 1972', *Sociology and Social Research*, 58(4), 1974, pp 353–60.

10 See in particular, J. M. Brohm, *Sport: A Prison of Measured Time*, Ink

Links, London, 1978; Bero Rigauer, *Sport and Work*, Columbia University Press, New York, 1981.

11 Levine, p. 359.

12 March L. Krotee, 'The Rise and Demise of Sport: A Reflection of Uruguayan Society', *Annals of AAPSS*, 445, 1979, pp 142–3.

13 From Krotee, p. 152.

14 Janet Lever, 'Soccer: Opium of the Brazilian People', *Transaction*, 7(2), 1969, p. 37.

15 Hoberman, p. 1.

16 Hoberman, p. 14.

17 Hoberman, p. 84.

18 Hoberman, p. 85.

19 Quoted from James Riordan, *Sport in Soviet Society*, Cambridge, 1977, in Hoberman, p. 198.

20 Hoberman, p. 208.

21 Hoberman, p. 231.

22 Hoberman, pp 84–5.

23 Cited by Hoberman, p. 92.

24 Hoberman, p. 202.

25 Brian M. Petrie, 'Sport and Politics', in Donald W. Ball and John W. Loy (eds), *Sport and Social Order*, Addison Wesley, Reading, Mass., 1975, p. 195.

26 Richard S. Gruneau, 'Sport, Social Differentiation and Social Inequality', in Ball and Loy (eds), p. 129.

27 Gruneau, p. 130.

28 Quoted by Gruneau, pp 131–2.

29 Graham Murdock and Peter Golding, 'Capitalism, Communication and Class Relations', in J. Curran, M. Gurevitch and J. Woollacott (eds), *Mass Communication and Society*, Edward Arnold, London, 1977, pp 37–8.

30 For some examples of writing on modern sport that explore this perspective see, Mary Jo Deegan and Michael Stein, 'American Drama and Ritual: Nebraska Football', *International Review of Sport Sociology*, 13, 1978, pp 31–42; Susan Birrell, 'Sport as Ritual: Interpretations from Durkheim to Goffman', *Social Forces*, 60(2), 1981, pp 354–76; Alice Taylor Cheska, 'Sports Spectacular: A Ritual Model of Power', *International Review of Sport Sociology*, 14(2), 1979, pp 51–72; Michael Real, 'The Super Bowl: Myth Spectacle', in Michael Real, *Mass Mediated Culture*, Prentice Hall, Englewood Cliffs, NJ, 1977, pp 91–117.

31 See, for example, the interpretations of the significance of American Memorial Day by W. Lloyd Warner. 'An American Sacred Ceremony', in *American Life: Dream and Reality*, rev. edn, University of Chicago Press, Chicago, Ill., 1962; and the coronation of Queen Elizabeth II by Edward Shils and Michael Young, 'The Meaning of the Coronation', *Sociological Review*, 1, 1953, pp 63–81. For a discussion of the changing historical role played by television with regard to civic rituals that has helped to transform them into 'media events' see David Chaney 'A Symbolic Mirror of Ourselves: Civic Ritual in Mass Society', *Media, Culture and Society*, 5(2), 1983, pp 119–35.

32 See the discussion of the television coverage of the marriage of Prince Charles and Princess Diana in Daniel Dayan and Elihu Katz, 'Electronic

Ceremonies: Television Performs a Royal Wedding', in Marshall Blonsky (ed.) *On Signs*, Basil Blackwell, Oxford, 1985, pp 16–34.
33 Richard Lipsky, 'Political Implications of Sports Team Symbolism', *Politics and Society*, 9(1), 1979, pp 72–3.
34 Lipsky, p. 86.
35 Lipsky, p. 86.
36 Claire Louise Williams, Geoffrey Lawrence and David Rowe, 'Women and Sport: A Lost Ideal', Paper presented to SAANZ Conference, University of Queensland, 30 August – 2 September 1985, p. 2.
37 Williams, Lawrence and Rowe, p. 3. Despite the ostensive influence of the feminist movement on intellectual and social life, it is important to note that such views remain firmly entrenched at all levels of society. At best, they may no longer be so openly and publicly expressed and rarely, within the academy, as uncompromisingly as in a recent paper by John Carroll, who writes,

women should once again be prohibited from sport: they are the true defenders of the humanist values that emanate from the household, the values of tenderness, nurture and compassion, and this most important role must not be confused by the military and political values inherent in sport.

'Sport: Virtue and Grace', *Theory, Culture and Society*, 3(1), 1986, p. 98.
38 Some indication of the comprehensiveness with which this policy of sexual apartheid in sport has been maintained emerges in the statistics reported by Williams, Lawrence and Rowe, (p. 4) that only fifteen of the 266 events contested at the Los Angeles Olympics permitted direct competition between the sexes.
39 Williams, Lawrence and Rowe, p. 8.
40 Harry Edwards, 'Sport Within the Veil: The Triumphs, Tragedies and Challenges of Afro-American Involvement', *Annals of the AAPSS*, 445, 1979, pp 116–27.
41 Edwards, p. 120.
42 See the discussion of television and sport by John Fiske and John Hartley in *Reading Television*, Methuen, London, 1978, pp 142–7.
43 This interpretation of the rise in the value of 'professionalism' in modern society owes much to the insights of Will Wright as presented in his innovative study of the Hollywood Western, *Six Guns and Society*, University of California Press, Berkely and Los Angeles, 1975.

6

Television and the commodification of high-performance sport

The shifting balance of control

In his pioneering book first published in 1971, William Johnson presents the following to illustrate the shift in the financial relationship between sport and the media. In 1936, the organising committee for the annual Orange Bowl—an end of season college football event held in Florida between two of the season's most successful teams—volunteered to pay CBS $500 to ensure a network radio broadcast of the game. In 1969 NBC paid the Orange Bowl Committee $500 000 for television broadcast rights.[1] The implication that could be drawn from this observation is that over the past decades sporting organisations have become healthy financial beneficiaries of television's programming requirements. The guardians of sport have, under their jurisdiction, a highly desirable commodity for which television organisations appear to be prepared to open their ample coffers and pay out staggering sums of money. Furthermore, the competitive bidding for exclusive rights has become so intense, the figures indicate a dizzying upward spiral in the shifting market value of the television rights to the most desirable sports events each time they are offered. As a prime example, the American rights to the 1960 Olympics in Rome were won by CBS for $660 000, the Munich Olympics in 1972 cost the ABC network $13 500 000 and the same network paid $255 000 000 for the 1984 Los Angeles Olympics. The price escalated over the twenty-four year period by a factor of 386. The probable asking price for television rights to the 1988 Olympics in Seoul has been reported as $US 700 million.

Increasingly large sums of money paid out to sport by television, which then go to the particular sporting organisations involved, make it appear that sport has benefited substantially from the largesse that television has generously bestowed upon it. This is a position that, as Johnson notes, executives in the television industry are not loathe to reinforce. In 1968, a high-level executive of the CBS network told him: 'Sports is quite a bad investment, generally speaking... the rights have gotten so damned costly that we almost have to do sports as a public service and just forget about its making a profit'.[2] While commercial television executives have been known on occasion to miscalculate the revenue earning potential of particular programming material they are not renowned for persisting with programmes that continue to lose money for their organisation, nor for their magnanimity in serving the public. One might be excused for expressing a certain amount of incredulity that the latter consideration played any significant part in stimulating the burgeoning growth of sport on television.

There would seem to be very little evidence of any 'public service' motivation, for example, for the American NBC network's decision to televise the 1986 Super Bowl—the biggest event on the American television sports calendar. After paying $17 million for the television rights they received $27.5 million from the sale of commercial time during the broadcast (at $1.1 million per minute) making it the highest grossing single television programme of the year for the network.

Certainly, given the economic logic of the industry, sports are sought after by commercial television because they provide some benefit to the media organisation, as the means of generating income directly or enhancing the general image of the station or network, thereby increasing the potential advertising revenue of other programmes in the schedule. But because television appears so keen to broadcast sporting programmes and thereby contributes considerable income to sporting bodies through the purchase of rights and the promotion of particular events and competitions, this has led some observers to nominate the relationship as one of symbiosis or interdependence.[3] One writer goes so far as to suggest that in recent times, '...a balance of bargaining power had shifted in the direction of sport'.[4]

However, it is argued here, that the basis of the relationship between television and sport is premised on the opportunity for television to benefit its own interests. In doing so this might result in some economic and status enhancement of sport but, ultimately, the control of the terms, conditions and arrangements remains with television rather than the sport.

The key development that effectively threw sport into the arms of television was the process of the transformation of sport itself, that began at the point of its emergence in its modern form in the middle of the nineteenth century. Writing thirty years ago, Gregory Stone encapsulated the essence of this process within sport as a shift in emphasis from 'play' to 'display'. It was the increasingly significant role of the spectator, he suggested, that was fundamental to this shift.[5]

The development of certain sports into commodity entertainment forms that facilitated the emergence of professionalism, heightened entrepreneurial activity and, particularly in the United States, the private ownership of sports organisations meant that the technology of television represented to the providers of sports entertainment a potent vehicle for increased 'market penetration'. Thus, it is no coincidence that the early 1950s saw the beginning of:

> ... the emergence of large-scale organisation and sophisticated administrative planning ... in American professional sport ... This was a time when those in control of professional sport were forced to confront the dual dilemma of decreasing attendance and the unknown impact of television. In this context a new sports entrepreneur stepped into the picture, one with less concern for the esthetic aspects of sports and more for sound business practices and the maximization of profits. These organisation persons have fundamentally transformed the character of sports ...[6]

By having built up loyal sporting audiences and broadly based sporting subcultures over some decades, certain sports were more attractive to television than others. The more popular sports, particularly those with already established national competitions, clearly had most to offer in terms of network television's marketing economics. Thus, it was those well established spectator sports such as baseball, football, basketball and hockey in the United States, all of which already featured full professionalisation of participants, private ownership of clubs and a broad based inter-city competitive structure that appealed most strongly to commercial television networks. It is not surprising, in turn, that economic and organisational control in these sports quickly passed into the hands of an aggressively entrepreneurial consortium of owners, administrators and business advisers who eagerly sought the financial advantages available from the sale of television rights as a viable base for unprecedented economic growth and increased profitability. A handful of other sports—some, such as boxing and wrestling traditionally promoted employing entrepreneurial marketing techniques, and others, such as roller-derby and demolition derby, bizarre creations constructed primarily for television —also established a firm niche in American television programming schedules of the late 1940s and early 1950s. The subsequent television history of these sports also provides us with evidence regarding the relative strengths of the institutions of sport and television. When the audience ratings figures began to decline by the mid to late 1950s, all of these sports were quickly and unceremoniously dumped by television. Boxing still appears on television, but not on a regular basis. Wrestling has made a recent revival as a television 'sport' but as a comic spectacle that employs outrageously contrived show business techniques. The level of authenticity of television wrestling as a genuine contest of skill is not convincing to a substantial proportion of the general public. It has often been suggested that the contestants are all paid-up members of actors equity, or if not, they definitely should be.

While the major American team sports mentioned above do not appear to have suffered the same fate, the developmental history of their ongoing relationship with television suggests that their relative autonomy as independent cultural institutions has become increasingly compromised to the extent that their future as professional sports is now inextricably linked to the logic and decision-making prerogatives determined by network television executives. The process of subjugation of these sports to television is evidenced by the extent to which they have consistently accommodated themselves to the requirements of television coverage and become economically dependent upon the revenue from television to continue to operate profitably at their present level.

With regard to the last point, as a number of observers have noted, the sale of broadcasting rights has become a critical factor contributing more than a third of the gross revenue returned to the teams in the four major American sporting leagues.[7] In the twenty years to 1972, the share of major league baseball revenues derived from television rights increased from 13 to 25 per cent. In major league football the figures show a more dramatic shift—from 9 per cent to 36 per cent.[8] Examining data for each year between 1952 and 1970 for all major sporting teams, Horowitz concludes that very few would have made any money without their share of the income from broadcasting rights, the most substantial part of which came from network television.[9] Furthermore, apart from the overall sum of money contributed by television, as multiple year contracts are the norm, this source of revenue is both more stable than ticket sales and one of the few areas of income that provides potential for a real increase in financial return as ticket prices 'are about as high as the market might bear'.[10]

A similar trend has developed in Australia over the past fifteen years. In the 1973–74 season, 62 per cent of the income to Australian tennis organisations from spectator events came from gate receipts, while they received nothing from the sale of television rights. Ten years later the respective figures were 31 per cent and 29 per cent.[11] Over the same period the contribution of television money to the coffers of Australian football and cricket organisations has continued to increase dramatically.

While referring primarily to the American context Altheide and Snow have pointed out,

Another way to examine the importance of television revenue to professional sports is to note the failures. The World Football League got off the ground with television support, but foundered when it was withdrawn. The American Basketball Association struggled for several years, but failed without television support. The recently developed World Team Tennis league is facing financial pressure since TV coverage has been cut. In each case the respective leagues have been unable to attract the number of viewers required for networks to make a profit, so TV executives have either reduced the size of contracts or cancelled them.[12]

More recently, and primarily for the same reasons, despite the investment of large sums of money to attract the involvement of a number of ageing European and Latin American former superstars, the North American Soccer League has suffered the same fate.

The significance of the television market has become the most important feature in determining both the granting of and the movement of club franchises from one city to another. Thus teams may be uprooted and relocated not because stadiums are unfilled by paying spectators but because location elsewhere means larger, more concentrated, more demographically desirable television audiences that translates into increased income to the networks from the sale of commercial time and, in turn, an increase in the amount they are prepared to pay the sports leagues for the rights to broadcast games.

The significance of a television contract for the potential profitability of sport as an entrepreneurial exercise has encouraged the growth of certain sports, and moved the ownership and administrative organisations further into the realm of big business operations. More and more it has become a profitable avenue for speculation and investment entered into primarily as an entrepreneurial and marketing venture in which the sport event itself is the saleable product, sportsmen and sportswomen highly paid labourers, and sports spectators paying customers. While publicly the sports entrepreneurs continue to pay lip service to the support and loyalty of paying spectators who attend the event and to the cities and communities that provide the 'home' for their team, the potential profitability of the enterprise has become largely determined by the size and characteristics of the home viewing audience. Television must produce a form of entertainment that ensures a maximisation of the sale of commercial time and therefore the staging of the sports event is increasingly susceptible to changes in structure and form that television professionals assess will be most favourable to this end. This has led to the most visible and widely commented upon influences on sport attributed to television — changes to the internal structure of sporting contests through manipulation of rules, scoring, conditions of play and control over decisions affecting time, place and duration of the event. While it must be recognised that sports were constantly changing and evolving prior to television's involvement, as one writer notes, in general such changes,

> were made to improve the sport itself either for 'sporting' reasons or to make it more interesting to spectators in order to stimulate attendance. Gradually, entrepreneur types of sportsmen saw an opportunity for greater profits by making slight changes within their sports to appeal to the desires of television . . .
>
> Tradition was often abandoned as rules, styles, and playing fields were changed so that organized sports would be more attractive to television. For example, networks like neat time packages to increase a program's saleability to prospective sponsors. So, to help them out, the NFL [National Football League in the US] cut the halftime intermission from 20 minutes to 15 minutes so that the program would fit more comfortably into a two-and-a-half hour time segment. Golf changed from match to medal or stroke play in order to guarantee prospective television sponsors attractive celebrity golfers for their telecasts in the final stages of an event. Tennis introduced the tie-breaker . . . NHL [The North American National Hockey League] hockey changed its center line to a broken line so it would show up better on television.[13]

One could continue with an enormous list of what, taken independently, might be considered essentially trivial changes effected in many different sports, almost all of which have been instigated for the benefits of television. But, more importantly, the general lack of resistance by sporting authorities to such changes indicates that they have voluntarily accepted or resignedly acknowledged that, to adapt an oft-cited aphorism, 'what's good for television is good for sport'.

But most significantly, the subservience to television's wishes is not confined to commercially based spectator sports, nor do the pressures for 'tinkering' with established sporting forms come solely from commercial television organisations. The general belief within the sporting world that getting one's particular sport or event on television is both desirable and necessary is so widely held that almost every type of sporting body, be they amateur, junior or representative of relatively obscure pastimes is more than happy to make whatever changes or modifications requested if the result will mean television exposure. The conventional wisdom in contemporary sport is encapsulated in the outspoken statement attributed to an American college football coach who explained: 'We think TV exposure is so important to our program and so important to this university that we will schedule ourselves to fit the medium. I'll play at midnight if that's what TV wants'.[14]

In Australia, a television sports producer proposed a significant rule change which would make coverage of a squash tournament, a sport rarely shown on television, more attractive to viewers. It was explained that, from a television point of view, it was very unsatisfactory to have a magnificent rally, 30 or 40 shots, at the end of which if the non-server won, all he gets as a reward for winning that rally is the service and the scoreboard stays the same.... (This is) not satisfying for the television audience that wants to see something for its money. So we devised a scheme where they had five services each and whoever won each rally scored a point and it went tick, tick, tick on the screen.

The authorities from the local squash association were quite happy to accept this fairly fundamental change to the structure of the game if it would help to 'drag in the telly'.[15]

In assessing the significance of the changes in various sports that television had managed to secure in the relatively brief time they had been on the scene, Johnson, as far back as 1969, concluded somewhat dramatically that the impact of the medium

has produced more revolutionary—and irrevocable—changes in sports than anything since mankind began to play organized games ...The geography, the economics, the schedules, the esthetics, the very ethos of sports has come to depend upon television cameras and advertising monies...[16]

Of course, it is true to say that once a sport is well established on television, whether it already had a substantial pre-television following that has been broadened by increased exposure from the medium, or a large following has developed primarily as the result of television's involvement, it is able to bargain more securely for substantial increases in rights' payments. It is in these circumstances that it may be accurate to suggest a certain level of interdependence exists between *particular* sports or sporting events and television. If the sports are prepared to instigate the necessary changes required to make the televising of their leagues or championships successful, in terms of consistently providing television organisations with satisfactory viewer audience ratings, this places strong pressure on television to pay what is being asked for the rights, and creates a competitive bidding situation between rival organisations for exclusive access to highly desirable programming material. These circumstances have led to the phenomenal escalation in the prices television organisations are prepared to pay for periodic single events such as the Olympic Games, Soccer's World Cup, the most prestigious championships on the annual calendar in golf, tennis and soccer, and, in North America the play-offs in final series of the major spectator sports, all of which past experience has demonstrated will be 'guaranteed winners' in attracting huge television audiences.

In this sense, high performance sport is in an analogous position to other forms of independently produced television programme material such as dramatic series or situation comedies. For as long as particular shows maintain their rating power, they establish a sound bargaining position for contractual renewal and increased remuneration for all concerned with the production. But their position deteriorates rapidly if the size and characteristics of their viewing audience do not match up to the television organisation's requirements.

It is important to note that the criterion commercial television executives employ for making such decisions is not based purely on the total size of the viewing audience. The public rationale aggressively and frequently reiterated within the commercial television industry is that programming decisions represent the ultimate in the application of democratic principles to the provision of mass entertainment, 'giving the people what they want'. As one commercial television executive proudly proclaimed.

Television is rated every fifteen minutes. I don't think there is any other industry in the world that is under so much scrutiny as television. Every fifteen minutes we know what the people are saying to us. We are a service industry.[17]

Such admirable rhetoric masks the fact that the demographic characteristics most closely associated with groups in society that are the primary consumers of the products sold by television advertisers are far more significant in determining the 'success' of particular programmes on commercial television than the absolute number of viewers. Thus, many shows that are still drawing large viewing audiences are cancelled by commercial stations because they tend to attract 'proportionately more elderly, lower-income rural audiences' while buying patterns for consumer goods direct advertisers towards seeking out 'the young, urban affluent audiences' who have more cash to spend and are also less likely to have developed well entrenched purchasing patterns.

In the United States, experience and research has sensitised television decision makers to the fact that,

Among the most difficult demographic segments of the population to reach are the adult males. Sports programming provides advertisers with vehicles to reach them in large numbers without the waste that would normally be realized through other types of prime-time programming. Thus the desirability of football for television programming can be attributed not only to its high audience ratings but also to the composition of its audience, for according to Nielson ratings, the television audience for football is the only TV sports audience which is composed of at least 50 percent adult males. In contrast, although baseball may be as popular as football, it reaches fewer, less affluent men and therefore is less attractive to advertisers.[18]

Thus, it has already been suggested that while baseball still appears on television, America's traditional 'national game' may eventually prove so unattractive to advertisers it will disappear from the small screen primarily because the composition of its still extensive following is made up of people with the 'wrong' combination of demographic characteristics.

Golf provides a reverse example. While it is one of the more popular sports in terms of active participants, on television it has never attracted viewers in large numbers. Yet, commercial television networks continue to annually telecast a significant number of golf tournaments primarily because this sport attracts a larger proportion of wealthy, high status males than any other programme on television and access to this group is eagerly sought after by those businesses and financial institutions seeking to reach this target population.[19] Advertising time for golf programmes can thus be sold at a high price because of the buying power of its viewing audience, while a sport consistently attracting an equivalent or larger viewing audience but one with less attractive 'demographics' would have been dropped by television long ago.

The potential income to sports with a high level of television exposure is further enhanced in that it is easier to attract direct sponsorship of teams and events, the money from which goes directly to the sporting body involved. In return for providing sponsorship money the company's name is linked to the name of the event, displayed on advertising hoardings in the arena or prominently on participants' clothing. Guaranteed television coverage ensures that the sponsors' name will receive commercially valuable exposure without the necessity of directly purchasing television advertising time, as well as prestigious publicity acknowledging the company's support and assistance to the sport.

Ultimately, then, television is in the position to largely determine the relative societal visibility of particular sports at local, national and even international levels. Given that sports compete against each other for adherents, followers and financial support and also operate within the leisure-entertainment market in competition with 'other forms of entertainment for the discretionary income spent on leisure time activities *outside* of the home',[20] access to television exposure has become a major factor in determining any sports' relative social and economic position in the crowded and intensive struggle for a share of the consumers' 'entertainment dollar'.

Thus inevitably the business-marketing mentality begins to predominate. The well established commercially oriented spectator sports with regular fat television contracts become the primary model and example of the pathway to success, encouraging, almost compelling, the administrators and controllers of less popular, obscure and little known pastimes to fall over themselves in a rush to secure a television contract. As Garrie Hutchinson has wryly suggested, the distinction between a 'major' and a 'minor' sport these days is simply that 'a minor sport is one that is not on television much'.[21] So a generalised belief has developed that for a 'minor sport', getting on to television is both essential to its continued survival and will help to propel it into the 'big-time', in terms of social prestige, popularity and if not incredible wealth for all concerned, at least significantly improved financial rewards. Amateur sports associations that for decades have been administering to the needs of small groups of dedicated enthusiasts on a modest scale find increasing pressures placed upon them to approach and employ business consultants, public relations experts and advertising agencies who will guide them towards a more 'business-like' approach to promoting their sport in the market-place. Many of these amateur sports administrators somewhat naively believe that television is merely a transparent medium that will display their sport to a wider public and reveal what they believe to be its intrinsic appeal to prospective participants and spectators. However, as should by now be apparent, television operates primarily as an independent institution with its own logic and its own set of dominant interests. As a number of the major sports whose administrators or controllers have already entered into the Faustian pact with television have discovered,

Television *buys* sports. Television *supports* sports. It moves in with its money and supports sports in a style to which they had hoped to become accustomed and then, like a bought lady, sports become so used to luxurious living they cannot extricate themselves. So, slowly at first, but inevitably, television tells sports what to do. It *is* sports and it runs them the way it does most other things, more flamboyantly than honestly.[22]

The sports professional: Playing for keeps

One of the most visible effects of both the infusion of substantial amounts of money into sport and the broad-based expansion of the audience for sport brought about by television's involvement has been the dramatic rise in social visibility of the sports professional. Until the middle of the nineteenth century, very few individuals attempted to earn their living by exhibiting their sporting skills. Apart from horse-racing which developed a formal organisation in both Britain and North America considerably earlier than most other sports, prize fighting was the other sport from which a skilled practitioner might be able to forge a brief but relatively lucrative 'career'. However, the basis for the modern form of sports professionalism only began to emerge in the mid-nineteenth century with the development of regular fixtures and competitions in a number of team sports such as soccer and cricket in England and baseball in the United States.

The principles of employment as a professional in these team sports developed very early and were adopted by a number of other sports such as football, hockey and basketball when they established their first professional leagues in North America in the late nineteenth and early twentieth centuries. The primary organisation to which the professional athlete was bound was the club, which in turn formed part of a league or association, the latter an overarching administrative body formed by selected representatives from the constituent clubs. The practice of tying the player's professional services to a particular club, until that club agreed to release them, emerged at a very early stage, and remained an unshakeable cornerstone of professional employment in most team sports until the 1960s. It was almost universally institutionalised even in sports that remained totally amateur and extended down to youngsters who played in inter-club junior competitions.

Ostensibly, the rationale for this, subscribed to by both amateur and professional sports bodies, was in order to ensure a stability and evenness to potential competition on the field between the clubs and to prevent attempts by more successful clubs to establish long-term superiority through continually enticing away talented personnel from the weaker clubs in the league. It was felt that this might create a permanent imbalance in the competition and thereby diminish spectator and participant interest in the weekly fixtures that cumulatively determined the champion club each season. In addition to the principle of the 'reserve clause', as it became known in America, some professional sports' leagues determined salary scales for all players based on years of service and even in some cases decreed a maximum wage in excess of which no player could be paid.

The effect of these regulations was to constrain sports professionals in a tightly controlled employment situation that soon provoked considerable discontent. Particularly when in this century the developing norm in most industrialised countries was towards the acceptance of more liberal legislation guarding against the exploitation of the workforce, such conditions appeared to many to be extremely antiquated, still rooted in the feudalistic assumptions of lifelong loyalty and obligation that bound serf to master. While it was in the interests of most professional sports leagues to ensure the mutual enforcement of the 'reserve clause' principle, the clubs themselves were also in perpetual competition with each other for supremacy in the annual battle for the championship and particularly in the United States, any notion of a universal salary scale and a maximum wage were very quickly undermined.

The more skilled players could bargain for better contracts, receive bonuses based on performance and other considerations, for it was in the club's interest to keep them reasonably happy and playing to the best level of their ability. Even where a 'maximum wage' stipulation was officially enforced such as in English soccer or Australian football, clubs and supporters developed a number of 'semi-legal' techniques to first secure the services of desirable players and to supplement the official remuneration of those considered vital to the club's on-field success. Unofficial 'incentives' for signing with the club in the form of cash or goods could be arranged; a lucrative year-round job connected with the club or in the employ of a wealthy supporter might be offered that provided the player with supplementary income while allowing him to concentrate most of his time during the playing season on training, preparation and competition. Groups of club supporters formed coterie organisations one of the primary purposes of which was to raise money to supplement the income of key players through 'gifts' for outstanding performances or regular under the table payments to selected individuals.

These and a number of other devices also operated within sports that nominally were wholly amateur including individual sports such as athletics, swimming, golf and tennis where sports organisations and tournament promoters were known to regularly offer 'appearance guarantees' secretly paid to particular players whose participation, it was considered, would enhance the status (and the gate takings) of their event. In the 1950s and 1960s this practice was so widespread in international tennis that the accusations of 'shamateurism' constantly alluded to by journalists and other critics led in 1967 to a surrender of the sport to full professionalism with the abandonment, after four decades, of a lengthy battle to keep this sport totally amateur up to its highest level of tournament competition.

Certainly while it is impossible to gather reliable statistics, it seems clear that despite the various unofficial sources of payment, until the last two decades, very few professional sports persons were paid or accumulated enough money from their playing exploits to make them outstandingly wealthy, although quite a number made a good and even relatively luxurious living during the few years they were at their peak.[23] However, the average as well as the few, widely publicised, outstandingly high sporting salaries earned by professional sportsmen in the United States between the 1920s and 1960s were consistently and substantially greater (again with a few isolated exceptions in Europe and Latin America) than those received by professionals in any other country. Thus, for example, although by the 1930s, soccer was long established as a professional sport in England and clubs were already making player transfer deals with each other of ten thousand pounds or more, when, in the mid-thirties American baseball star Babe Ruth met Bill Dean, a leading English soccer player of the period 'Ruth was astonished to learn that Dean was paid a basic wage of only [eight pounds] a week'.[24]

Again, with the obvious exception of privately owned teams, most sports clubs did not seek to make profits. Many of the weaker ones were only able to scrape by with the assistance of fund-raising efforts among supporters and short-term assistance from the leagues of which they were members when they found themselves in financial difficulties. In many professional team sports, the playing personnel were recruited predominantly from the working class and lower middle class. Coming from such backgrounds, the players' elevated community status and respectable income, which was often considerably more substantial than the wages received by those of their social peer group not involved in professional sports, was sufficient to ensure that there was little effective group agitation to improve salaries.

While there was a well developed transfer system of players from one club to another, in the main this involved the weaker and more marginal players or older players whose skills and abilities were beginning to decline. The typical experience of most participants in team sports—both amateur and professional—was to play out their entire career with the same club.

It is perhaps no coincidence that substantial changes to these patterns first began to take place in the 1950s and early 1960s at about the time that television's involvement with sports increased dramatically. The injection of large and well publicised amounts of money into sport from the sale of television rights did not go unnoticed by the players. Their longstanding feelings of discontent and exploitation erupted into active agitation—sometimes through existing or newly formed players' associations—to secure better payments and conditions for the sports labourer. In North America, their bargaining position for successfully achieving such changes was strengthened by a number of other connected developments that took place around the same time. First, the transformation of many sports from small localised diversions into large-scale lucrative enterprises, a change greatly encouraged and almost demanded by television, brought a 'new breed' of owners and managers into particular clubs and into sports administration in general. Both for pragmatic and ideological reasons, these individuals sought to run their organisations as a business enterprise within the service and entertainment industry. As Furst has observed:

> Formerly sport franchise owners were men who generally approached the administration of teams with a mixture of deep emotional commitment to the sport and the belief that financial operations were a necessary adjunct to a successful season. Imbued with the organizational ethos, the new owner thinks primarily of maximizing profit through calculated business procedures. This new type of sports entrepreneur still appreciates the spectacle of sport but only as a secondary consideration. Consistently increasing revenues are the primary consideration.[25]

Particularly in North America where private team ownership was the established norm, but soon spreading to sports administration generally, it became almost mandatory to draw upon the sophisticated cost accounting, managerial and administrative techniques available and to employ or contract highly qualified professionals from all of these areas to advise, analyse, report upon and occupy key positions in the running of sports organisations. Such advisors were quick to identify the critical variables involved and employing rationalistic free-enterprise economic models, to isolate the importance of such factors as the maintenance of relatively even competition between all teams in a league, the establishment of orderly incentive scales to encourage an increased employee productivity, and the calculation of the relative value of each employee's contribution to the profitability of the enterprise. It was necessary to ensure that the most effective players both in terms of skill and audience appeal (live and television) were rewarded sufficiently so that they would perform at their best and not be lured away by the opposition. Despite the desire to maintain competitiveness within a league and to redistribute income to assist the poorer clubs, the more successful clubs inevitably were also the most profitable. Substantial variation in players' salaries were seen as necessary to secure the consistent high level performance by contracted personnel, to create a larger, more competitive pool of prospective players and to attract necessary talent from other clubs.

The continual leap-frogging of maximum salaries that has evolved from this reflects the considerable economic expansion of the sports industry leading eventually to the perceived need by players to also secure professional advice, personal managers and agents to bargain for their contracts and conditions.

Furthermore, the longstanding collusion between team managements that had successfully restricted players' attempts to squeeze more money from them became less effective, at least in North America, with attempts by various business interests to establish rival leagues in three of the four major sports, thus operating in direct competition for players, supporters and television coverage with the traditional competitions. Throughout the 1950s and 1960s, in basketball, football and hockey, the existing leagues expanded by issuing franchises tied to particular cities, considered suitable to the competition and capable of supporting a major-league team. Successful bidders for the available franchises had to demonstrate they were capable of running a major sports team and pay the league a hefty 'joining fee' of several million dollars for the privilege. In each sport there were also a number of unsuccessful bidders some of whom became convinced that they were being irrationally or unfairly excluded and determined, in association with other entrepreneurs and business interests in various cities, to start their own leagues. They created the American Basketball Association, the American Football League and the World Hockey Association between 1960 and 1972. In each case the new organisations successfully plundered the existing leagues in their respective sports capturing, by lucrative salary offers, a handful of notable 'stars' and numerous lesser lights. But, by attracting television coverage, the newly formed basketball and football leagues quickly developed strong followings and eventually negotiated successful merger agreements with the established leagues. The World Hockey Association failed to negotiate a major television contract. After only a couple of years many of its franchises were in serious trouble and the disbandment of the league imminent. The floundering enterprise succumbed to a takeover offer by the established National Hockey League, which then incorporated a small number of the remaining franchises into their existing competition.

The effect on players' salaries during these 'wars' was understandably beneficial as it broke the 'traditional' circumstances whereby all of the successful American 'professional sports leagues have a remarkably complex set of rules and practices that all but eliminate business competition among their members'.[26]

Also, the new leagues did not feel bound by the reserve clause which also came under challenge in the courts. As a result of a number of cases, involving all four of the major American team sports, the perpetual reserve clause system whereby the club first signing a player had virtual control of his career for life was abandoned, returning some personal autonomy to the sports professional.

In summary, the financial rewards paid to professional athletes in North America have increased significantly since the early 1960s, at a much faster rate than average salary movements among the general population. A detailed analysis of average and maximum salaries in 1977 over seven sports compiled by Loy et al. is reproduced in Table 6.1 below. In this year there were a few individuals in each sport earning annual salaries in excess of $250 000. The average salaries

Table 6.1 Estimated average and maximum annual salaries for professional sport [in North America] 1977

Sport	Approximate number of players	Estimated average salary	Estimated maximum salary
		$	$
Baseball	600	95 000	500 000
Football	1200	50 000	450 000
Basketball	200	120 000	600 000
Hockey*	600	75 000	250 000
Golf	300	30 000	300 000
Tennis	200	50 000	600 000
Horse-racing (jockeys)	2500	10 000	450 000

* This is the only sport in which there are two leagues competing for playing personnel.

Source: John W. Loy, Barry D. McPherson and Gerald Kenyan, *Sport and Social Systems*, Addision-Wesley, Reading. Mass., 1978, p.268.

(with the possible exception of horse-racing) were also well above the national median. For the four major team sports with national network television contracts the lowest average salary was $50 000 for football and the highest $120 000 for basketball.

Of course since this time, salaries have continued to escalate. Thus, by 1985, average major-league salaries in the United States were reportedly $150 000 in football, $332 000 in basketball and $363 000 in baseball. In baseball, the highest 1985 salary was $2 130 000 with thirty-six players earning $1 000 000 or more. But there continues to be great variation 'in salaries between sports, between leagues in a given sport, and within clubs depending on the position played, the level of ability, and the degree of "charisma" generated'.[27]

Similar developments have occurred in professional sports outside of North America, notably soccer in Europe and Latin America and football and cricket in Australia. Thus, for example, between 1965 and 1984, the average annual payment to each senior club player in the Victorian Football League rose from $290 to $22 000. By 1984, the highest paid player in the league was on an annual salary of $66 000.[28] In individual sports such as golf and tennis, where a player's earnings are primarily dependent upon prize money won (with the exception of the most successful who often make more from commercial endorsements), the number of tournaments and overall prize money available have both increased dramatically, resulting in a rapid growth in the number of professional participants travelling the international circuits. Thus, top ranking tennis player, Ivan Lendl, has won more than $2 000 000 in a single year. In 1984 the leading money winner on the American golf circuit earned $476 260 with the player ranked fiftieth making $133 445. Once again these developments have been largely facilitated by the increased money directly available from television, and indirectly through the attractiveness of business sponsorship for events guaranteed television exposure.

However, apart from increasing the earning potential of professional athletes, television has brought about a dramatic change to a number of dimensions of their social role. While a few of the more outstanding professional athletes of the past have become 'public figures' and even major celebrities, regular television coverage of sport has brought many more into public prominence. The major thrust of the televisual style of sports coverage as outlined in Chapter 4 involves a strong bias towards personalisation through extensive use of close-up shots. This is reinforced by constant monitoring and recapitulating by commentators of many aspects of the sportsperson's public and private life as well as strong pressure on players to participate in on-camera interviews, all of which have led to the incorporation of sporting professionals into the ever-changing cast of international media 'celebrityhood'.

Simply by being regularly seen on television the professional athlete comes under constant and intense scrutiny and is expected to co-operate in the process of characterisation through which the dramatic narrative structure of television sports is constructed and packaged to the public.

A full complement of character roles is created including 'super star', 'rising champion', 'solid reliable performer', 'fading former champion', 'villain', 'local hero' or just 'personality' into which particular players are directed. The colour and toning of the roles relies upon the individual psychology and temperament of the performer as signified by their on-field manner and style and in the way they present themselves in on-camera interviews. To this is added background concerning their pre-professional sporting career, social and educational background, family life, hobbies, interests and numerous other personal attributes so that a fully developed media persona is created.

Television feeds on and amplifies the eccentric, the unusual and the 'controversial' and therefore tends to hone in on sportspersons who exhibit such characteristics. Unusual physical appearance, sexual proclivities, ethnic or class background, flamboyant dress, speaking style, accent, mannerisms, vocabulary, are all considered to contribute positively to the personalisation process. Players who naturally or calculatingly project such attributes are eagerly cultivated and further encouraged by the extent to which they are singled out on camera, commented upon, sought out for interviews, provided with colourful nicknames and generally transformed into minor or even major celebrities. Such 'characters' are adopted and vigorously promoted by television into 'cult' figures. Their television audience drawing power is often perceived to be far greater than a highly skilled but 'colourless' player, and there are strong pressures for their inclusion in a contest on grounds other than their sporting ability.[29]

Through the widespread coverage of sports, when such individuals emerge they become candidates for incorporation into the television 'celebrity' market. Sports have become another branch, together with cinema, light entertainment, the arts and politics, from which television recruits, creates and exploits 'celebrities'. Once adopted by television, the source of 'celebrityhood' becomes irrelevant, and the particular roles assigned to the celebrity may bear little or no relationship to the particular skill for which they first gained media recognition. This allows new hybrid genres of television to be created — football coaches host nature documentaries; film and television 'celebrities' play at mock sporting contests with tennis and golf 'celebrities'. Sports 'celebrities' become part of the 'talk show' circuit, are often guests on variety shows and make rock video clips.

The involvement of television in sport has meant that almost all players are expected to develop appropriate techniques of impression management which will be of benefit to the image that sporting authorities and television interests wish to present to the paying spectators and viewers. As they may be interviewed by the media, players are encouraged to become more articulate, to learn basic 'communication' techniques, ways of deflecting tricky questions and a set of responses that are consistent with the public image professional sport seeks to project.[30]

Inevitably this means the separation of 'front-stage' and 'back-stage' regions, the latter being carefully shielded from the media and other outsiders including fans and supporters. As one American baseballer wrote in a book severely critical of modern professional sport,

> On camera or within earshot of working reporters, the behaved player is an actor who projects blissful contentment, inexhaustible optimism, and abiding gratitude. 'I'll sweep out the clubhouse to stay here', he says. 'I love the game. I owe everything to baseball. I am thankful to this grand organization for giving me my big chance. I am in love with this town and its wonderful fans'.[31]

This is not to say that professionals are never critical of many aspects of the sports scene, but in general such dissatisfactions are not aired publicly, at least not while they are still actively involved.

In a study of professional baseballers, the majority of those interviewed revealed strong contempt for the average fan, few considering that the public had much understanding or appreciation of the game. The writer suggests that many players 'view adult fans in much the same way Howard S. Becker (1963) reports that jazz musicians perceive non-musicians. In plain words, adult fans are "squares", people who lack understanding of the sport of baseball or the men who play it. They are seen as naive, uninformed and fickle'.[32]

Players are also expected to maintain certain practices off-field which sporting authorities consider will assist in preserving the necessary belief by the public that sport is clean, wholesome and authentic. For example, in baseball there exists a strong taboo against fraternisation with players on opposing teams in public because it is considered that this might undermine the belief in 'unadulterated competition'.[33]

However, on the field there also develops a set of peer group norms that recognises the common group position of sporting professionals, and therefore concerned with not undermining an opponent's capacity to earn a living. In the baseball study cited, the players acknowledge that, for example, they try never to make opponents appear inept or unprofessional in a one-sided game, nor 'subject opposing players to the risk of injury unless such a risk might have an effect on the outcome of the game'.[34] Such sentiments extend to sports traditionally renowned for hard physical contact. As one Australian footballer remarked, players saw no point in knocking each other's teeth out, now they were all professionals.[35]

Thus, while professional athletes as a group, have their own set of interests that at times cut across those of management, television and spectators—as indicated by the recent emergence of militant player associations and increasing number of players' strikes—the circumstances within which professional sports operate present outstanding athletes with the opportunity for greater material and social benefits if they are prepared to comply with the requirements of 'putting on a good show' for paying spectators and the television audience.

Thus, authenticity of striving and performance, which lie at the root of sports' essential attraction to both participants and empathic spectator, are often submerged by the pragmatic interests of entrepreneurs, promoters, and television. The latter are better served by the creation of spectacle, pre-structured and technologically manipulated excitement and by encouraging the participants to play to the crowd (and camera) rather than in the exhibition of the more subtle skills appreciated most by other players and dedicated followers of the sport.[36] As the benefits accruing to sports professionals are so closely tied to the continued growth and profitability of the sport-television nexus, it is inevitable that the players' priorities, approaches and personal values become more aligned to these powerful, institutionalised interests. As Alan Ingham has written,

> Professionalization and commercialization have enslaved the athlete into fulfilling the commercial and cathartic needs of others rather than those within himself...The agonistic experience is transformed into a service occupation; sport ceases to be ennobling; the athlete is viewed as an entertainment commodity.[37]

Television rules — OK? Two Australian case studies

Over the past ten years, the two most popular team sports in Australia —cricket and Australian rules football—have entered into lucrative alliances with commercial television. The reasons behind television's increased involvement and the effect this has had on both sports— their organisational structure, the players and the general subculture of supporters and spectators—provides useful case study material illustrative of many of the processes outlined above.

Television's commodification of cricket

The game of cricket has been popular in Australia from the time of the first European settlement when, for a period of more than one hundred years, Australia consisted of a number of geographically separated colonial settlements, almost entirely populated by expatriates from the the British Isles and their descendants. As an indigenously English sport, cricket found a firm root in Australian culture. Representative matches were already being played between the colonies by the middle of the nineteenth century and 'national' teams competed against touring English sides whose intermittent visits were sponsored by private entrepreneurs. By the beginning of the twentieth century, at the time of Australian Federation, there existed a highly organised hierarchical cricket structure from the local club level through to interstate and international competition. The latter was institutionalised between Australia and England in the form of a series of test matches which formed part of the reciprocal 'tours' undertaken every few years by a representative team selected from the nation's top players. Opportunities for international cricket matches increased as gradually more countries, all of them at some time British colonies, were granted admission to the membership to the ICC (International Cricket Conference) a roof body administering and controlling the sport. In England there were already professionals playing the game in the early part of the nineteenth century. As already noted, cricket was one of the first sports to accommodate professionals playing together with amateurs, distinguished by the respective apellations of players and gentlemen. However, in keeping with the importance of class distinctions in English society, a gentleman always captained the English side and there were even separate dressing-rooms to reinforce this separation. The conservative nature of the English cricketing culture can be gauged by the fact that it was only in 1954 that the first professional captained an English team and only in 1962 that the last vestiges of the gentleman/player distinction was finally put to rest, mainly because by this stage almost all the top players were professionals. Professional cricketers were not paid particularly well and, in earlier times, tended to be,

> working class players who found cricket preferable to working down the mines. They played cricket for only 5 months of the year, and for the rest of the year had to find some other means of support, quite often in recent years the dole.[38]

In Australia, full professionalism did not exist in cricket up until the 1970s. Players chosen for state or national teams were paid a modest amount per game with travelling and accommodation expenses covered by the relevant association when they were touring. Spectator interest was predominantly focused on the international test matches played over five days (sometimes longer in the early years) and the interstate matches played over four days. These together with the English games between counties and equivalent interregional matches in other cricket playing countries were given the status of 'first class' matches, one of the stipulations being that such contests must be played over at least three days and within a two innings per side match structure.

Gate money from paying spectators contributed the bulk of the income to the cricket organisations to finance the various competitions at the first class level. Radio broadcasts of first class matches began in the 1930s. The BBC in Britain and the ABC in Australia—both state funded national broadcasters—became the traditional carriers of cricket commentaries and routinely received the *non-exclusive* broadcasting rights from the cricket authorities which were generally contracted for relatively small sums. This policy was extended to television although in the early years, loss of attendance revenue was guarded against by restrictions on the number of hours that could be telecast in the city in which the match was being played.

Despite cricket consistently attracting large crowds over many years, particularly to test matches played in Australia (over 90 000 attended one day of a 1961 test played in Melbourne between Australia and the West Indies), the financial organisation was still operating at a modest semi-professional level in all the major cricketing countries well into the 1970s. To give some indication, the county players in England in 1977 received less than $5000 for five months cricket; in the same year English internationals earned about $12 000; Australian internationals in 1975–76 were paid $5000 less expenses for a test series, while those playing at state level earned $2000 for the entire season.[39]

There had been some discontent brewing among top-level cricketers with regard to their relatively low income when it was well publicised that the controlling bodies, particularly in England and Australia were accumulating large surpluses. A major crisis occurred directly because of the intervention of the chairman of one of the commercial broadcasting organisations, Kerry Packer, whose extensive media holdings included control of stations GTV-9 in Melbourne and TCN-9 in Sydney. The Nine network, of which these two stations were the dominant sources of locally produced programme material, had not held a particularly high profile in television sport up to this time. It is reported that Packer was interested in obtaining the rights to test cricket after the ABC's telecast of an international one-day cricket final, played in England, and shown in Australia late in the evening, rated extremely highly—more than the average prime-time ratings normally obtained by commercial stations.[40] In 1976, he offered a large sum of money to the ACB (Australian Cricket Board) for exclusive rights to televise Australian cricket for the next five years. The Board continued its policy of granting *non-exclusive* rights to the ABC for a fraction of what the Packer organisation had bid, but offered the latter the commercial rights. This was rejected and Packer embarked on a path that rocked the cricketing world and changed the entire face of the game.[41]

Packer decided to secure the services of as many as possible of the world's best cricketers to play in his own competition, which he called World Series Cricket. The offers were extremely lucrative and consequently, in 1977, thirty-five top players including most of the Australian and West Indian Test teams signed contracts.

World Series Cricket got under way in the Australian summer of 1977 amidst strong opposition from the 'official' cricketing organisations, legal writs, and mutual vilification on both sides. The 'rebels' scheduled a series of 'Tests' and a one-day cup competition between three sides (Australia, the West Indies and the 'World'—meaning the rest), mostly played on grounds not normally used for cricket as the ACB successfully put pressure on those controlling traditional venues to deny the use of these grounds for 'Packer Cricket'. The entire schedule was televised nation-wide through the Nine network.

The 'official' Australian team debilitated by the loss of most of its top players performed disastrously in international competition over the next two years. World Series Cricket due to the hostility from the supporters of traditional cricket and much of the rest of the media had poor attendances for its first season and the Nine network had trouble selling the commercial time for its telecasts.

World Series Cricket introduced numerous gimmicks such as coloured uniforms, night games, white balls, special rules to stimulate high scoring and a revolutionary style of television coverage.

> the use of 8 cameras allowed each over to be shot from behind the bowler thereby showing the batsman front-on, a greater number of replays from more angles were made possible, and the practice was introduced of interviewing players as they returned to the pavillion.[42]

The last practice was quickly discontinued, mainly due to the hostility of the players to the idea. The commentator and cameraman would be standing at the gate as the player walked from the ground and asked the recently dismissed batsman something to the effect of 'Why did you play that stupid shot?' As Ross Edwards, who played in the early World Series Cricket games commented,

> the hapless interviewer nearly got killed on a number of occasions ... The last thing you want to do is have some gorilla with a microphone asking you why did you do that dumb thing when you've just been asking that of yourself in the last hundred yards as you've walked off the pitch.[43]

Despite losing money on the first year of the venture, World Series Cricket continued the following season with attendances, ratings and sponsorship gradually improving—particularly for the one-day contests. After a number of meetings between the warring factions, and following a British High Court case in which the Packer organisation won $250 000 in damages on the grounds of restraint of trade, the cricket establishment finally caved in.

> That happened in April 1979: PBL Sports, a Packer subsidiary, was awarded, by the Australian Cricket Board, a 10 year contract to organise the marketing and sponsorship of official cricket, and Packer was awarded exclusive Australian television rights for 3 years in the first instance.[44]

This has since been renewed and there is little reason to doubt that a strong influence on the direction of Australian cricket will remain firmly in the hands of the Nine network for the foreseeable future.

And the preferred direction of cricket, for television at least, lies in the promotion of the one-day match over test cricket. The one-day game as a contest for first class cricketers began in England in 1963 as a response to declining attendances at test and county fixtures in that country. Its structure differs significantly from that of traditional cricket. One-day cricket is unabashedly spectator oriented, geared towards providing excitement, tight finishes, big hitting and aggressive play. Many cricketing traditionalists argue that it diminishes the importance of many of the skills, strategies and subtleties intrinsic to the game as it has developed over the past 150 years. As Ross Edwards (who at the time of my interview with him was in charge of selling the Nine network's cricket telecasts to potential sponsors) commented, from the point of view of someone who had played most of his first class cricket in the traditional form, the structure of the four or five day game

> is based on the balance between the bat and the ball. That's the one thing that's ignored in one-day cricket. One-day cricket is not a balanced game. It's a one-sided game — it is for the batsman only.

He continued by suggesting that 'if we don't do something about it shortly, I think [it] will degenerate into a game that is recognised as something being totally different from traditional cricket'.[45]

But there is no doubt that one-day cricket is ideally suited for television. It is commercially lucrative because the structure of the game and the style in which it is covered by television attracts viewers, many of whom would not watch traditional cricket. It is advertised and promoted to emphasise aggression, speed and danger, rather than grace, patience and subtlety; a twentieth century gladiatorial sport, rather than a leisurely nineteenth century rural pastime.

The point is not whether crowds like it — judging by attendances at one-day games compared to test matches played in Australia in the 1985–86 season — they obviously do. But a lot of people liked and still like test cricket too. In the three years before World Series Cricket entered the scene, attendances in Australia for interstate and test cricket averaged 1 088 000 each year. In the three seasons between 1982 and 1984 when there were about 60 per cent more days of top-level cricket played — the addition being mainly one-day matches — the average annual attendances increased by less than 100 000.[46] But both the television take-over of cricket marketing and cricket promotion has consciously assisted the rise of the one-day game. The primary enticement is of course more money for everyone — cricketers earn more money, the organisations administering cricket get a bigger share of the spoils, the Nine network increases its advertising revenue by selling more commercial time in the summer period, traditionally a 'dead' season for commercial television.

Yet the experience is a classic example of the overpowering of sporting autonomy by television because of its greater capacity for the commercial exploitation of a cultural commodity. The outcome of the confrontation between the traditional cricketing organisations, represented by the ICC and the ACB, and a commercial television network epitomises the continuing process whereby the remaining vestiges of the 'English conception of sport' are easily swept aside by 'those who think along more American or capitalist lines'.[47]

If the present trends continue it seems quite conceivable that test cricket might soon decline to the status of a 'minor sport', banished from commercial television schedules. If this is the case then the calculated intervention by commercial television interests into the game's organisation and administration will have been a critical and possibly decisive factor. The oft repeated view of television's influence on sport, as typified by the following, is that 'the direction of sports would not have been greatly impeded if television were not present', so television's effect has been merely to increase the 'tempo of change . . . rather than acting as a prime determinant in the evolution of sports'.[48] While in general this seems accurate, it is suggested that the example of the intervention of television into cricket as outlined above provides convincing evidence that it can, and does, play a determining role in the developmental history of a popular sport.

Selling Victorian football to the world

In the 1850s in Melbourne, a peculiarly localised code of football evolved and quickly took root in the community. It drew some elements from the vaguely similar game played in Ireland with a round ball, but within a few years adopted the use of an oval shaped ball, similar to rugby. It had no 'off-side' rule unlike most of the other football codes and a unique scoring system that involved four upright posts placed at each end of an oval shape field. Played between two teams consisting of eighteen players it incorporated kicking, catching the ball in the air, running while bouncing the ball, passing by either hand or foot and vigorous tackling of the player in possession of the ball. It very quickly became the most popular football code in the colonies (later States) of Victoria, Tasmania, South and Western Australia, but made little impact in New South Wales and Queensland where the two rugby codes predominated. Soccer, which took firm root to become the dominant football code of most countries throughout the world (with the exception of North America) has always remained a decidedly minor sport in Australia.

Under the name of Australian Rules Football (although derisively referred to as 'Victorian Rules' by many in the northern States) the game quickly developed an extensive infrastructure of inter-club competition. By late in the nineteenth century, games between a number of Melbourne suburban clubs organised under the name of the Victorian Football Association were already attracting a large spectator following. As a result of some organisational infighting within the Association, in 1897 a few of the stronger clubs broke away to form the Victorian Football League which gradually emerged as the strongest and most popular competition. More clubs were added (some from the Association which has continued as a separate organisation to the present day) until in 1925, the League settled into a twelve team competition. Eleven of the clubs were named for, and identified with a particular suburban area of Melbourne in which their 'home ground' was situated and the twelfth was centred in Geelong, Victoria's second-largest city — but with a considerably smaller population — some sixty kilometres away. In the early part of this century the eleven suburban clubs covered the city of Melbourne's major population areas. From the 1920s onwards the stature of VFL football as the major winter-season spectator sport continued to grow with each of the six matches played every Saturday consistently drawing several thousand spectators. Total attendances for the series of four finals played in September to decide the season's champion team in the city's largest stadium, the Melbourne Cricket Ground, were consistently over 200 000 by the early 1920s. A gate figure of more than 50 000 at an inter-club match during the regular season became a commonplace occurrence by the 1930s.

The economics of league football depended upon income from gate receipts and club membership. Loyal supporters bought an annual membership ticket from their club which then entitled them to attend all games for the season. Major organisational, financial and administrative decisions were determined by the league's board of directors, consisting of a delegated representative from each club. Most players in the teams received some payment for playing, but the league stipulated a standard fee per game which was extremely modest, and in theory no player could be paid more. The competition between the clubs and supporters was fierce and winning the annual premiership has always been the primary goal of each club. Paying extra money to potentially valuable young recruits or in order to secure the services of stars from opposing clubs is not unknown, but until the 1970s this practice had little major impact on what was basically a parochial semi-professional sport. As late as 1965, the average payment to each player in the league was $16 per game.[49]

Until the 1980s football was merely a source of a little extra income for players, coaches and trainers who had other jobs, professions, or businesses from which they made their living. At least until the 1950s, the entire character of each club — administration, players, supporters — broadly reflected the socio-economic and demographic characteristics of its 'home' territory. League football was the centre of a tribalistic culture in which loyalties were passed down through family and neighbourhood from one generation to the next. There were similar localised competitions elsewhere in Australia, with the strongest in the three other states of Australia in which the game had developed considerable popularity as a spectator sport. Interstate games were regular fixtures with teams made up of the best club players from each State, but these were of passing interest to Victorians as their State usually won such matches very easily. The games were made even more one-sided as many of the better interstate players were recruited by Victorian clubs and did not play for their 'State of origin' until recently when the rules were changed thereby making the contests more evenly matched. Despite a steady trickle of interstate recruits, the basis for the continuity of the VFL relied predominantly on recruiting potential players from local junior competitions supplemented by the occasional 'finds' by club 'scouts' whose role was to scour the Victorian country regions to sign up talented youngsters whom they considered had a future in league football.

From its very foundation, the VFL has had expansionist aims, firmly committed in the belief that Australian rules is the 'greatest game in the world' and should be exported to the whole of Australia if not the entire world. There were early attempts to develop the game in the northern States but these came to very little. A body called the National Football League (NFL) was formed in 1906, one of the founding aims of which was to 'promote and develop the game on a national basis'.[50] This organisation has operated primarily as the nominal roof body for Australian Rules Football to which all the football associations in the States and Territories of Australia, including amateur leagues, are affiliated. But apart from controlling the laws and rules of the game, its major function until recently, has been to organise interstate matches and periodically, national carnivals in which representative teams from all the States (including New South Wales and Queensland where competitions exist but receive little spectator support) take part. But the NFL has always been dominated by the VFL and the latter in turn has reflected the fierce parochialism of its constituent clubs and their supporters. The administrators invariably consisted of long term club stalwarts — former players and coaches, occasionally a few local businessmen — who were elected by the membership because of their commitment to the club's success on the football field. Almost nothing else really mattered.

In the 1950s and 1960s there were significant changes to the demographic make-up of the Melbourne suburbs. A substantial immigration programme and a thriving economy stimulated the geographic expansion of a huge suburban sprawl. The nexus between many of the football clubs and their traditional neighbourhoods was weakened. The descendants of those who had formed the core of loyal supporters of a number of the inner-city working-class clubs moved to the outer suburbs. A few clubs moved to new grounds further removing themselves from their original geographic base. The game still maintained enormous popularity as a spectator sport but signs were beginning to appear that it was undergoing significant changes. A further blow to the traditional mores was affected by a personal decision made by one player. At the end of the 1964 season, the captain of the Melbourne Football Club, Ron Barassi, a charismatic figure and inspiring footballer who had been an instrumental part of that club's domination of the competition for the previous decade, accepted the position of captain and coach of the rival Carlton Club. Players had transferred from one club in the league to another before, but for a player of Barassi's stature and position in the club, such a move was virtually unprecedented.

An almost religious-like edict within Melbourne's traditional football culture that had nurtured the expectation of life long loyalty to the club had been broken. Not that Barassi's personal image or reputation suffered any permanent damage. He was successful at his new club and also, as a coach, led his third club to their first ever premiership. But more money was beginning to enter the game and the players began to see themselves as professionals, more and more prepared to offer their services to the highest bidder.

Once again television had a critical role in expanding the financial base of the sport. Originally, the league had been very cautious of allowing live televising of matches. For a while they permitted a last quarter to be shown live, but after a few years there were fears that this was responsible for declining attendances. In Melbourne only edited highlights were permitted, but both the ABC and the commercial Seven network who became the major carriers of televised football were permitted to show a complete game live through their interstate affiliates. As the VFL had by far the highest standard of football these telecasts attracted significant viewing audiences throughout Australia. Visions of a national competition began to surface again. In 1976, the VFL entered into a five year contract with both networks selling the rights to replay portions of regular season's games for a total of $3 000 000, three times the amount they had received for the previous five years.[51] A further cog in the expansion came with the VFL building its own stadium, VFL Park, situated in one of Melbourne's outer eastern suburbs. The aim was to become independent of the MCG, the traditional home of football, the arena where all the finals games were played, but which was controlled by a Board of Trustees nominated by the State government. The VFL had to pay to lease the MCG and they were also unable to derive income from the seats in the ground reserved for Melbourne Cricket Club members, substantially cutting into revenue from finals matches. Their aim in building VFL Park was to eventually switch the finals to this venue. The first game was played there in 1970 and the venue became a permanent fixture on the weekly schedule of league games. In 1977 a national cup competition including all VFL teams and the leading clubs in South and Western Australia was introduced. It was played at VFL Park and televised live by the Seven network who paid $200 000 for the rights during the first year.[52] The games were played on Tuesday nights, invariably in damp and chilly conditions that were typical of Melbourne's winter. Attendances were miniscule compared to the regular Saturday games. Coaches did not help the status of the competition when they consistently used them to try out players who would not have normally made the first team and left out key stars rather than risk them being injured for the following week's game.

Clearly the media were becoming an increasingly important source of both publicity and funds for the VFL. The VFL was therefore responsive to the demands of Channel 7 in particular.

This was evident with the organisation of the night football series . . . The night games were conveniently arranged to commence at 8.30 p.m., the middle of prime viewing time for the commercial stations. (Indeed, umpires were instructed not to start play until advertising commitment had been cleared.) Playing time was cut down to ensure that the game would end before 10.45 p.m.[53]

A familiar pattern typical of the American television-professional sports alliance previously outlined began in earnest. More money came into the hands of the administrators; bigger payment demands from players (the average match payment across the league had risen to $272 by 1978); the richer, more successful clubs were becoming more so; there was an increasing involvement with corporate sponsors because of the national television exposure; there was a noticeable entry of leading businessmen and corporate executives into club administration; the calls began for 'economic rationalisation' of the competition; the weaker clubs were getting further into debt because of the increasing cost to remain competitive.

Clubs were moved from their traditional home grounds in the name of 'rationalisation' because it was deemed the venues were 'not up to expected standards of spectator comfort'. The football public in general — the paying spectators — were not consulted. The long cherished dream of bringing the wonders of Australian Rules Football to the people of Sydney was finally acted upon by a VFL decision to permanently relocate South Melbourne (one the least successful and financially most troubled clubs of the post-war era) there from the beginning of the 1982 season. This emanated from a proposal by the club's chairman, but was pushed through by the VFL, despite strong opposition by a significant group of the club's members and supporters. However, the move was supported by most of the senior players who argued that it was their only chance to recoup the substantial sum of money still owed to them by the club for past services on the field.

The arrangement was for the Sydney Swans (as the team became known) to play their home matches at the Sydney Cricket Ground on Sunday afternoons. This overcame another impasse that the VFL had faced in Melbourne where the State government had, for some years, refused their requests to schedule league games on Sundays. The ostensive aim of moving the South Melbourne club to Sydney was to attract a following in that city for Australian rules, as the necessary base for a projected national competition. It was also clear that the commercial television networks would only be interested in a national competition that included both of the two largest population markets. The Seven network was granted rights to televise the Swans home games live, throughout the rest of Australia. While the games played in Sydney drew only modest crowds, the live Sunday telecasts attracted a huge audience in Melbourne. The Swans performed poorly in the league competition over the next three years and attendances at their home games remained disappointingly low. Despite the Swans receiving a substantial amount of media publicity, the people of Sydney continued to show almost no interest whatsoever in their new 'home' team or in Australian rules generally. The meagre crowds that attended the Swan's games appeared to consist of football starved expatriate Victorians bolstered each week by a small contingent of supporters of the Swan's opponents who travelled from Melbourne on weekend jaunts organised by the VFL and by their own clubs.

The Sydney venture continued to lose money which required heavy subsidies from the VFL, meaning the other eleven clubs. The major beneficiary was the Seven network who were able to turn the normally dead Sunday afternoon time-slot into a lucrative commercial money spinner.

Amid mounting discontent over the VFL's handling of the Swans, bolstered by surveys that showed little public support for the way the organisation was running league football, in 1983 a decision was made by the league's directors to appoint a five-man independent 'task force' instructed 'to examine and make recommendations on the future direction of the League, including possible alternatives to its eighty year old organisational and administrative structure'. With regard to the latter the major recommendation of the final report, completed in 1984, was to appoint a board of commissioners, not directly connected to any of the clubs, who would act as an independent decision-making body determining the overall policy direction and thereby overcoming the 'parochial' club interests that had dominated the previous arrangements. Signficantly, when appointed, the five-man commission included a director of one of Australia's leading companies and a 'prominant merchant banker who drives a silver Rolls-Royce'.[54] Thus, from its origins as a communal form of recreation, which for more than a century had its base and support in the working class culture of the city, the 'people's game' had somehow evolved into a world of corporate planning and rational marketing strategies in which decision-making control was being ceded to men who drove silver Rolls-Royces.

One of the first decisions made by the new commissioners when they took office early in 1985 was to consider the viability of selling the Sydney Swans into private ownership. After several months of procrastination and consideration of rival bids, in August of 1985 the ailing Sydney Swans was sold to Dr Geoffrey Edelsten, a flamboyant Sydney doctor for the reported sum of $6.3 million, about half of which was to be divided among the other eleven clubs. Afterwards one of the commissioners suggested that the sale was considered a 'one-off', but that 'the commission would look at any proposal for the sale of another club with an open mind'.[55]

Subsequently, proposals were put forward for a fully national league to incorporate the existing clubs with the addition of others drawn from the other States. Games could then be spread over Fridays, Saturdays, Sundays and possibly one other week night, undoubtedly attracting the interest of one of the commercial television networks. The Seven network retained the television rights for the 1985–86 seasons but it was reported that both of the other commercial networks would be extremely interested in bidding for the right to telecast Australian rules 'when the League decides to form a national league'.[56]

Corporate sport in which television operates as the principle entrepreneurial force seems poised to swallow up VFL football, closely following the pattern set in North America. Inevitably the lure of a hefty television contract will hasten the formation of a national competition, which,

> will complete the transformation of the local club game into national, professional sporting entertainment... The latest lot of good old days are gone and there doesn't seem any way to go back to any of the ones that existed B. T. — Before Television.[57]

The entire process seems to have been largely engineered by an alliance of small groups with specific economic interests — the players, the administrators, the corporate sponsors and the television networks. The grass roots football supporters of Melbourne, of which there are hundreds of thousands, were not consulted. In an interview with a former footballer and well known media commentator for the past thirty years, Lou Richards, I suggested that there were signs that a considerable number of those traditional supporters did not whole-heartedly endorse the direction the VFL Commissioners seemed to be taking. He replied,

> We should never neglect them... As long as we look after the ordinary guy that is out in the outer, it's okay to have the corporate sponsors and the coteries and all that jazz and give them the fine lunches. But don't forget the guy that goes out there in the outer with his wife and couple of kids, once he is neglected, that's the end of football.[58]

If this is true, then the end is indeed near, because there seems little doubt that the commercial television networks who have already become 'football's most lucrative paymaster'[59] are considerably more interested in keeping 'plenty of guys' in the living room watching the sponsors' messages rather than worrying too much about neglecting the 'guy and his family in the outer'.

These two case studies demonstrate the economic and social power of television that enable it, for its own purposes, either in alliance with, or against the wishes and desires of any particular sport's administrative trustees, players and supporters, to undermine the institutional autonomy and cultural unity evolved within that sport over many years. What has happened to cricket and Australian Rules football in Australia over the past decade or so is also indicative of the way in which the more powerful groups in this society appropriate what are essentially collective cultural resources for their own personal or corporate ends with little regard for the feelings, wishes or interests of those in the community less able to exert any influence on such decisions. Thus, privately controlled media corporations, advertising agencies, larger business and commercial organisations, management companies hired to represent the financial interests of elite sports professionals combine and negotiate to determine the future direction of 'their' sport. In the process they arrogantly sweep aside any consideration of the organic significance of these games, as collective social and cultural resources, representing to many people deeply meaningful community traditions, identities and relationships. To those who appropriate sport as their own property, it is just another potentially lucrative entertainment commodity.

Television's wide world of sport

In the late 1970s and even more effectively in the 1980s, it has become possible to achieve a direct interconnection between the various television transmission sources throughout the world, by relaying a signal containing both picture and sound via stationary communication satellites floating hundreds of miles above the earth. This has meant, in effect, that there are increasingly more occasions when world-wide audiences, numbering in the hundreds or even thousands of millions are simultaneously being presented with identical television images and sounds. This can occur in circumstances where there are significant events taking place considered internationally newsworthy. In 1985 such technology was harnessed for an international humanitarian cause when hundreds of millions watched a televised concert featuring numerous well known musicians and pop groups, organised for the purpose of raising money to aid those dying of hunger in Ethiopia. But in the main, the available technology is increasingly employed to transmit top-level sports events such as the World Cup in soccer, the Olympics, the major tennis and golf tournaments and the like which consistently attract enormous world-wide television audiences. This provides an even greater potential for financial benefit to all of those involved in promoting sport as an entrepreneurial entertainment commodity. It further extends to the area of high-achievement sport a more general process of the international rationalisation of popular culture or as John Alt has put it,

> the corporatisation of social life worlds once under communal and normative control... The social agents of corporatisation are those experts — the 'new class' — who expropriate the moral and skilful resources of people under cover of scientific progress and enlightenment, and fragment and administer to discrete spheres of people's lives.[60]

As the case studies above have sought to demonstrate, the communal and ritual elements of spectator sport are swept away to be replaced by sport as commodity spectacle. Thus inevitably,

> The national media take over the mass distribution of the new games, and interject an entertainment ethic and technical fetishisation, replacing that traditional commentary once important to the meaning of ritual.[61]

The gap between participating in sport for relaxation, fun, physical health, sociability — which millions of people throughout the world still enjoy doing — and the rarified world of high-achievement sport dominated by an elite corp of specialists whose abilities bring them substantial economic and status rewards, and who help facilitate the gigantic entertainment and marketing structure that has grown around them, signifies that sport has become two distinct entities, 'sport which is designed to be watched, and sport which is designed to be played'.[62]

The recruitment of personnel from one into the other forms a prime connecting link between them. Parents, teachers, coaches, government funded sports institutions and the mass media still operate as if sport is a unified entity to stimulate this process of recruitment. The economic and status potential of a successful sporting career have become seductive arguments to channel youthful physical energy and skill into psychological drive and ambition in order to reap the rewards that accrue to those few who can 'become a champion.' The values of monomanic discipline, body-numbing training, ruthless desire to succeed that are required to reach the ultimate levels of sporting achievement are positively inculcated at a young age. Parents and coaches impose an earnest and intensely serious quality to the playful endeavours of nine and ten year old children urging them to demon-strate the fierce competitiveness and uncompromising aggression typi-cal of the elite athlete.

Most fall by the wayside. A few who have the talent and respond appropriately to the socialising values of competitive achievement and material rewards continue to channel their physical and psychological energies into a specialised sporting career. For some the transition from playful child to high-earning professional is rapid and dramatic. Sometimes the costs are great. In women's tennis, Andrea Jaeger and Tracy Austin reached the top rankings in their early teens and withdrew from the sport 'burnt out' before they were twenty. Playful sport is fun — professional sport is often anything but fun. The incredible expectations for continuing success from all around and the obssessive attention of the media can be oppressive and draining. Television in particular feeds off the rise and fall of celebrities and is often ruthless in exploiting both. Bjorn Borg retired from tennis at twenty-five, partly, it is reported, because the media refused to allow him to be just a great tennis player but continually sought to exploit him as a celebrity — a commodity to be used for their own ends — a role he had no wish to play. At the time of writing it appears that John McEnroe is about to follow a similar road for similar reasons.

Finally then, for television, sporting events, participants, spectators are all basically vehicles for producing 'good television', this is tele-vision that is dramatic, colourful, exciting and makes full use of the available technology thereby attracting as many people as possible to tune into these programmes and then keeps them from tuning out. Television already promotes its own sporting events — exhibition tennis or golf matches for example — which the players appear not to take as seriously as regular tournaments. This is very apparent to the fans, so consequently spectator attendance at such events is generally low, but to television this does not really matter. Furthermore, after one or two generations, it seems conceivable that the mediated ex-periences of sport on television will come to represent the real thing. Perhaps as Donald Parente speculates, in the future,

> as television technology becomes more sophisticated and TV screens become significantly larger, we may begin to see some sports

existing as studio sports, with only token live audiences for background and atmosphere, where in fact as well as effect the new stadium is TV.[63]

However, while this projected scenario would appear to be workable for some sports, there is the difficulty that with stadium events, it is not possible for television to present the necessary component of excitement without the presence of a sizeable 'live' audience of involved spectators. One approach to solving this problem lies in the recent trend towards the construction of gigantic video screens in sports stadiums thereby effectively turning them into gigantic television studios. Thus, while in the past, watching televised sport was generally considered a secondary and therefore a relatively impoverished version of direct spectatorship, the defining power of television as the authoritative interpreter of the sporting experience has successfully inverted the social validity of this assumption. The view of the sporting contest mediated by television has established itself as the primary experience. The giant video screen is there to attract people to the stadium event and to ensure that by attending they will not be deprived of the 'television experience'.

The effectiveness of television in convincing the general sporting public of the superiority of the mediated view of the event is reinforced by observing the pattern of preferred spectator seating in those stadiums that incorporate the giant video screens. As the crowd builds prior to the sporting event, the points in the stadium that provide the clearest and most direct view of the video screen are occupied first. Those areas of the stadium which often provide excellent vantage points from which to view the contest on the field, but offer no direct line of sight to the video screen, are invariably the last to be occupied. If the game is not 'sold-out' they tend to be almost completely empty of spectators.

Thus, the triumph of television is complete and sport becomes just another source of programming material with the spectators occupying the role of the 'studio audience' necessary to provide a convincing atmosphere to the viewers at home, a technique television has successfully employed in the presentation of variety and comedy programmes. Ultimately, television has extended even further the historical movement of high-performance sport from 'play' to 'display' by incorporating the spectators, who are conveniently transformed into television extras, more than happy to pay for the privilege of playing their role in the performance.

Notes

1 William O. Johnson, Jr, *Super Spectator and the Electric Lilliputians*, Little Brown & Co, Boston, 1971, p. 50. To extend the perspective further, for the television rights to the 1983 Rose Bowl—the premier US college

football event of the season—NBC paid $7 000 000. See Benjamin G. Rader, *In Its Own Image*, Free Press, New York, 1984, p. 77.

2 Johnson, p. 71.
3 See, for example, Donald E. Parente, 'The Interdependence of Sports and Television', *Journal of Communication*, 27(3), 1977, pp 128–32; Susan L. Greendorfer, 'Sport and Mass Media', in Günther R. F. Lüschen and George H. Sage (eds), *Handbook of Social Science of Sport*, Stipes Publishing Co., Champaign, Ill., 1981, pp 160–80.
4 Greendorfer, p. 176.
5 Gregory P. Stone, 'American Sports: Play and Display', in Eric Dunning (ed.), *Sport: Readings From a Sociological Perspective*, Frank Cass & Co., London, 1971, pp 47–65.
6 Howard L. Nixon II, *Sport and Social Organisation*, Bobbs-Merrill, 1976, p. 56.
7 Such statistics have been independently reported in a number of studies of North American sport, see Richard Harmond, 'Sugar Daddy or Ogre? The Impact of Commercial Television on Professional Sports', in F. J. Coppa (ed.), *Screen and Society*, Nelson Hill, Chicago, 1979, pp 81–105; Barry D. McPherson, 'Sport Consumption and the Economics of Consumerism', in Donald W. Ball and John W. Loy (eds), *Sport and Social Order*, Addison-Wesley, Reading, Mass., 1975 pp 239–75; Ira Horowitz, 'Sports Broadcasting', in Roger G. Noll (ed.), *Government and the Sports Business*, The Brookings Institution, Washington D.C., 1974, pp 275–323; Nixon II, Parente.
8 Peter R. Shergold, 'The Growth of American Spectator Sport: A Technological Perspective', in Richard Cashman and Michael McKernan (eds), *Sport in History*, University of Queensland Press, St Lucia, 1979, p. 35.
9 Horowitz, p. 290. In Baseball, he notes, writing in 1974, 'only one team would have shown a book profit in either 1952 or 1970, the first and last years for which relatively complete data are available'. Ironically, of the four major team sports, only in hockey, the sport least favoured by television, would a majority of teams in the competition 'operate profitably without broadcasting'.
10 Parente, p. 129.
11 See Department of Sport, Recreation and Tourism: Australian Sports Commission, *Australian Sports, A Profile*, AGPS, Canberra, 1985, p. 199.
12 David L. Altheide and Robert P. Snow, 'Sport Versus the Mass Media', *Urban Life*, 7(2), 1978, p. 194.
13 Parente, pp 129–30.
14 Quoted by James A. Michener, *Sports in America*, Random House, New York, 1976, p. 298.
15 Personal interview with Australian ABC sports producer, J. Murray Ashford, 9 November 1984.
16 William Johnson, 'TV Made It All A New Game', *Sports Illustrated*, 31 (22 December), 1969, p. 88.
17 Personal interview with David Hill, Vice-President in Charge of Sports, Nine network, Sydney, 16 November 1984.
18 Parente, p. 130.
19 Altheide and Snow, p. 194.
20 Parente, p. 130.
21 Garrie Hutchinson, 'Canned Crowds', *Metro*, No. 62, 1983, p. 4.

22 The quote is from Leonard Shecter, cited in Harmond, p. 88.
23 For example, it is reported that, in general, professional careers in American sport, 'have often been far more characterised by a short spurt of economic success followed by an inevitable drop in status... than by any enduring "embourgeoisement" or objective change in living conditions'. This is supported by statistics up to the end of the 1960s that show,

After the peak earning years of 25 to 35 the average salaries of all players without college degrees descends to a rate far lower than the median income for comparable non college members of the American labor force. In the case of players with college degrees, the inflated peak earning rate drops to a level approximately compatible with comparative college educated members of the labor force.

See Richard S. Gruneau, 'Sport, Social Differentiation and Social Inequaltiy', in Ball and Loy (eds) p. 157 and footnote 34.
24 Stephen Wagg, *The Football World: A Contemporary Social History*, Harvester Press, Brighton, UK, 1984, p. 65.
25 R. Terry Furst, 'Social Change and the Commercialization of Professional Sports', *International Review of Sport Sociology*, 6, 1971, p. 161.
26 Roger G. Noll, 'The U.S. Team Sports Industry: An Introduction', in Noll (ed.), p. 9.
27 John Loy, Barry D. McPherson and Gerald Kenyon, *Sport and Social Systems*, Addison-Wesley, Reading, Mass., 1978, p. 268. Because of successful legal challenges to the 'reserve clause', in recent years clubs have begun to consider it safer to sign 'super-stars' to mammoth long-term contracts of fifteen, twenty-five and even forty years.
28 Reported in *The Age*, 24 June 1985.
29 A prominent example of this has been the 'career' of Mark Jackson, an Australian rules footballer of modest ability, but a real 'character' complete with a face that has been described as one 'that only his mother could love'. Despite a turbulent footballing career that has seen Jackson traded from club to club, frequently suspended for both on-field and off-field infractions, his commercial appeal has been carefully promoted to create a 'cult phenomenon', both locally and even in Britain and North America where replays of this internationally little known sport are carried on television.
30 In addition they are expected to assist in television promotions. It is reported that when commercial television interests first sought to take control of Australian cricket in the mid-1970s, the Nine network's marketing organisation hired Sydney's leading theatrical talent agency. 'Its task was to improve the television commercial image of Australia's leading cricketers, some of whom had difficulty negotiating their lines and/or expressing them with conviction'. See Brian Stoddart, 'Sport, Television and Sponsorship in Australia, 1975–1983', Paper presented to Conference on the History of Sporting Traditions, Melbourne, August 1983, p. 1.
31 From the book by Curt Flood, *The Way It Is*, Trident, New York, 1971, cited by Alan G. Ingham, 'Occupational Subcultures in the Work World of Sport', in Ball and Loy (eds), p. 371.
32 Harold Charnofsky, 'Ballplayers, Occupational Image and the Maximiza-

tion of Profit', in Phyllis L. Stewart and Muriel G. Cantor (eds), *Varieties of Work Experience*, Wiley, New York, p. 268.

33 Charnofsky, p. 267.
34 Charnofsky, p. 269.
35 Reported by Stoddart, p. 11. Ironically, however, the Australian footballer to whom this comment was attributed, Leigh Mathews, was himself subject to a four-week 'deregistration' as a player and a police charge resulting from a 1985 on-field incident in which he broke an opponent's jaw in two places. This was done behind the backs of the umpires, but in front of millions of television viewers.
36 Thus the fine irony in the conviction with which the Nine network's top executive in charge of sport asserted to me that his primary motivation for becoming involved with sports' television was because 'what happens out there in the middle, 99.9% of the time, is sheer honesty'. He firmly believes that sport remains 'the last bastion of reality on television'. From personal interview with David Hill, Sydney, 16 November 1984.
37 Ingham, p. 380.
38 Bill Bonney, 'Packer and Televised Cricket', *Media Papers*, No. 2, NSW Institute of Technology, Sydney, 1980, pp 5–6.
39 These figures are reported in Bonney, p. 8.
40 Bonney, p. 4.
41 For more detailed accounts of the ensuing turmoil see Henry Blofeld, *The Packer Affair*, Collins, London, 1978; C. Forsyth, *The Great Cricket Hijack*, Widescope, Melbourne, 1978.
42 Bonney, p. 16.
43 Personal interview with Ross Edwards, Sales Manager, Nine network Sport, Sydney, 19 November 1984.
44 Bonney, p. 19.
45 From the interview with Ross Edwards, Sydney, 19 November 1984. Although Mr Edwards concluded that 'you have to recognise the fact that it [one-day cricket] may not be a bad idea' if the game was made more 'balanced'.
46 These figures are reported in Richard Cashman's book, *Australian Cricket Crowds: The Attendance Cycle*, History Project Incorporated, Kensington, NSW, 1984.
47 Richard Cashman, 'Crisis in Contemporary Cricket', in Richard Cashman and Michael McKernan (eds), *Sport: Money, Morality and the Media*, NSW University Press, Kensington, NSW, 1980, p. 309.
48 Furst, p. 164.
49 From the VFL Taskforce Report, June, 1985 as reported in *The Age*, 24 June 1985, p. 27.
50 Bob Stewart, *The Australian Football Business*, Kangaroo Press, Kenthurst, NSW, 1983, p. 27.
51 Stewart, p. 122.
52 Stewart, p. 122.
53 Stewart, p. 122.
54 *The Age*, 13 December 1984.
55 *The Age*, 20 August 1985. Prior to the commencement of the 1986 season, it came to light that Dr Edelsten was only a minority shareholder in a new company, Powerplay International Pty Ltd, formed to control the Swan's

licence. About a third of the company's shares were held by a Western Australian investment company. Powerplay would be listed on the stock exchange and 46.4 per cent of its shares offered for sale to the public. On 19 March 1986 a meeting of VFL club directors formally approved the new ownership structure. The press reports of the meeting also revealed that the sum paid for the Swans was $2.9 million and not $6.3 million as originally widely reported at the time of the sale. *The Age*, 20 March 1986.

56 *The Age*, 14 December 1984. After much speculation, the VFL administrators decided, late in 1986, to expand the competition to fourteen teams for the 1987 season. Licences have been granted to privately owned consortiums to field teams based in Brisbane and Perth. The major television networks are expected to offer up to $30 million for the rights to televise games over the next five years.

57 Garrie Hutchinson, *The Age Green Guide*, 31 May 1984.

58 Personal interview with Lou Richards, Melbourne, 25 November 1984.

59 Michael Carrick, *The Age Green Guide*, 17 January 1985.

60 John Alt, 'Sport and Cultural Reification: From Ritual to Mass Consumption', *Theory, Culture and Society*, 1(3), 1983, p. 98.

61 Alt, p. 99.

62 Mungo MacCallum, 'The Future', in Department of Sport, Recreation and Tourism: Australian Sports Commission, *Australian Sport: A Profile*, AGPS, Canberra, 1985, p. 163.

63 Parente, p. 132. This should not be dismissed as mere idle academic speculation. As Peter Shergold (p. 38) reports;

On the afternoon of 24 December 1976, at Yonkers, New York, an unusual trotting meeting was held . . . The reason was that not a single spectator was present. It was the first 'TV meeting'; a sporting contest recorded by camera and played into households later that same evening.

References

Alt, John (1983) 'Sport and Cultural Reification: From Ritual to Mass Consumption', *Theory, Culture and Society*, 1(3), pp 93–107.

Altheide, David L. and Snow, Robert P, (1978) 'Sport Versus the Mass Media', *Urban Life*, 7(2), pp 189–204.

Ashcraft, Richard (1972) 'Marx and Weber on Liberalism as Bourgeois Ideology', *Comparative Studies in Society and History*, 14, pp 130–68.

Bailey, Peter (1978) *Leisure and Class in Victorian England: Rational Recreation and the Contest for Control, 1830–1885*, Routledge & Kegan Paul, London.

Ball, Donald W. (1972) 'Olympic Games Competition: Structural Correlates of National Success', *International Journal of Comparative Sociology*, 13, pp 186–200.

Barr, Charles (1975) 'Comparing Styles: England v West Germany', in *Football on Television*, British Film Institute, London, pp 47–53.

Betts, John R. (1953) 'Sporting Journalism in Nineteenth-Century America', *American Quarterly*, 5(1), pp 39–56.

—— (1967) 'Mind and Body in Early American Thought', *Journal of American History*, 54(3), pp 787–805.

Birrell, Susan (1981) 'Sport as Ritual: Interpretations From Durkheim to Goffman', *Social Forces*, 60(2), pp 354–76.

Blofeld, Henry (1978) *The Packer Affair*, Collins, London.

Bonney, Bill (1980) 'Packer and Televised Cricket', *Media Papers*, No. 2, NSW Institute of Technology, Sydney, June.

Bourdieu, Pierre (1978) 'Sport and Social Class', *Social Science Information*, 17(6), pp 819–40.

Boyd Barrett, O. (1977) 'Media Imperialism', in James Curran, Michael Gurevitch and Janet Woollacott (eds), *Mass Communication and Society*, Edward Arnold, London pp 116–41.

Brohm, J. M. (1978) *Sport: A Prison of Measured Time*, Ink Links, London.

Bryant, Jennings, Comisky, Paul and Dolf Zillmann (1977) 'Drama in Sports Commentary', *Journal of Communication*, 27(3), pp 140–9.

Bryant, Jennings, Dan Brown, Paul W. Comisky, and Dolf Zillmann, (1982) 'Sports and Spectators: Commentary and Appreciation', *Journal of Communication*, 32(1), 1982, pp 109–19.

Burke, Peter (1978) *Popular Culture in Early Modern Europe*, Temple Smith, London.

Caillois, Roger (1972) 'The Classification of Games', in Ellen W. Gerber (ed.), *Sport and the Body: A Philosophical Symposium*, Lea & Febiger, Philadelphia, pp 36–43.

Cantwell, Robert (1973) 'Sport was Box-Office Poison', in John T. Talamani and Charles H. Page (eds), *Sport and Society: An Anthology*, Little Brown & Co., Boston, pp 440–54.

Carroll, John (1986) 'Sport: Virtue and Grace', *Theory, Culture and Society*, 3(1), pp 91–8.

Cashman, Richard (1980) 'Crisis in Contemporary Cricket', in Richard Cashman and Michael McKernan (eds), *Sport: Money, Morality and the Media*, NSW University Press, Kensington, pp 304–12.

_____ (1984) *Australian Cricket Crowds: The Attendance Cycle, Daily Figures, 1877–1984*, History Project Incorporated, Kensington, NSW.

_____ (1984) *'Ave a Go Yer Mug!: Australian Cricket Crowds From Larrikin to Ocker*, Collins, Sydney.

Chaney, David (1983) 'A Symbolic Mirror of Ourselves: Civic Ritual in Mass Society', *Media, Culture and Society*, 5(2), pp 119–35.

Charnofsky, Harold (1974) 'Ballplayers, Occupational Image and the Maximization of Profit', in Phyllis L. Stewart and Muriel G. Cantor (eds), *Varieties of Work Experience*, Wiley, New York, pp 262–73.

Cheek, Neil H. Jr and William R. Burch, Jr (1976) *The Social Organisation of Leisure in Human Society*, Harper & Row, New York.

Cheska, Alice Taylor (1979) 'Sports Spectacular: A Ritual Model of Power', *International Review of Sport Sociology*, 14(2), pp 51–72.

Clarke, Alan and John Clarke (1982) '"Highlights and Action Replays"—Ideology, Sport and the Media', in Jennifer Hargreaves (ed.), *Sport, Culture and Ideology*, Routledge, London, pp 62–87.

Comisky, Paul, Bryant, Jennings and Dolf, Zillmann (1977) 'Commentary as a Substitute for Action', *Journal of Communication*, 27(3), pp 150–3.

Cunningham, Keith (1980) *Leisure in the Industrial Revolution c1780–c1880*, Croom Helm, London.

Curran, James (1977) 'Capitalism and Control of the Press, 1800–1975', in James Curran, Michael Gurevitch and Janet Woollacott (eds), *Mass Communication and Society*, Edward Arnold, London, pp 195–230.

Dayan, Daniel and Elihu, Katz (1985) 'Electronic Ceremonies: Television Performs a Royal Wedding', in Marshall Blonsky (ed.), *On Signs*, Basil Blackwell, Oxford, pp 16–34.

Deegan, Mary Jo and Stein, Michael, (1978) 'American Drama and Ritual: Nebraska Football', *International Review of Sport Sociology*, 13, pp 31–42.

Delves, Anthony (1981) 'Popular Recreation and Social Conflict in Derby, 1800–1850', in Eileen Yeo and Stephen Yeo (eds), *Popular Culture and Class Conflict 1590–1914: Explorations in the History of Labour and Leisure*, Harvester Press, Sussex, pp 89–127.

Department of Sport, Recreation and Tourism: Australian Sports Commission (1985) *Australian Sport: A Profile*, AGPS Canberra.

Dulles, Rhea Foster (1974) 'In Detestation of Idleness', in George H. Sage (ed.), *Sport and American Society*, 2nd edn, Addison-Wesley, Reading, Mass., pp 64–80.

Dunning, Eric (1971) 'The Development of Modern Football', in Eric Dunning (ed.), *Sport: Readings From a Sociological Perspective*, Frank Cass & Co., London, pp 133–51.

Edwards, Harry (1979) 'Sport Within the Veil: The Triumphs, Tragedies and Challenges of Afro-American Involvement', *Annals of A.A.P.S.S.*, 445, pp 116–27.

Eliot, T. S. (1948) *Notes Towards a Definition of Culture*, Faber, London.

Fiske, John (1983) 'Cricket/T.V./Culture', *Metro*, 62, pp 21–6.

_____ and Hartley John, (1978) *Reading Television*, Methuen, London.

Forsyth, C. (1978) *The Great Cricket Hijack*, Widescope, Melbourne.

Furst, R. Terry (1971) 'Social Change and the Commercialization of Professional Sports', *International Review of Sport Sociology*, 6, pp 153–70.

Gans, Herbert J. (1974) *Popular Culture and High Culture*, Basic Books, New York.

Goldman, Robert and Wilson John, (1977) 'The Rationalization of Leisure', *Politics and Society*, 7(2), pp 157–87.

Greendorfer, Susan L. (1981) 'Sport and Mass Media', in Günther R. F. Lüschen and George H. Sage (eds), *Handbook of Social Science of Sport*, Stipes Publishing Co., Champaign, Ill., pp 160–80.

Gruneau, Richard S. (1975) 'Sport, Social Differentiation and Social Inequality', in Donald W. Ball and John W. Loy (eds), *Sport and Social Order*, Addison-Wesley, Reading, Mass., pp 117–84.

_____ (1976) 'Sport as an Area of Sociological Study: An Introduction to Major Themes and Perspectives', in Richard S. Gruneau and

John G. Albinson (eds), *Canadian Sport: Sociological Perspectives*, Addison-Wesley, Don Mills, Ont., pp 8–43.

Guttman, Allen (1978) *From Ritual to Record*, Colombia University Press, New York.

Hargreaves, John (1982) 'Sport, Culture and Ideology', in Jennifer Hargreaves (ed.), *Sport, Culture and Ideology*, Routledge, London, pp 30–61.

Harmond, Richard (1979) 'Sugar Daddy or Ogre? The Impact of Commercial Television on Professional Sports', in F. J. Coppa (ed.), *Screen and Society*, Nelson Hill, Chicago, pp 81–105.

Hoberman, John M. (1984) *Sport and Political Ideology*, Heinemann, London.

Horkheimer, Max (1964) 'New Patterns in Social Relations', in E. Jokl and E. Simon (eds), *International Research in Sport and Physical Education*, Charles C. Thomas, Springfield, Ill., pp 173–85.

Horowitz, Ira (1974) 'Sports Broadcasting', in Roger G. Noll (ed.), *Government and the Sports Business*, The Brookings Institution, Washington, D. C., pp 275–323.

Huizinga, Johan (1971) 'The Play Element in Contemporary Sport', in Eric Dunning (ed.), *Sport: Readings From a Sociological Perspective*, Frank Cass & Co., London, pp 11–16.

—— (1972) 'The Nature of Play', in Ellen W. Gerber (ed.), *Sport and the Body: A philosophical Symposium*, Lea & Febinger, Philadelphia, pp 54–7.

Hutchinson, Garrie (1983) 'Canned Crowds', *Metro*, 62, pp 3–5.

Ingham, Alan G. (1975) 'Occupational Subcultures in the Work World of Sport', in Donald W. Ball and John W. Loy (eds), *Sport and Social Order*, Addison-Wesley, Reading, Mass., pp 333–89.

Inglis, K. S. (1983) *This is the ABC: The Australian Broadcasting Commission 1932–1983*, Melbourne University Press, Melbourne.

Johnson, William O. Jr (1969) 'TV Made It All A New Game', *Sports Illustrated*, 31 (22 December).

—— (1971) *Super Spectator and the Electric Lilliputians*, Boston, Little Brown & Co.

Kamper, Erich (1972) *Encyclopedia of the Olympic Games*, McGraw Hill, New York.

Kando, Thomas M. (1975) *Leisure and Popular Culture in Transition*, C. V. Mosby Co., St Louis.

Krotee, March L. (1979) 'The Rise and Demise of Sport: A Reflection of Uruguayan Society', *Annals of A.A.P.S.S.*, 445, pp 141–54.

Kuntz, Paul Grimley (1977) 'Paul Weiss on Sports as Performing Arts', *International Philosophical Quarterly*, 17, pp 147–65.

Langer, Beryl (1985) 'The Culture Industry: High Culture as Mass Culture', Paper presented to SAANZ Conference, Brisbane, August.

Lever, Janet (1969) 'Soccer: Opium of the Brazilian People', *Transaction*, 7(2), pp 36–43.

Levi Strauss, C. (1966) *The Savage Mind*, Weidenfeld & Nicholson, London.

Levine, Ned (1974) 'Why Do Countries Win Olympic Medals? Some Structural Correlates of Olympic Games Success: 1972', *Sociology and Social Research*, 58(4), pp 353–60.

Lipsky, Richard (1979) 'Political Implications of Sports Team Symbolism', *Politics and Society*, 9(1), pp 60–88.

Lowenthal, Leo (1968) *Literature, Popular Culture and Society*, Pacific Books, Palo Alto, Calif.

Loy, John. W., McPherson, Barry D. and Kenyon Gerald, (1978) *Sport and Social Systems*, Addison-Wesley, Reading, Mass.

Lüschen, Günther R. F. (1970) 'Sociology of Sport and the Cross-Cultural Analysis of Sport and Games', in Günther R. F. Lüschen (ed.), *The Cross-Cultural Analysis of Sport and Games*, Stipes Publishing Co., Champaign, Ill., pp 6–13.

McIntosh, Peter C. (1963) *Sport in Society*, C. A. Watts & Co., London.

_____ (1981), 'The Sociology of Sport in the Ancient World', in Günther R. F. Lüschen and George H. Sage (eds), *Handbook of Social Science of Sport*, Stipes Publishing Co., Champaign, Ill., pp 25–48.

McPherson, Barry D. (1975) 'Sport Consumption and the Economics of Consumerism', in Donald W. Ball and John W. Loy (eds), *Sport and Social Order*, Addison-Wesley, Reading, Mass., pp 239–75.

Maheu, René (1962) 'Sport and Culture', *International Journal of Adult and Youth Education*, 14(4), pp 169–78.

Malcolmson, Robert W. (1973) *Popular Recreations in English Society 1700–1850*, Cambridge University Press, London.

Marx, Karl (1973) *Grundrisse*, Penguin, Harmondsworth.

Mason, Tony (1980) 'Football and the Workers in England: 1889–1914', in Richard Cashman and Michael McKernan (eds), *Sport: Money, Morality and the Media*, NSW University Press, Kensington, pp 248–71.

Meyer, Heinz (1973) 'Puritanism and Physical Training: Ideological and Political Accents in the Christian Interpretation of Sport', *International Review of Sport Sociology*, 8(1), pp 37–52.

Michener, James A. (1976) *Sports in America*, Random House, New York.

Moorfoot, Rex. (1982) *Television in the Eighties: The Total Equation*, BBC, London.

Mosely, Phil (1983) 'Factory Football: Paternalism, Profits or Plain Exhaustion?', Paper presented to Conference on History of Sporting Traditions, Melbourne, August.

Murdock, G. and Golding, P. (1977) 'Capitalism, Communication and Class Relations', in James Curran, Michael Gurevitch and Janet Woollacott (eds), *Mass Communication and Society*, Edward Arnold, London, pp 12–43.

Nixon, Howard L. II (1976) *Sport and Social Organisation*, Bobbs-Merrill, Indianapolis.

Noll, Roger G. (1974) 'The U. S. Team Sports Industry: An Introduction', in Roger G. Noll (ed.), *Government and the Sports Business*, The Brookings Institution, Washington, D.C., pp 1–32.

Nowell-Smith, Geoffrey (1978–79) 'Television-Football-The World', *Screen*, 19(4), pp 45–59.

Okner, Benjamin A. (1974) 'Subsidies of Stadiums and Arenas', in Roger G. Noll (ed.), *Government and the Sports Business*, The Brookings Institution, Washington, D.C., pp 325–47.

Parente, Donald E. (1977) 'The Interdependence of Sports and Television', *Journal of Communication*, 27(3), pp 128–32.

Parker, S. (1976) *The Sociology of Leisure*, George Allen & Unwin, London.

Petrie, Brian M. (1975) 'Sport and Politics', in Donald W. Ball and John W. Loy (eds), *Sport and Social Order*, Addison-Wesley, Reading, Mass., pp 185–237.

Rader, Benjamin G. (1984) *In its Own Image: How Television Has Transformed Sports*, The Free Press, New York.

Real, Michael (1975) 'Super Bowl: Mythic Spectacle', *Journal of Communication*, 25(1), pp 31–43.

—— (1977) *Mass Mediated Culture*, Prentice-Hall, Englewood Cliffs, N. J.

Reisman, David and Denney, Reuel (1971) 'Football in America: A Study in Culture Diffusion', in Eric Dunning (ed.), *Sport: Readings From a Sociological Perspective*, Frank Cass & Co., London, pp 152–67.

Rigauer, Bero (1981) *Sport and Work*, Columbia University Press, New York.

Riordan, James (1982) 'Sport and Communism—On the Example of the U.S.S.R', in Jennifer Hargreaves (ed.), *Sport, Culture and Ideology*, Routledge, London, pp 212–31.

Roberts, John M., Arth, Malcolm J. and Bush, Robert R. (1974) 'Games in Culture', in George H. Sage (ed.), *Sport and American Society*, 2nd edn, Addison-Wesley, Reading Mass., pp 138–48.

Rosenberg, Bernard and White David M. (eds) (1957) *Mass Culture: The Popular Arts in America*, Free Press, New York.

Schiller, Herbert I. (1969) *Mass Communications and American Empire*, Augustus M. Kelley, New York.

Schmitz, Kenneth L. (1972) 'Sport and Play: Suspension of the Ordinary', in Ellen W. Gerber (ed.), *Sport and the Body: A Philosophical Symposium*, Lea & Febiger, Philadelphia, pp 25–32.

Shergold, Peter R. (1979) 'The Growth of American Spectator Sport: A Technological Perspective', in Richard Cashman and Michael McKernan (eds), *Sport in History*, University of Queensland Press, St Lucia, pp 21–42.

Shils, Edward and Young, Michael (1953) 'The Meaning of the Coronation', *Sociological Review*, 1, pp 63–81.

Snyder, Eldon E. and Spreitzer, Elmer A. (1983) *Social Aspects of Sport*, Prentice-Hall, Englewood Cliffs, N. J.

Stewart, Bob (1983) *The Australian Football Business*, Kangaroo Press, Kenthurst, NSW.

Stoddart, Brian (1983) 'Sport, Television and Sponsorship in Australia 1975–1983', Paper presented to Conference on History of Sporting Traditions, Melbourne, August.

Stone, Gregory P. (1971) 'American Sports: Play and Display', in Eric Dunning (ed.), *Sport: Readings From a Sociological Perspective*, Frank Cass & Co., London, pp 47–65.

Strenk, Andrew (1979) 'What Price Victory? The World of International Sports and Politics', *Annals of A.A.P.S.S.*, 445, pp 128–40.

Sutton-Smith, Brian (1981) 'The Social Psychology and Anthropology of Play and Games', in Günther R. F. Lüschen and George H. Sage (eds), *Handbook of Social Science of Sport*, Stipes Publishing Co., Champaign, Ill., pp 452–78.

Tatz, Colin (1982) 'The Corruption of Sport', *Current Affairs Bulletin*, September.

Tudor, Andrew (1975) 'The Panels', in *Football on Television*, British Film Institute, London, pp 54–65.

Tunstall, Jeremy (1977) *The Media Are American*, Constable, London.

Tyrell, Ian (1980) 'Money and Morality: The Professionalization of American Baseball', in Richard Cashman and Michael McKernan (eds), *Sport: Money, Morality and the Media*, NSW University Press, Kensington, pp 86–103.

Unesco Statistical Yearbook, 1982.

Vamplew, Wray (1980) 'Playing for Pay: The Earnings of Professional Sportsmen in England 1870–1914', in Richard Cashman and Michael McKernan (eds), *Sport: Money, Morality and the Media*, NSW University Press, Kensington, pp 104–30.

Veliz, Claudio (1983) 'A World Made in England', *Quadrant*, 27(3), March, pp 8–19.

Wagg, Stephen (1984) *The Football World: A Contemporary Social History*, Harvester Press, Brighton, UK.

Walvin, James (1975) *The People's Game*, Allen Lane, London.

Warner, W. Lloyd (1962) 'An American Sacred Ceremony', in *American Life: Dream and Reality*, rev. edn, University of Chicago Press, Chicago.

Wheeler, Robert F. (1978) 'Organised Sport and Organised Labour:

The Workers' Sports Movement', *Journal of Contemporary History*, 13, pp 191–210.

Whitson, David (1986) 'Structure, Agency and the Sociology of Sport Debates', *Theory, Culture and Society*, 3(1), pp 99–107.

Williams, Brien R. (1977) 'The Structure of Televised Football', *Journal of Communication*, 27(3), pp 133–9.

Williams, Claire Louise, Lawrence, Geoffrey and Rowe, David (1985) 'Women and Sport: A Lost Ideal', Paper presented to SAANZ Conference, Brisbane, August.

Williams, Raymond (1965) *The Long Revolution*, Penguin, Harmondsworth,

—— (1974) *Television: Technology and Cultural Form*, Fontana, London.

—— (1981) *Culture*, Fontana, Glasgow,

Wren-Lewis, Justin and Clarke, Alan (1983) 'The World Cup — A Political Football', *Theory, Culture and Society*, 1(3), pp 123–32.

Wright, Will (1975) *Six Guns and Society*, University of California Press, Berkeley and Los Angeles.

Index